3/2000

Riding the Rails

*Teenagers on the Move
During the Great Depression*

Errol Lincoln Uys

New York

CATALOGING-IN-PUBLICATION DATA
Uys, Errol Lincoln.
   Riding the rails : teenagers on the move during the Great Depression / Errol Lincoln Uys.
      p. cm.
   Includes bibliographical references and index.
   ISBN: 1-57500-037-7

   1. Tramps—United States—History—20th century. 2. Tramps—United States—Interviews. 3. Depressions—1929—United States. 4. Poor teenagers—United States—History—20th century. I. Title.
   HV4505.U97 1999   305.5'68
                                             QBI99-15

The publisher has made every effort to secure permission to reproduce copyrighted material and would like to apologize should there have been any errors or omissions.

TV Books, L.L.C.
Publishers serving the television industry.
1619 Broadway, Ninth Floor
New York, NY 10019
www.tvbooks.com

Interior design by Rachel Reiss.

Manufactured in the United States.

Contents

———•———

To my grandsons
Jeremy Lovell Uys
Alexander Porter Uys

Preface

The story of the 250,000 boxcar boys and girls of the Great Depression is one of the vital sagas of America in the 1930s. Often as young as thirteen, each one came from a different background, each left home to ride the rails for different reasons, and each had unique experiences. They shared at least one thing: They knew the hardships and danger of life "on the road" during this almost-forgotten epoch. It was hard times—and none forgot how hard—but it was also a time when they were fearless and free. It was the beginning of a life's journey.

Their story has seldom been told, and firsthand accounts of individuals who endured these trying times are even more scarce. As they grew older, some survivors shared reminiscences with family and friends: bittersweet remembrances mixed with wistful longings for youth. Some kept their memories locked up, for they had been ashamed of their lives as "bums." Some never regarded their freight train odyssey as the stuff of history.

This book has as its primary source thousands of letters sent to Michael Uys and Lexy Lovell, coproducers of the documentary film *Riding the Rails*. Some three thousand respondents, a majority answering to a notice in *Modern Maturity*, the bimonthly magazine of the American Association of Retired Persons, wrote letters about their life on the road between 1929 and 1941. Some sent handwritten memoirs as long as sixty pages, with evocative passages detailing their childhood wanderlust. Some letters are only a paragraph or two in length, fragments of memory that are raw and powerful—and sometimes bitter.

Follow-up questionnaires were sent to fifteen hundred of these letter writers, seeking data on their backgrounds and asking a series of questions about their hobo days. For example: "What led you to leave home?" "How old were you, and how did you survive?" "What rewards or disappointments did you have when trying to find work?" "Did you witness, or were you involved in, racially charged incidents while riding the rails?" "Were you injured or did you see anyone injured or killed?" "How did your experience shape the rest of your life?"

The information gleaned from the questionnaires facilitated a further sifting of respondents, with some five hundred people selected for telephone interviews conducted over a two-month period in fall 1993. From these personal contacts, twenty men and women were chosen as potential candidates for the documentary. They were interviewed on film at various locations around the country in late spring and early summer 1994. A total of forty hours of interviews were filmed, only a fraction of which could be used in the final documentary.

The pages that follow juxtapose these oral histories, with four narrative sections woven from the rich and varied reminiscences in the letters and questionnaires: "Catching Out," "Hard Travelin'," "Hitting the Stem," and "The Way Out." Included with the book are photographs from the Library of Congress and other archival sources. These include classic images of the 1930s by such WPA/FSA photographers as Dorothea Lange, Walker Evans, and Carl Mydans.

Not long ago, a former boxcar boy was telling a young man about his trials in the Depression: how he went without food for a day and a half; how he unloaded a truckload of threshed wheat and was given a rotten ham sandwich; how he was thrown off a train in the Nevada desert. The young man told Walter Miletich that it couldn't be true, something like that could never happen in this country. As this century itself passes and the years of the boxcar boys and girls draw to a close, these memories of a landscape of ruin stand as a reminder to those who might forget the lessons of history.

Introduction

————•————

At the height of the Great Depression, 250,000 teenage hoboes were roaming America. Some left home because they felt they were a burden to their families; some fled homes shattered by the shame of unemployment and poverty. Some left because it seemed a great adventure. With the blessing of parents or as runaways, they hit the road and went in search of a better life.

A boy's or girl's decision to leave home was intensely personal, often spurred by naïveté and hope. Many held grand visions of finding work and sending money home. Like their parents, many sought jobs that simply did not exist.

Public perceptions of the road kids differed. There were people who saw the American pioneer spirit embodied in the young wanderers. There were others who feared them as the vanguard of an American rabble potentially as dangerous as the young Fascists then on the march in Germany and Italy.

What was indisputable, and what was highlighted by a series of government inquiries that addressed the "Youth Problem," was that crumbling family structures were not the only reason these children left home. Across the nation, school doors were locked or classrooms hours drastically reduced. Four out of ten youths of high school age were not in school. Many so-called vagrant boys had looked for work in their home town for two or three years before they hit the rails.

The young nomads of the Great Depression struggled to survive in a country "dying by inches," in the words of Franklin Delano

Roosevelt. Resourceful, adventurous, and brave, they met joy and terror, loneliness and grandeur on their journeys. A lost generation seeking to find itself, they would be profoundly influenced by what they saw and experienced on the road.

An Army of Children on the Loose

Arvel "Sunshine" Pearson was nine years old when he quit school to work as a waterboy in the Arkansas coal mines in 1924. When he was thirteen, he was old enough to go underground with his stepfather. In 1930, the Great Depression sealed the fate of the mines around Clarksville, Arkansas, throwing twelve hundred miners out of work—including Arvel and his stepfather. There were no jobs for experienced miners, much less for young boys. Arvel left home with fifteen cents in his pocket, went down to the Union Pacific railroad yards at Clarksville, and caught a freight going west.

Sixteen-year-old Jim Mitchell's decision to leave his Kenosha, Wisconsin, home was two years in the making. It began on a day in 1931, when Jim witnessed his father break down and sob uncontrollably after losing his factory job. In the following year, his father would land the occasional day job for a dollar or two. His mother went to work in a restaurant. One winter morning in 1933, Mitchell slipped out of bed, dressed swiftly, and packed a rucksack with a change of underwear, socks, shirt, a pair of pants, and his favorite book, Thoreau's *Walden*. He placed a note on his pillow. "I'll write," he promised.

John Fawcett was the son of a prosperous ophthalmologist in Wheeling, West Virginia, where he did not want for anything during the years that brought poverty and destitution to so many American families. John attended the Linsly School at Wheeling, then a boys-only military institute. In high school, he rebelled against the strict discipline and punishment meted out to the boys. On February 7, 1936, with the ground covered by snow and the temperature below zero, Fawcett ran away. "Mom and Dad were good, loving parents, so I didn't run away because of my home life. Why do boys run

away? For adventure, I guess because it's exciting and dangerous."
That night, seventeen-year-old Fawcett swung onto the blinds—the
narrow wooden ledge between the coal tender (behind the locomotive) and baggage car—of Train Number 77, which had made a stop
at Wheeling on its run from Pittsburgh to West Virginia.

By the winter of 1931–32, in the third year of the Great Depression, hope and desperation drove an army of boys and a scattering
of girls to swell the ranks of the migratory idle moving across
America riding the freights or hitchhiking. Small towns in Texas,
New Mexico, and Arizona along the route of the Southern Pacific
reported two hundred transients a day coming into their communities, the number of boys among them estimated at 20 to 25 percent. The superintendent of a soup kitchen in Yuma, Arizona, fed
7,500 boys between November 1 and March 15 that winter.

In January 1933, C. C. Carstens, executive director of the Child
Welfare League of America, told the LaFollette-Costigan Committee of the Senate, then holding hearings on federal aid for unemployment relief, that the number of wandering boys and girls was
variously estimated from two hundred thousand to one million.

> MR. CARSTENS: I don't believe anyone knows what the num-
> ber is.
> SENATOR CUTTING: You are talking of children now?
> MR. CARSTENS: Yes, sir; quite so. I think it is somewhere in be-
> tween. They are drifting from place to place mostly in
> the southern section of the country, in the wintertime in-
> evitably so, but they can be found in the north as well.

D. O'Connell, Chief Special Agent of the Southern Pacific Company, reported that in 1927 78,099 trespassers had been ejected from
the company's trains and property. In 1930, that figure climbed to
170,641. By 1932, the number of trespassers had soared to 683,457
on this railroad, one of ninety major companies existing at that time.

"In 1927, more than 50 percent of these trespassers were men
of middle age and older; in later years these older men have

largely disappeared," O'Connell reported. "I estimate that 75 percent of the 1932 trespassers ranged in age from sixteen to twenty-five years. The figures of ejectment tell only part of the story, as there were many trespassers whom it was impossible for our men to interfere with."

As the number of illegal riders soared, so did accidents involving trespassers. In 1932, the Interstate Commerce Commission recorded 5,962 trespassers killed and injured in the first ten months of the year, 1,508 of them under twenty-one. On the Missouri Pacific Railroad line alone, in the three years from 1930 to 1932, 330 trespassers lost their lives and 682 were injured.*

The public's opinions of the "Children's Army" differed widely. As superintendent of police in Washington, D.C., General Pelham D. Glassford had witnessed the rout of the Bonus Marchers in August 1932, who were dispersed by the tanks of General Douglas MacArthur and scattered to the winds behind the smoke of Anacostia Flats. Openly sympathetic to these veterans who had trekked to the capital to ask for their World War I bonus—many arriving by freight train—Glassford made a special study of the transient problem in late 1932, traveling for ten weeks in the East, South, and Northeast.

General Glassford was amazed by the intelligence and resourcefulness he found among the young men and boys on the road, some of them as young as fourteen. "They come from substantial respectable families," Glassford told the La Follette-Costigan Committee's hearings on relief for unemployed transients. "Usually they

---

* "Trespassers" are not limited to freight train riders in the Interstate Commerce Commission reports, but include other trespassers such as people walking their dogs along the tracks, casualties at grade crossings, and so forth. Significantly though, the ICC reveals a sharp increase in accidents described as "getting on or off cars or locomotives"—fatalities rising from 253 in 1929 to 425 in 1932, and injuries climbing from 706 to 1,344. A similar increase occurred in the "miscellaneous" group, which included such classes of accidents as "standing, walking, or running alongside trains," "falling from locomotives and cars," and "load shifting"—fatalities rose from 305 in 1929 to 455 in 1932, injuries from 533 to 890.

give their ages much higher than they actually are, believing they will get along better, but many are boys who ought to be in grammar school, and boys who have not completed high school."

Glassford compared the boys riding the freights and traveling the roads with those unemployed youths who had remained in their home towns. "The more venturesome take to the road. Those without ambition, content to remain in their communities, idle and hanging around street corners and pool rooms, and picking up a little food here and there, with a few hours of employment, are not in any way comparable with the young men on the road today.

"The spirit of the boys is splendid. They will travel a thousand miles just on a rumor that there is work to be had, and many rumors are running around. A boy will say he is going to New Orleans to ship out on a vessel. If he cannot get that work, he travels on a rumor about work at some other place."

"The wandering boys hail from every section of the United States," wrote A. Wayne McMillen of the University of Chicago. In spring 1932, acting on behalf of the Children's Bureau, a federal child welfare organization, McMillen visited communities in New Mexico, west Texas, California, Arizona, Nevada, and Utah. At the Community Lodge in Los Angeles, 623 boys who applied for shelter in the five months ending March 31, 1932, came from forty-five states and the District of Columbia.

A considerable proportion of the youths had a high school education, and some even college. In Atlanta, 5,438 transients were registered between November 1, 1931, and February 20, 1932: 1,641 had attended high school and 194 had been in college. In Washington, of 7,512 transients served by the Salvation Army in the first quarter of 1932, 1,866 had an eighth-grade education, 2,060 had been in high school, and 258 were college trained.

"It is a striking fact that when you see knots of young men and boys waiting around for freights, almost every one has a small valise," observed McMillen. "They are the types of men and boys who have standards of personal cleanliness which make them think it is worth while to carry a small bag with them on the journey. The old style hobo sometimes carried a few possessions wrapped in a bandanna handkerchief, but never a valise."

Not everyone viewed the young nomads in a positive light. Mario Lapenta, who owned a summer camp below Bear Mountain, near Peekskill, New York, was critical of a *New York Times* rotogravure section on the boy wanderers in October 1932. In a letter to the paper, he wrote that five years earlier he made a journey of eight thousand miles to see for himself the condition of these "homeless boys." "I traveled, slept, and ate with them and got to know them well. The majority had left home for the greater glamour and adventure of traveling about the country on other people's money and sympathy. Most of them came from middle class families and had left home of their own free will and still had homes to return to. Most of them are slackers and think the world owes them a living. I remember when about fifteen of us were given supper by a Minnesota farmer on condition that we would work in his grain fields the next day at $3 a day. That night we slept in the barn and in the morning there were three of us. The others had sneaked off."

Herman Schubert studied twenty thousand transients at the Federal Transient Center in Buffalo, New York, from December 1933 to August 1935. One-third were in the fifteen-to-twenty-four age group. Suggested Schubert: "These men and women, or perhaps even better, these boys and girls are close to becoming gypsies, if not bandits and criminals. They have had only a few years of being practically outcast. What will they be like when they have had a score or more in which to develop their unusual habits and allegiances?"

The knowledge that an army of 250,000 "wild boys" was on the loose in America brought comparison with the *bezprizorni*, the street children of Russia left homeless in the civil strife and famine after the 1917 revolution. The 750,000 *bezprizorni* banded together and hunted in packs like wolves; thieves, pickpockets, and robbers, as young as seven, sallying forth with homemade weapons to attack their victims.

"In America such a grave crisis has not yet come to pass," wrote Lowell Ames Norris in *Scribner's Magazine* in May 1933. "But the army of the American *bezprizorni* continue their hope-killing march. Hitch-hiking when they can, many are killed or injured by hit-and-run drivers as they tramp the highways. Many more are killed or crippled while riding the freights."

Grace Abbott, chief of the Children's Bureau, warned that the boys were getting accustomed to the nomadic life. "They get used to the dangers and hardships; to the lack of opportunity for cleanliness; they overcome their abhorrence of begging. Their interest is in 'getting by,' and they come to make a game of beating the authorities. The danger is not only what is happening to them now, but they can easily become confirmed in the habit of vagrancy and become what is called the American hobo."

Rugged Individualists

The new nomads were following a well-beaten path taken by earlier generations of Americans heeding Horace Greeley's admonition to "Go West, young man!" Penniless, out-of-work youths clung to the old ethos of pioneering, with the belief that westward, across the plains, today's pauper could be tomorrow's millionaire. Even if a youth set his sights lower, maybe hoping only for a dollar-a-day harvest job, the lure of the West persisted. But by then, for forty years, there'd been no new land to homestead and precious little hope of finding quick and easy riches in the wilderness with gold, silver, or oil.

John Levy, a psychiatrist at Columbia University, interviewed homeless boys passing through New York in 1933. Four years of harsh discomforts had made the boys "rugged individualists" who saw the future as something to work out for themselves. Levy found that dissatisfaction had given the boys clear-sighted initiatives. They were all set to start a career of independence and responsibility—the hallmarks of mature adulthood.

"Without waiting to be told, these fellows were putting into practice the slogan that their ministers might have given them half a century or so ago: 'Go West, young man,'" wrote Levy. "The place and the boy were adequate. The time was wrong. The adolescent army found itself going nowhere. Discovering that Atlanta, Georgia, had no more work to offer than Erie, Pennsylvania, they pushed on to Phoenix, Arizona. The only improvement was the air."

The tramp life held a powerful attraction for boys. A decade before the Great Depression, estimates of the number of boy tramps rose as high as one-fourth of the total tramp population of two million. Nels Anderson, author of *The Hobo* (1923) interviewed four hundred tramps in transit between Chicago and the West Coast during the summer of 1921: fifty-one of the boys were under nineteen, and one-third of the entire group told Anderson that they had left home before they were twenty. Anderson himself had quit school and spent five years on the road. He worked as a mule skinner, a lumberjack, and a miner before finding a job on a ranch in Utah that allowed him to go back to school. He wrote *The Hobo* as a graduate student in sociology at the University of Chicago.

"Who has not felt that urge to cast off all responsibility and strike out for parts unknown?" Anderson asked, continuing:

> No grownup can feel it more than the average red-blooded boy who has access to the railroad and confidence to do what other boys do. The boy who lives in a dream world where he is constantly building air castles, only to see them toppled by the stern realities of the daily routine, is strangely attracted by the tramp's life. No other life offers such charm and fascination. The tramp is the only person whom he regards as having the ideal philosophy. He sees him as does the poet:
>
> > We are the true nobility;
> > > Sons of rest and outdoor air;
> > Knights of the tide and rail are we,
> > > Lightly meandering everywhere.
> > Having no gold we buy no care,
> > > As over the crust of the world we go,
> > Stepping in tune to this ditty rare;
> > > Take up your bundle and beat it, 'Bo!'
> > > > —H.H. Knibbs

Poets painted a bucolic picture of the hobo life. "Tramp writers" fired the budding road kids with their stories. Fifteen-year-old Jack London joined a "push," a teenage gang of freight riders, in 1891, later chronicling his experiences in his novel *The Road*. London's vagabond companions dubbed him "The Sailor Kid," and taught him the "delights of drifting along with the whimsicalities of Chance."

London wrote lyrically of the freedom he felt beating his way across the West on the railroads, on occasion riding on the deck of a night freight: "Above me the stars were winking and wheeling in squadrons back and forth as the train rounded curves, and watching them, I fell asleep. The day was done—one day of all my days. Tomorrow would be another day and I was young."

Jim Tully was the second of a trio of writers who filled the minds of Depression-era youth with wanderlust. Tully was a cocky, streetwise Irish kid from St. Mary's, Ohio. He had slugged it out as a prize-fighter for four years in his late teens, until he was once knocked out for twenty-four hours. From the age of eleven, when he ran away from an orphanage, until his mid-thirties, he rode the rails as a hobo and circus roustabout. He was a "literary bum,' reading Dickens, Goldsmith, Dostoyevsky, Balzac, Zola, and Shakespeare on his boxcar journeys, books he often borrowed permanently from libraries en route. Tully told the story of his travels in *Beggars of Life* (1924), which became a bestseller.

Ray Hinkle, a road kid in the Depression, remembers first coming across Tully's book when he was staying at a transient center in Memphis in 1935. "I knew Jim Tully had penned the words straight from his heart. I was living in a world that he wrote about. I was able to look at life in the same manner. I read his book three times during my stay in the shelter."

In contrast to the fighting Tully, Richard Halliburton was the scion of a Tennessee planter's family, a member of the class of 1920 at Princeton. Immediately upon graduation, Halliburton hit the road, not to hop freights, but to live the trailblazing adventures that later made him a hero to a generation of American youth. In his travels, the intrepid Tennessean climbed the Matterhorn, Parnassus, Olympus, and Mt. Fujiyama; he plunged through the jungles of Malaysia, wandered down to Bali, trekked up to Peking, and invaded Siberia in sub-zero temperatures. He swam the Panama Canal, emulated Hannibal riding an elephant through the Alps, and followed the Odyssey of Ulysses. On his last journey in 1939, Halliburton set out to cross the Pacific in a junk from China to San Francisco; after twenty-three days at sea, he was never seen again. *The Royal Road to Romance* and three other books by Halliburton entranced stay-at-home boys for twenty years, never more appealing than in those dreary days of the Depression, when Halliburton lived what so many only dreamed.

Charley Bull was nineteen when he left home in California in the summer of 1930. He crewed on tramp steamers in the Gulf of Mexico, and in boats on the Mississippi; he was a "pearl diver," washing pots and dishes in restaurants, and worked as a ranch hand for six dollars a month. This was not exactly the "royal road" that had propelled Charley on his travels, but Richard Halliburton remained his inspiration. "Thousands of us left home on account of Halliburton's book," he recalled. "He wrote of a new life, romantic and adventurous, which was better than sitting around at home. Naturally I thought of myself not as a bum or a tramp, but as a vagabond."

For hundreds of thousands of young men and boys, the new trails they sought led them through a wilderness of unemployment. "We're foraging animals in thin pastures and we have to cover an incredible lot of territory to keep alive," Frank Bunce wrote in *The Forum* in February 1933. The son of a deputy sheriff, Bunce had worked as a mechanical draftsman in Chicago, until he was laid off in 1931. Unable to find a job, he confessed to readers of *The Forum* that after two years on the road, he had lost his loyalties to his country, to God, and to mankind. "Having lived like an animal, I am taking on the ethics of an animal. I have become, in short, a public menace."

It was a tragic paradox that most of the wandering boys, whose rugged individualism was to be lauded, were actually penalized for their spirit. For once they hit the road without a legal or habitable residence behind them or ahead of them, they had to cross as many frontiers as if they were traveling in foreign lands. "Half a million American boys set out to look for the pot of gold at the end of the rainbow. They found it, but instead of gold it contained only traces of mulligan stew," said Kingsley Davis in a contemporary pamphlet on Depression-era youth.

Otto Mullinax, a student at the University of Texas, put it another way: "Horace Greeley is supposed to have unwittingly indicted the whole Capitalistic order back in 1870 when he said, 'Go West, young man!' Now he would say as readily, 'Go on relief, young man!' But for the lack of a Horace Greeley, we must depend on the railroad bulls to say, 'Keep moving, keep moving.'"

When School Was Out

By summer 1932, the "roving boy" had become a fixture on the American landscape. The occasional girl was sighted too, mostly passing unrecognized in male garb. When field-workers of the United States Children's Bureau confirmed that hundreds of thousands of young people were "on the road," newspapers and periodicals seized on the story. *The New York Times* rotogravure section of October 23, 1932, depicted "A Tragic Aftermath of the Days of Prosperity: The Army of Homeless Boys Now Roaming the Country." The *Detroit News* sent reporter Daniel Robert Maue across the United States with the young nomads. Wrote Maue: "The migratory youth is a product of these times which have upset a whole world. His elders, his friends, his teachers, his parents have failed to understand a perplexed youth. They have driven him from his home into the physical and moral hazards of transiency."

Dramatic images of a youthful horde swarming over the countryside captured the headlines. The invasion of Washington by twenty-five thousand veterans of the Bonus Army in summer 1932 remained fresh in many minds. Some observers suggested that this new army of the disaffected, young, and impetuous, carried the seeds of rebellion. Psychiatrist John Levy found no "group consciousness" among the wandering boys, but he wondered about the future: "As these young men get older and reflect on the raw deal that life seems to have given them, stolid egocentricity will give way to more serious personality twists, more one-sided points of view, tensions and restlessness."

The wandering boys and girls served to focus national attention on the "Youth Problem." In 1923, Nels Anderson had identified the main types of boy tramps, including the adventure-seeker; the boy rebelling against his parents; the boy fleeing a broken home; the work seeker; the mentally handicapped boy who drifted into the tramp class. The youth who hit the road in down-and-out America in the 1930s frequently did so for reasons totally beyond his control.

Many of the youngest, who should have been in the classroom, found their school doors locked. For millions of children, the 1933–34 school year ended on January 1 because reduced local resources made a full term impossible; for 175,000 children, school did not open at all.

One disheartened fourteen-year-old living on a prairie farm wrote to her cousin: "With the school closed (I feel like crying every time I see it with the doors and windows boarded up) I'll be too old before I am ready to go to high school. Do you think that you could get on without a school or even a set of books? Grace has the Arithmetic VIII and I have the Grammar. Teacher let us borrow these books when school closed. I guess she had a hunch how this year was going to be."

In 1934, schools had twenty-five thousand fewer teachers than in 1930, with a million more pupils. Terms had been shortened in one out of every four American cities, and five thousand schools had closed altogether. By 1935, of ten million youths of high school age, four million were out of school. The worst situation was in the Southern states: in Arkansas and Mississippi, fewer than 5 percent of African American youth of high school age were in school. Throughout the rural areas of the United States, non-attendance at high school rose as high as 60 percent.

The Hoover presidency, with its reliance on individualism, private enterprise, and grass-roots volunteerism, had failed to address the escalating school crisis. A "go-getter" ethos endorsed by auto-maker Henry Ford in his personal response to the youthful vagabonds captured the political mood: "Why it's the best education in the world for these boys, that traveling around! They get more experience in a few weeks than they would in years at school."

In February 1933, a militant session of the National Council of Education appealed to president-elect Franklin Roosevelt to give educators a role in a national body on socioeconomic planning. Among the teachers' resolutions was one calling on the federal government to entrust a program for nomadic unemployed youth not to the War Department, as some people were suggesting, but to a recognized educational agency.

In May 1933, President Roosevelt's Federal Emergency Relief Administration (FERA) funded a college work-study program, expanded in 1935 under the National Youth Administration (NYA), which gave aid to needy secondary school, college, and graduate students between the ages of sixteen and twenty-five. Eleanor Roosevelt made the youth problem a personal crusade. "I have moments of real terror, when I think we may be losing this generation," said the first lady. "We have got to bring these young people into the active life of the community and make them feel that they are necessary." Mrs. Roosevelt appealed to parents and teachers to see the lives that youth led not as they wished they were, but as they existed: "It is not purely a question of the education of youth; it is a question of the education of parents, because so many have lost their hold on their children."

Six million children under eighteen, one in seven of the youth of America, were living on relief, a catch-as-catch-can subsistence in insecurity and pauperization. Aubrey Williams, who became the director of the NYA, reflected on the lives of these children: "On the farm, in the village and city, these young people are woven into family life like a plaid into a bolt of woolen goods. They room with their little brothers and sisters. They help to further subdivide food that is already not enough. If they want to read a book, they fight for quiet. If a different mood is on them, they yell down their grandmother's request for peace in the sitting room. For two-thirds of them come from a class that never was decently housed. Now they have been doubled up, poured in, and congested like so much cheese in a rind."

Celeste Strack, an official of the American Student Union, visited one hundred high schools in 1935, interviewing students and teachers. She found the picture even darker when the number of high school graduates was taken into account. In 1930, the Office of Education estimated that less than one-third of youths entering high school received diplomas. By 1935, the percentage of graduates was even lower. "Five to eight million of our youth aged sixteen to twenty-four are neither in school nor at work," said Ms. Strack. "Hundreds of thousands belong to those transient youth who have been called 'boys and girls of the road,' wandering aimlessly about the country, without family ties, without funds, living a hand-to-mouth existence."

A 1934 survey of two hundred thousand Pennsylvania youths under twenty who were seeking work showed that 71 percent had never been employed. In New York, nearly 80 percent of sixteen-year-old job seekers were unable to find work. "These young men and women cannot, like cotton, pigs, or wheat be considered as 'surplus,'" said Phil Schiff, head worker at Madison House on New York's Lower East Side, which housed five hundred young people ages sixteen to twenty-five. "They cannot be held in reserve or put in cold storage, and they cannot remain idle forever."

The New York Committee on Unemployed Youth published a handbook, *Youth Never Comes Again*, highlighting the plight of the jobless boy, deprived of all that youth had meant to American boys in the past: "He has dressed in rags since the second year of the Depression. His gay young predecessors drove fast cars. He rides blind baggage. His family has moved from a house to a flat to single room, which, until he takes to the road, he shares with all the generations of his clan. Like as not he spends weary night's decline in a boxcar on a railroad siding. He has nothing to dream on. No past, no present, no future."

Young men and women lucky enough to have a job frequently found themselves "bewildered, baffled, and engulfed" noted Carol Brooke of the Cook County Bureau of Public Welfare in Chicago. Circumstances forced them to support unemployed fathers, brothers and sisters, and others living in the home. "Food isn't the only thing I'm worried about," Stella Munn told a social worker at the bureau. "I had hoped that I could buy a few things for the house and a few clothes. But now I realize that I am working for the grocer and the landlady, and I'm thoroughly discouraged. I have two dresses on my back, for work and Sundays too. If I knew this existence was only for a short time I wouldn't feel this way, but it's been like this for over three years, ever since I started working, and we're worse off now than when I started."

James Scott was earning ten dollars a week, of which he gave seven dollars to help his family. "There isn't any reason for me to stay home any longer. My parents find it impossible to keep our imitation home together because they lack sufficient food, clothes, rent, and other necessities. Continually moving, eating according to statistics, and having empty rooms to bring my friends to is not my idea of home." James was leaving within the week. "I am hoping for the best, but am prepared for the worst."

The plight of rural youth, of whom six hundred thousand were on relief in October 1935, was compounded by the joblessness in the cities. For decades prior to the Depression, young people had left the country to seek opportunity in the nation's industrial towns and cities. At the onset of the Depression, farm youth were entering the productive age at the rate of about two hundred thousand a year. This was the approximate number who migrated to the cities in the five years from 1930 to 1935, making the yearly increase almost five times as rapid as the migration. "This is some indication of the speed at which youth have been piling up in rural territory," wrote Homer P. Rainey, director of the American Youth Commission.

When the New York Stock Exchange crashed in 1929, Donald Newhouser was a thirteen-year-old Nebraska farmboy. "I saw children coming to school in zero weather with holes in their shoes, thin coats, and no gloves. We would have a bucket of snow ready to put their frozen hands in, as they came screaming into the schoolhouse after walking two miles to get there. One little girl came in, her eyes swollen from crying. She said that her father had tried to kill her because there was nothing in the house to eat. Her father held her over the cistern by her fingers, ready to drop her in; only her mother's praying and begging saved her.

"I was one of the few boys who got through grade school and high school. I took a job on a cattle ranch that paid ten dollars a month and my room and board. After a few months, I realized that I would get nowhere fast. I took the only means of transportation I could afford and hopped a freight train to follow the harvests through the West."

In March 1936, Congressman Thomas Amlie of Wisconsin, testifying before a Senate committee on a proposed American Youth Act, said that he lived in Elkhorn, a small country town with a population of twenty-five hundred. His office overlooked the courthouse square. Congressman Amlie observed that since the Civil War, the square had been a gathering place for retired farmers, who would meet in the morning and afternoon, sit around and watch the traffic, and discuss one thing or another.

"When the Depression came along another group began to make the square their hangout—the youngsters who were graduating from school. In June, when they got out of school, they would be restless, playing baseball, football, one thing and another. As the summer wore on, they would play less vigorously, and pretty soon they would pull up the chairs in another part of the square. So for about four or five years, the thing that has impressed me in this little town has been that in one part of the public square the young people will gather in the morning, hang around, just sit there until it is time to go home for dinner or for supper, very much the same as the retired farmers have been doing for over eighty years."

"I Knew I'd Made a Mistake"

"The damp smell of steam mixed with the acrid odor of hot oil drifted through the morning air. The train gained speed. My buddy Poke and I moved at precisely the same moment. Poke grabbed the handrail of the tender and leapt on; I followed without missing a beat," said Jim Mitchell, recalling how he caught his freight when he ran away from home in 1933. "Oh, hell, I don't think I was twenty miles down the road when I knew I'd made a mistake. But you're young and foolish and you don't go home crying."

The road kids' first weeks away from home could be euphoric. "I experienced a feeling of freedom, such as I'd never felt before," wrote Earnest L. Best. Boys who'd never left the town of their birth logged thousands of miles on the railroads and highways of America. They crossed the Continental Divide and thrilled to their first sight of the Rockies; they roared through the Sacramento Valley and down to the coast, many who'd never seen the sea coming to gaze in wonder at the Pacific.

George Phillips rode the rails from the age of eleven until he reached seventeen, first catching local freights out of his home town of Princeton, Missouri, and later traveling by boxcar throughout the West. "There is no feeling in the world like sitting in a side-door Pullman and watching the world go by, listening to the clickety-clack of the wheels, hearing that old steam whistle blowing for crossings and towns," Phillips reminisces. Riding at night, in the pitch dark, he'd see the lights of farmhouses. "I'd imagine those lucky people sitting down to supper. I might have nothing but some dry doughnuts. It was no big deal, because I was going somewhere. Wanderlust really had me."

City kids fetched up in small country towns, as happened to John Fawcett, who landed in Marshall, Arkansas. He listened to dirt-poor farmers talk about "Ruzafelt" and the "Giverment," the cost of feed and seed, and the drought. John left Marshall in a quandary of despair that there was so much going on in life that he'd never heard about at home or in school.

Boys coming from the country braved the streets of New York and Chicago, gawking at skyscrapers and seeing the "World of Tomorrow" laid out before their eyes at the Chicago World's Fair. The fair, which opened in 1933, became a mecca for thousands of footloose youth.

Sooner or later, however, the romance and adventure dwindled and the boy and girl tramps entered a new stage of their journey. In summer 1932, Thomas Minehan, a graduate student of the University of Minnesota, dressed as a young hobo and rode the rails with the nomads. Minehan observed that after six months on the road, the boys and girls lost their fresh outlook and eagerness. Trips across the continent were no longer educational, but were quests for bread. Towns and cities were remembered not for their historic past, but the hostility of their "heavy-foots." Wrote Minehan: "There comes a day when the boys are alone and hungry, and their clothes are ragged and torn; breadlines have just denied them food, relief stations an opportunity to work for clothes. A man of God at a mission has kicked them into the street. A brakie (brakeman) has chased them from the yards. An old vagrant shares his mulligan (stew) with them and they listen."

When A. Wayne McMillen of the University of Chicago undertook his research for the Children's Bureau in spring 1932, he visited a hobo "jungle" at Belen, a small town thirty miles southwest of Albuquerque, New Mexico. The hobo encampment was at the north end of the railroad yards, immediately contiguous to the yardmaster's residence. McMillen interviewed the yardmaster's wife, who told him that except on snowy days there were never less than fifty and often as many as two hundred men and boys in the jungle. One-fourth of them were under twenty-one. She had seen one boy eight years old, and literally hundreds who were fifteen to eighteen years old.

During the Senate committee hearings on the American Youth Act in March 1936, a nineteen-year-old road kid, William Fields of Brooklyn, New York, testified on behalf of the "Untouched Youth of America," an organization representing the transients. Fields said they had signed up six hundred members, though he admitted theirs was a very loose group, its adherents all on the road. Most of these homeless youth had become migrants because of the Depression; a minority being runaways from the brutalities of orphan homes and reform schools, a few looking for adventure who didn't last long when they came face to face with the tragedies and troubles of life on the road, and a very insignificant number of petty criminals.

Howard Gee, chief juvenile probation officer at Salt Lake City, Utah, kept records of 352 male transients under twenty-one who applied for shelter in June 1932. More than 75 percent were novices who had been on the road less than five months. Only 96 boys had a definite destination, 84 of them claiming to be on their way home. Eleven boys said that they were going to promised jobs, though one eighteen-year-old from Ohio revealed that this was at the invitation of a friend who wrote, "Come out to Los Angeles and I will get you a job at a hot dog stand."

The number of girls who rode with the army of boys was difficult to determine because the majority traveled in disguise for their safety. A sample census of the nation's homeless taken on three days in January 1933 revealed that among 256,000 persons reported 11,323 were women, of whom 35 to 40 percent appeared to be under twenty-one. Hobo expert Nels Anderson said that five years earlier there would have been less than 10 percent of that number of transient females. "We built up the West with boy transients and never worried about them until the last two or three years. The problem of homeless women is more recent and their number is increasing more rapidly than the number of boys," reported Anderson in 1933.

Riding with the road kids, Thomas Minehan estimated that 10 percent of those he met were girls. They traveled in pairs, sometimes with a boyfriend, and not infrequently with a tribe of ten or twelve boys. Minehan described "Kay," who was fifteen: "Her black eyes, fair hair, and pale cheeks are girlish and delicate. Cinders, wind, and frost have irritated but not toughened that tender skin. Sickly and suffering from chronic undernourishment, she appears to subsist almost entirely upon her finger-nails, which she gnaws habitually."

There were less scrupulous girl tramps, who made themselves available to all men and boys. "They enter a boxcar or jungle and without more ado, the line forms to the right," said Mine-han. "In one hobo camp in the grain belt, a pair of girls received thirty or forty men and boys in a boxcar, some men doubling back on the line. Promptly at six o'clock, the girls quit, de-manded their supper, divided seventy cents in nickels and dimes, and caught a night freight for the East."

The Wrong Side of the Tracks

On March 25, 1931, a freight train half a mile or so in length sped westward from Chattanooga toward Memphis. Two young women dressed in men's overalls and their seven male compan-ions, all white, occupied a gondola partially filled with crushed gravel. The freight stopped at Stevenson, Alabama, where a group of African Americans climbed aboard, among them nine boys who ranged in age from twelve to twenty years. Taunted by the white boys, the African American youths rushed them, with the result that six of their tormentors hastily leapt from the train. One of the six fell between two cars and was pulled back by an African Amer-ican youth, thereby most likely saving his life. Alerted by the van-quished white boys, a sheriff and an armed posse stopped the train at Paint Rock and ejected the trespassers, hauling them all to Scottsboro jail. The two girls, Ruby Bates and Victoria Price, fab-ricated a tale of rape by the nine young African Americans.

Barely a month passed when the accused, who would become known as the "Scottsboro Boys," stood in the Jackson County courthouse to hear an all-white jury pronounce its verdict after a farcical trial: Eight boys were found guilty and sentenced to death. The prosecution asked for life imprisonment for the twelve-year-old. Nevertheless seven jurors were adamant that the boy should also suffer the supreme penalty.

"If I leave my mother, it will mean one mouth less to feed," said Eugene Williams, thirteen, one of the condemned youths, explaining how he happened to be on the Memphis-bound freight that night. The Scottsboro Boys had their convictions overturned by the U.S. Supreme Court, only to be reconvicted by the Alabama courts. The four youngest, including Williams, were freed after spending six years in jail; four others were later paroled. Haywood Patterson, who was sentenced to seventy-five years, escaped in 1948 and fled to Michigan. Three years later, he was convicted of manslaughter. He died in prison.

Clarence Lee, a sharecropper's son, was living in Baton Rouge, Louisiana, when he left home in 1929 and rode the rails until 1931. He recalled how white hoboes were treated better than African Americans when it came to seeking the kindness of strangers. "When you went to people's homes to ask for food, if your skin was white you were fed better. They might let a white boy stay in the house with them, but me? I could sleep in the barn with the mules and hay."

In 1931, Lee narrowly escaped the summary justice of a Southern lynch mob: "I was leaving from Baton Rouge to go to Denham Springs, Louisiana, and this train made a stop in between. A man climbed aboard and spoke to the conductor. 'There's been a rape between here and Denham Springs,' I heard him say. 'That boy has to be put off here. They're going to lynch him.' He put me off right in the middle of a swamp. Probably saved my life."

The 1935 survey of twenty thousand transients conducted by Herman Schubert in Buffalo, New York, was one of the rare studies to tally African American youths. While the figures only give a picture of transients passing through a northern city, they are revealing. Schubert interviewed 2,308 whites and 662 African Americans in the fifteen to twenty-four age group.

The young African Americans had been on the road longer than the whites, the median age of wandering for the former about six months as compared with three months for the latter. Eighty-five percent of the white youths said they were seeking work; for the African Americans the amount was even higher, at 98 percent. Fifty percent of the African Americans had been unemployed for two years or longer.

"Are they bums? Not unless one wants to classify a goodly section of the remainder of the country's population as such," Schubert concluded.

In Harm's Way

Riding the freights brought constant peril, regardless of race or gender. As late as October 1937, five years after the wandering boys first hit the headlines, *Life* magazine published a primer for hobo "gaycats." A gaycat was a novice hobo, who was encouraged to follow the rules depicted in *Life*'s picture spread if he wanted to grow up to be a real "dingbat," a seasoned hobo. The magazine offered advice on safe ways to ride boxcars, gondolas, and "reefers," or refrigerator cars. It warned against riding on loose loads like scrap iron that could shift and crush a rider. As a cautionary example, the editors published a gory photograph of a rider cut in two by a train at Detroit Lakes, Minnesota.

The Interstate Commerce Commission's annual reports show that during the years 1929 to 1939, 24,647 trespassers were killed and 27,171 injured on railroad property. Since railroad agents placed the percentage of minors at one-third, there can be no doubt that thousands of young nomads met a gruesome fate on the rails.

Gene Wadsworth was seventeen, riding freights in California and Arizona. He teamed up with a boy he knew only as Jim. One freezing night, they were riding back-to-back on the ladders between boxcars. Recalled Wadsworth: "All of a sudden the train gave a jerk. I heard Jim let out a muffled moan as he fell. I whipped around and made a grab for him. I got his cap and a handful of blond hair. Jim was gone. Disappeared beneath the wheels. I felt so sick I had to climb up and lie on the catwalk. From then on, I was a loner."

At Phoenix, Arizona, that same winter, thirty-five young men and boys were removed from boxcars, some in advanced stages of pneumonia. One record showed seven transients killed while boarding moving trains within a period of ten days. Edward Vezolles was struck by a train in the railroad yards at Knoxville, Tennessee. When taken to a hospital, he wouldn't say who he was or where he came from. "Labeled a runaway," he recalls, "they paid me little attention. On the third day, since I was a nobody from nowhere, my leg was amputated. I was fifteen."

When General Pelham Glassford was surveying transient youths in the South, he met a seventeen-year-old boy who had been on the road for five months. The boy had just been released from a free hospital in Atlanta, where he had had an emergency appendectomy. The hospital turned him loose without a cent, four hundred miles from his home in Lacota, Florida. "He had not had anything to eat on the day I found him, and his condition was too awful to believe," said the general, who, to the lad's good fortune, drove him to his home.

Hospitals treated transients only if they were seriously ill. Hoboes suffered diseases due to exposure, lack of cleanliness, vermin, contagion, or infection. Ill-clad and undernourished, they sometimes went days without food. "I was hungry all the time. Dreadfully hungry," remembered John Fawcett. "I'd never been hungry before. I went two or three days without anything to eat. In a short time on the road, I lost fifteen to twenty pounds. Your hunger hurts physically."

Minehan reported that much of the conversation of young "tramps" concerned food, though the signs of malnutrition might not be evident to the casual observer. "But if the observer is critical, he will note the too prominent ribs, an abdomen too concave, and legs and arms on which the skin is loose and baggy. He will notice, too, the tired, hungry eyes, the nervous mannerism, and the habitual posture of weariness and want," said Minehan.

William Fields of the Untouched Youth of America was critical of missions, where half-starved road kids often sought handouts. According to Fields, most of the religious were made up of out-and-out racketeers, who used God and the Bible as a "front" for soliciting funds and clothes. A very small amount of each of these

was allotted for the care of the homeless. The result: vermin infested, foul-smelling, unhealthy lodgings; half-cooked, indigestible
slop called food; second-hand clothing received in return for many
hours' work at the woodpile or in the kitchen. "All this enveloped
in a maze of red tape and questionnaires," added Fields.

Physical hardships left many youths demoralized and vulnerable.
Famished and lonely, a wandering boy could become easy prey of
an older man. The "yeggs," master tramps of criminal bent, had
traditionally chosen runaway orphan boys or bright hobo kids and
schooled them Fagan-style in the yeggs' "specialty" of safe blowing, or "cracking a box." Their safecracking activities were well on
the wane during the Great Depression, so new apprentices were
schooled in the arts of petty crime, stealing, and borrowing.

There were older men variously referred to as "wolves,"
"airedales," or "jockers" who rode the freights to pick up young
boys. Nels Anderson found that any boy who had been on the
road long without being approached many times was an excep-
tion. "Mother Jones," a man in his fifties, told Anderson: "I never
saw a boy I couldn't get next to." The boy who was away from
home without money and who did not have the courage to beg
was the easiest to win over. More experienced boys would travel
with other boys to avoid the approaches of older men.

Minehan's boy tramp informants told him that every trainload
of transients had a wolf waiting to seduce boys. At times, the wiles
succeeded. The older man obtained clothes and food for the boy,
later teaching the boy how to get both for himself. "Far from being
miserable, the boy did not want to be separated from his friend. He
resented and refused all efforts at his 'rescue,'" said Minehan.

James Pearson was thirteen when he went on the road in the
summer of 1931. One night around 3 A.M., he was on a freight
train that pulled into a yard somewhere in Texas. Pearson told the
hoboes riding with him that he was going to find an empty boxcar
and sleep. A man in his thirties said he would go with him. "As
soon as we were inside the boxcar, the man said he was going to
have sex with me. I kept my cool. I told him I had to pee. When I

reached the door, I shoved it open and hit the ground running. I stayed in town three days to give the man time to move on. I was still scared when I went back to the freight yard to catch out."

The average American community, struggling to cope with their own welfare and relief burden, opted for a system of "passing on" transients. In the winter of 1931–32, the four thousand citizens of Deming, New Mexico, confronted a human flood as 125 transient men and boys descended on the small town each day. They arrived by Southern Pacific freight or by hitchhiking on the Bankhead Highway. It was sixty miles across the desert in either direction to the next town, making Deming an oasis for the nomads. Signs in the stores warned transients not to ask for help: "You can be fed and slept at the jail in return for ten days' hard labor." The travelers were given a night's lodging and a meal and told to move on by the police.

Getting in and out of town often brought a run-in with both the railroad police and the local officers. It was the railroad bulls' duty to eject trespassers from railroad property, which would send them down main street, where the town cops were equally unwilling to welcome them. At Tucson, Arizona, where 250 transients were arriving on the trains daily during the winter of 1931–32 (a majority considered by Southern Pacific special agent C. L. Meyers to be under twenty-one), the two branches of the law clashed over the intruders. Meyers arrested and handed over twenty-five or thirty trespassers to the town police. They were sentenced to twenty days, but were released after serving two days. Police Chief Dyer marched the transients down to the railroad yard and told them to get out of town. When Meyers objected, Dyers issued an ultimatum: "You brought them into town and you will take them out of town if it takes the whole force of Tucson to see that they go." They went. According to A. Wayne McMillen, who related this incident to the LaFollette-Costigan Committee, "the general rule of the police is to visit the jungles and shelters each morning and escort to the city limits those who show some tendency to stay longer than a day."

The city of Weatherford, Texas, went one step further: WPA

authorities reported that "when a person comes through town who is very much diseased, the city does not attempt to give such a person medical aid. Instead he is driven six or eight miles out of town and left on the highway." Writing in *The Nation*, John Kazarian, who called himself one of the "Starvation Army," told of one city in southern Florida where a vagrant had been placed in a chair to be questioned. In the midst of the examination, an electric current wired to his chair was turned on: "If the victim jumps a few feet out of his chair and demands an explanation, he is told, 'That's a present from this town! We want you to remember it and not come back here again.'"

Every state, city, town, and village threw up its defenses against those they called "unsettled persons," legalese for the desperate and hungry people on the march across America. Until the federal government's Temporary Emergency Relief Act of 1933 recognized the plight of the wanderers, communities depended on ancient vagrancy laws influenced by medieval attitudes toward a class of "locusts"—"beggars and vagabonds, who imitated the mendicant friars in wandering up and down the country with lying tales of distress, either of mind or body," as Martin Luther described in his preface to the *Book of Vagabonds* in 1528. "I have myself of late years been cheated and slandered by such tramps and liars more than I care to confess."

H. T. Roach was eighteen in 1935, riding the rails in search of work. What stood out most vividly for him years later was the wide differences in attitude in the different regions he passed through. "The Midwesterners were the most empathetic. The Atlantic region shunned the floating population of hoboes; job opportunities were absolutely nonexistent for outsiders. The people in the Southeast were the least helpful, and the cops were often cruel and brutal. The mountain states and interior California offered us work, but Los Angeles declared war on us. I was on a freight train that was stopped at the Arizona-California border. A small army of railroad agents swept down the train and kicked off upwards of six hundred of us. They left us standing in the silent desert."

In 1936, the Los Angeles police blockaded a section of the California border to turn back jobless transients. Colorado gave its national guardsmen the duty of stopping the influx to its sugar beet fields. Armed sentry posts were set up to meet trains, buses, and cars crossing state lines.

Boys caught in freight yards were summarily beaten by notorious railroad bulls like Texas Slim, who ruled the yards at Longview, Texas. Denver Bob was reputed to have shoved trespassers beneath the wheels of moving trains. At Niland, California, a gun-toting bull robbed Henry Koczur and his two companions of a total of $2.70, Henry himself unable to contribute a cent to the man's pickings.

Many young riders reported being put in jail, not for a night's rest, but to do forced labor on the local pea farm or chain gang. John C. Lint of Virginia had been riding a freight train all night with two friends, when they got off to stretch their legs at a stop in Cottondale, Florida. A plainclothes bull took them into custody and drove them to Marianna, where a judge sentenced them to sixty days on a county farm. "We were fourteen, fifteen, and seventeen years old," says Lint. "When we were discharged, the warden handed us each four dollars. His son offered to drive us to Marianna for that sum. The ride was declined."

Though often shunned and sent on their way, the wanderers also experienced countless acts of kindness. Roger Brown had been riding the rails for three years since leaving high school, when he arrived in Fargo, North Dakota, one night in July 1933. He walked down Broadway Street, where a passing train was blocking a crossing. As he waited, he struck up a conversation with a neatly dressed young man, telling him he'd come from Ohio to look for work in the harvest fields.

"The young man asked if I was hungry," Brown recalls. "Of course, I was, but when he took me to a hotel coffee shop, I said I was too dirty to enter. He insisted, and told the waitress to serve me a chicken dinner complete with dessert. When the man left, the waitress told me that he was her boss, Tom Powers. He'd also instructed her to give me a room for the night. It was the first time in my life that I stayed at a hotel. The next morning breakfast was waiting for me in the coffee shop.

"I knew the shame of going door to door begging for food. Tom Powers gave me more than a place to stay that night. He gave me dignity."

Bitter Harvest

In summer, boys followed the harvests in the West. They called themselves "bindle stiffs," from the migratory hoboes who carried their wares in a rolled-up bundle from job to job. A young hobo might start with the hay harvest in California and the Rocky Mountain states in early summer. Later on there was corn and wheat in the Midwest; and in the early fall, hops, berries, and fruits in the Pacific Northwest. Winter could be spent in the cotton fields of Texas and the Southwest. In early spring, a harvester might drift into Southern California for the vegetable and citrus crops.

It was backbreaking work at starvation wages, and sometimes no wages at all. For three weeks in 1934, Burton Williams, sixteen, and his brother Vic, fourteen, picked cotton for a grower in Elk City, Oklahoma. "We worked hard and thought we had made enough money for some clothes and shoes," said Burton. "When we told the cotton grower we were quitting and going home, he said, 'You have thirty-five cents each coming.' That's all we got for three weeks' work."

Thousands of young men and boys working on the land for a pittance were refugees from drought-stricken regions and farms where they'd been "tractored out of a job." Predominant were the Dust Bowl migrants—"people in flight from the terror behind," as John Steinbeck described them in *The Grapes of Wrath*. While families of rural pilgrims like the Joads struggled west in their jalopies, unattached Okie youths preferred by far the relative luxury of a free ride on a Southern Pacific freight.

As the human flood rolled on unabated, even ill-paid seasonal agricultural work became hard to find. Farming communities first looked to their own unemployed for harvest hands. Families often had one, two, and sometimes three unmarried people at home, with little hope of obtaining outside jobs. A long-time migratory worker told Lurene Irwin, an Iowa tenant farmer's wife, of the appearance of firearms among the young. "In my day, guns were almost unheard of," he said. "It is different now. You find high school kids on the road armed. They can't get work, and they're sick of begging the old man for cigarette money. They're out for what they can get while it lasts."

The rootless existence of the migrant laborers held scant security. A boy who got started on the roving life going from job to job—with a couple of months idleness in between—could become a drifter and a floater, never able to learn a skilled occupation, keep a steady job, or establish a home.

"It took a long time to make a Wise Stiff out of me," Frank Bunce said in the *Forum*, when he wrote about his futile search for work. He described a "Wise Stiff" as one who had resigned himself to the futility of looking for more than the merest means of sustenance. He knew the good pastures, such rare places as Des Moines and Dallas, where the one-night-only rule was not tightly enforced. "In the coldest weather he hugs the Gulf Coast and the lower Rio Grande Valley and blandly boos the boys who are going sleepless and trying to get to Toledo and Detroit where things are picking up."

Psychiatrist John Levy once suggested to a transient he interviewed in New York that adversity was good for character development. The young man responded with a cynical laugh. "Hell," he replied, "you might be able to come back after the first defeat, but what happens after four straight years of it?"

In testimony to the Senate Committee on Education and Labor hearings on the American Youth Act in March 1936, Texas university student Otto Mullinax warned of "wasted youth roaming the streets searching for enough work to keep body together, forgetting soul entirely, and developing a bitter, cynical attitude on life."

As America's ragged army of boys marched into the conscience of the nation, they stirred fears about a different movement of disaffected youth. The young men and boys of Germany, the *wandervögels*, who'd looked for the meaning of life around the camp fire, now crowded the beer halls and stadiums to hear a message of salvation from Adolf Hitler. Fueled by anger and bitterness, with no hope of employment as unemployment rocketed after 1929, the German youth movement went political. The majority split between the two extreme parties, communist and Nazi. When Hitler gained control of the government in 1933, his brown-shirted boys stood ready to combat the enemies of the "Aryan" race—Jews, communists, and socialists—on their path to rule. In Italy, too, ragged mobs who had molested people in the streets became the regimented Fascisti behind Mussolini.

A New Deal for Youth

On March twenty-one, 1933, barely two weeks into his presidency, Franklin D. Roosevelt sent a message to Congress. It stated in part: "I propose to create a Civilian Conservation Corps to be used in simple work, not interfering with normal employment and confining itself to forestry, the prevention of soil erosion, flood control and similar projects. I estimate that 250,000 men can be given temporary employment by early summer if you give me authority to proceed within two weeks." Before the close of his first month in office, FDR signed an act creating the Civilian Conservation Corps (CCC), in which unemployed and unmarried men between the ages of eighteen and twenty-five were eligible to enroll. They were to be paid thirty dollars a month, of which twenty-five dollars was to be sent directly to their needy and dependent families.

So urgent and volatile did the administration view this youth crisis that the first camp was set up on April 17, 1933—just twelve days after the CCC was officially inaugurated. Two hundred CCC enrollees were trucked to "Camp Roosevelt" in the George Washington National Forest near Luray, Virginia, to begin work under the supervision of the United States Forestry

Service. By early July, 250,000 young men were settled in 1,468 forest and park camps. They were supervised by 25,000 war veterans and 25,000 experienced woodsmen.

In ten years, the CCC took 2.5 million youths from the ranks of the unemployed and put them to work planting 200 million trees, building dams, fighting forest fires, and clearing beaches and campgrounds. FDR provided youth with a new frontier to pioneer.

Gene Lamb rode freights across the states before joining the CCC. "I was on trains with families of migrants, mom, dad, and the children. When we stopped, the women would get off and go into stores like Piggly Wiggly. They took food off the counter, not a lot, just enough to feed the kids. I know in my mind that the CCC and the WPA saved this country from a revolution."

The National Youth Administration (NYA) provided fifty camps for five thousand young women and girls, for periods of three to four months. These camps offered job training and education. The girls earned their subsistence on work projects such as making visual aids for public schools and supplies for hospitals and state institutions, and working in tree nurseries of the Forest Service. The young women received a monthly payment of five dollars to meet personal expenses.

The NYA had been created in January 1935 to provide work-study jobs of a maximum of six dollars a month for needy high school students. College students could earn twenty dollars and graduate students forty dollars. Out-of-school youths were given employment on work projects. At its peak of operations in late spring 1936, the NYA was giving direct cash benefits to 581,320 young people between the ages of sixteen and twenty-five, over 45 percent of them females.

Critics levied the charge that the $50 million allotted to the NYA was insufficient to minister to five to eight million young people. In Virginia, for example, of 180,000 unemployed youths, only 25,000 were eligible for NYA assistance. Of these 5,000 at most could be cared for, with 2,400 high school students receiving aid. In May 1935, 400,000 African American children between the ages of fourteen and sixteen were on welfare rolls: the NYA had 19,000 African American youths on its list throughout the entire United States.

Critics also charged that NYA work-study projects were merely robbing Peter to pay Paul. Students were doing day jobs formerly held by school clerks, janitors, and gardeners. High school students in Rochester, New York, complained that they were doing forty hours work for six dollars a week, or just fifteen cents an hour. "To young Americans living in what should be the heyday of life, the period of golden youth, is offered in the seventh year of economic crisis, the privilege of working for candy and cigarettes," said William W. Hinckley, chairman of the American Youth Congress.

Hinckley was speaking at the March 1936 hearings on the American Youth Act, which was designed to replace the NYA. The Act was not to be restricted to members of families on relief. It provided for free public education for students in high school and vocational school and called for living expenses to needy students of not less than fifteen dollars a month. Political constraints and budget cuts led to the American Youth Act's being killed "in committee," prompting a "Youth Pilgrimage on Jobs and Education" to march on Washington in February 1937. The protests succeeded in saving the NYA, itself under siege by cost-cutting conservatives on both sides of the House.

The American Youth Congress, a federation of youth and student organizations based in New York and claiming to represent 1,300,000 young people, issued a Declaration of Rights of American Youth: "Our country, with its natural resources and mighty industries, can more than provide a life of security and comfort for all. We want to work, to produce, to build, but millions of us are forced to be idle. We graduate from schools and colleges equipped for careers and professions, but there are no jobs. You can find us along the highways, or in Army supervised camps, isolated from friends and family. We refuse to be the lost generation."

Despite a new deal for young people spearheaded by the CCC and the NYA, tens of thousands of young men and women continued to ride freight trains and hitchhike on the highways.

The CCC was primarily aimed at enlisting boys over the age of eighteen. Those who were younger, or ineligible to enroll, were free to continue wandering.

In May 1933, the government established a Federal Transient Relief Service to help the multitude of destitute people of all ages. By May 1934, the migrants were being catered to in 283 federal transient centers and camps.

At the Los Angeles Transient Intake Bureau in Griffith Park, ten thousand boys under age twenty-one registered between December 1933 and November 1934. This was an influx of nearly one thousand young nomads a month, more than in any other city in the country. Southern California established separate facilities for these young people. After registration and a physical examination, each boy was interviewed by a counselor, who tried to induce the boy to return home. Those wishing to go back were sent to one of two work camps, where they were able to earn the cost of their return transportation. Boys were not forced to go back against their will, for this would probably result in their becoming migrants soon thereafter. Attempts were made to find them work, educational fellowships, or a place in the CCC.

Thomas Minehan, who had joined the boy and girl tramps, believed the Federal Transient Service was itself contributing to the problem. It was possible for a boy aged sixteen to travel from Maine to Florida, stopping off at transient camps where the food was fair and conditions often excellent. A boy could stay two or three days without doing any work, perhaps inveigle the director into giving him some new clothes, and then hit the road again. Rarely would such a vagabond have to travel more than a day before reaching another camp.

But George Outland, the boys' welfare supervisor for the Los Angeles Transient Service, reported on the cases of 3,352 young migrants registered at Los Angeles in 1934–35. Exactly one hundred boys said they left home because they wanted to experience life in a transient camp. Of these one hundred, ninety-four were Mexican boys from the two cities of El Paso and Phoenix. A third of their families were on relief. Those who had stayed at the Los Angeles transient center returned home with glowing tales of the royal treatment they received and encouraged their friends to make the trip. The El Paso boys were touring at government expense, but the great majority had left home for economic and social reasons.

Outland did a follow-up study of 251 boys who were sent home from Los Angeles. Their home agencies were contacted five months after the boys had left California. All but three had returned to their homes. Of the 251 boys, 43 had been unable to make a go of it at home and had hit the road again.*

"As there's no single answer to why boys leave home, there's no single answer to what will keep them there after—and if—they go back," said one case worker. "But if I had to make such an answer it would be jobs. Just that. Honest-to-goodness jobs that would let a fellow feel that he's a man, running his own life."

Those jobs would only come when the Great Depression ended as the country prepared for war. For millions of young people who had found no place in the country's schools, fields, or factories, there would be a place on the battlefields. In 1942, even as the CCC camps were winding down, thousands of "Depression Doughboys," who had served in FDR's "Tree Army," were on their way to Europe and Africa. As trains carrying troops and matériel crossed the country day and night, the occasional rider could still be glimpsed in a boxcar door or sitting on the catwalk. It was the end of the last hobo era. The boys and girls who rode the rails had gone to war.

---

* One hundred forty-three boys were still at home; 23 were living with friends or relatives; 28 were in the CCC; 2 were in jail; 9 had moved elsewhere. Fifty-two boys had found full-time jobs; 28 were working part-time; 23 had gone back to school. Seventy-six boys had no occupation. Three had died.

Catching Out

L eaving home was often the most wrenching decision the boxcar boys and girls faced in their young lives. They had witnessed the slow impoverishment of their families, as fathers went from half time to no time at all, and mothers struggled to put food on the table for them and their siblings. Some had always known poverty: children whose fathers earned starvation wages in depressed coal-mining regions of West Virginia, or whose families eked out a living as tenant farmers sharecropping in the South.

There were traditional runaways, like those fleeing an abusive stepfather or cruel stepmother, and orphans escaping institutions that treated their wards with Dickensian ferocity. There were runaways from happy homes, still enjoying all the comforts but hankering for a life of adventure, "for the magic carpet—romance—the click of the rails."

Girls especially never took the decision to hit the road lightly, for they knew they were stepping into a world filled with danger. It was the same for young African Americans, for whom the beckoning rails could be doubly perilous should they lead into towns where the color of their skin would make them outcasts.

Whatever the reason they left home, they each faced a defining moment when they had to "catch out" and hop their first freight. From that point on, there was no turning back.

Camelot Crashed and Burned

"Glens Falls, New York was my Camelot. Toboggan slides and skating at the park in winter. Swimming at the lake in summer. My father was so smart. He put in the first phones, working with Western Electric and AT&T. My mother was beautiful. My little sister was fun."

Edward Vezolles cherished his boyhood memories of growing up in the small town of Glens Falls on the Hudson River. He was nine years old when Western Electric laid off his father at the height of the Great Depression. "Camelot, as I knew it, crashed and burned. We had family at Louisville, Kentucky, and moved there. My Dad supervised a WPA project for a year. Mother took in boarders at Derby time. My dad got sick. TB was the killer then. Dad died."

Edward, his mother, and his sister were living with his grand-parents when the Flood of 1937 drove two hundred thousand Louisville residents from their homes. Even more relatives sought shelter with his grandparents. Eleven people were staying in three bedrooms. Edward fell ill, half-blinded by an infection in his optic nerves. At fourteen, he was old enough to have a paper route with the *Louisville Times*. His mother helped him deliver morning papers by reading the house numbers. At Christmas, Edward won a live turkey in a subscription drive. Presented with the bird, he tied its legs together and rode his bicycle home, the bird flopping on his back.

"'There must be something better than this,' I told myself. I hung around the rail yards to find out how to catch a freight train to Florida. I wanted warmth, sun, something exciting and free. I picked up and left."

The private crash of Edward Vezolles's world was repeated in millions of American homes amid the human catastrophe un-leashed by Wall Street in the five days from October 24 to October 29, 1929. The panic on the New York Stock Exchange on Black Tuesday convulsed preexisting fault lines of the American economy, society, and culture.

Through the Roaring Twenties, agriculture, energy, and soft-coal mining had been on shaky ground. In that decade the value of farm land fell 30 to 40 percent, even as farmers' indebtedness soared. Bank failures averaged six hundred a year. Mergers swallowed up six thousand previously independent companies, leaving over half of American industry controlled by two hundred corporations. By 1929, the richest .01 percent of Americans had a combined income equal to the bottom 42 percent. More than half of all Americans lived on the edge of—or below—the minimum subsistence level.

The productivity of industrial workers rose 43 percent from 1919 to 1929, but while American producers could deliver the goods, they were finding it increasingly difficult to sell their products at home or overseas, where a fragile European consumer market was already shrinking.

The boom-and-bust land rushes in California and Florida in 1923 and 1926 were indicators of the speculative mania abounding throughout the nation. The stock market began its spectacular rise in those years. When the day of reckoning arrived, a million people held shares, not only the financiers of lower Manhattan, but small-town merchants, farmers, schoolteachers, and clergymen, all gambling on getting a piece of heaven on earth.

The tsunami that hit Wall Street in October 1929 swept everything in its path until the economy hit rock bottom in 1933. About nine thousand banks failed and $2.5 billion in deposits was lost. Unemployment rose from 1.5 million in 1929 to nearly 13 million, or about one in four of the labor force. Not since the Civil War had the American nation stared so deeply into the abyss.

In the eyes of the young, what mattered was the odd dime or nickel for a movie matinee or a few "coppers" to toss away on Tootsie Rolls and licorice sticks. Even an enterprising go-getter like Edgar Bledsoe, who had his own business at eleven, didn't have the foggiest notion of the goings-on on Wall Street. Edgar lived in Ardmore, Oklahoma, where a thousand people danced at the city bandstand on Saturday nights, reveling in the prosperity brought by oil and cotton. His parents' having divorced, Edgar stayed with his mother and sister. In March 1925, fire destroyed their home, forcing them to accept help from others. "It was a while before I realized that charity was not a disgrace, but an old Latin word for love," mused Edgar, reflecting on those days.

One day, Edgar was admiring the new lawn mowers in the window of Lane's Hardware, when the owner came out and offered to sell him a mower. "Heck, Mr. Lane, I'm only a kid. I don't have that kind of money," Edgar said. Lane asked for two dollars down, the balance of eighteen dollars to be paid out of Edgar's earnings mowing lawns. He never missed a payment. Over the next four years, he built up a lawn-mowing business that supplemented his mother's earnings as a seamstress: They never lacked for the necessities.

Then, one day in October 1929, Edgar heard a newsboy yelling, "Extra! Extra! Stock Market collapses."

"I ran home and told Mother that a cattle auction barn had collapsed. It must've killed many cattle and some people, too, because the newsboy sounded like it was pretty serious. That's what a stock market meant to me at the time."

By next summer, Edgar knew it was more serious than a barn caving in. Many local people had lost their jobs or were forced to take a salary cut. Others tightened their purse strings for fear the ax could drop on them at any time. Edgar's customers began to cut their own lawns or reduce his pay by half.

"When I was sixteen, I couldn't earn as much as I could at twelve. When it got to where the money I was bringing in could not pay for the food I was consuming, I grew more and more restless."

Leo Truscon's father worked at Ford's River Rouge plant in Dearborn, Michigan. He had a sure indicator of when times were good or bad. The smokestacks of the River Rouge power plant were visible from all parts of Dearborn. When the stacks were pouring out smoke, it meant full production, as happened with the changeover from the Model T to the Model A in 1927. On a day in June 1931, when Truscon was fifteen, he saw but two stacks clouding the sky. A notice appeared on workers' time cards: "Do not punch time card unless you agree to a 50 percent cut in your salary."

Truscon's father was laid off. "Our mortgage payments couldn't be met. We lost the house and moved to a small rented place," Leo recalled. "Later my father was assigned work as bricklayer on a WPA sewer project and received a food and rent allowance." When two friends sent Leo a postcard from Los Angeles, the road beckoned.

James San Jule's father was a successful businessman in Tulsa, Oklahoma. James graduated from Tulsa Central High School in 1929 at sixteen; he'd already been accepted at Amherst College in Massachusetts, and was planning to go on to Harvard Law School. Because of his youth, his father wanted him to wait a year and arranged for him to work as an office boy in the Exchange National Bank at Tulsa, where the father was on the board of directors.

"I didn't think much of money in those days. It was just something we had," said San Jule. "My father was probably a millionaire. We owned fancy cars, a fancy house, fancy everything. I led the ordinary life of a wealthy kid, nothing spectacular." He was working in the bank in October 1929 when the debacle began. "Of course, you didn't believe it. 'This is something that happens,' you thought. 'It will pass.'"

The Crash wiped out San Jule's father financially and physically. "It was a horrible, horrible period, about which I understood little. What's a kid to do? You have no worries about anything. You're going to Amherst and Harvard. All of sudden your life is blasted out of existence. It felt like being de-princed."

In the winter of 1930, San Jule ran away from home, not quite sure where he was going, or even why he was leaving. It just seemed the right thing to do.

There Was Never Any Money

For the young boy or girl born on the other side of the tracks, Black Tuesday darkened an already bleak existence. William Wallace was twelve years old in 1933, staying in Okmulgee, Oklahoma, with his mother, stepfather, and fifteen-year-old sister, Fannie. Looking back on that awful year, Wallace states bluntly, "Living didn't seem to be for me."

Wallace's stepfather, Evert Stubblefield, worked for Oklahoma governor W. B. Pine, on the governor's hog ranch. Bertie Frances, his mother, was employed in the Okmulgee city cannery, where hog meat and produce was canned for families on relief.

"Fannie and I would walk to the grease-rendering plant, where they cooked the hog meat. They gave away the rinds for free, all you could carry. We would take balloon jars to a sugarcane mill and buy sorghum molasses for fifty cents a gallon. We collected fruit and vegetables thrown out at a warehouse. My mother would can these for winter."

Wallace's flight from Okmulgee began in the winter of 1933, when Bertie Frances received a letter from her brother in California. He offered Frances and Evert jobs, provided they arrived within two months. The family decided to leave that night, each member dressing in two sets of clothing and taking whatever possessions they could carry. They had $4.50 to get to the promised land.

Christine Wolfrum's father was a miner for seventeen years until the Depression. "There was never any money," recalled Christine, who was born in Kentucky in 1921. "School paper cost thirty-five cents a year. It would take me all year to get the money, a few cents at a time. Teachers would embarrass you continually asking when you would bring it in. You figured, 'probably never.'" When Christine was eleven, she went on the road with her family, including her nine-year-old brother and her sickly mother. They trekked through Kentucky, Tennessee, North Carolina, and Ohio on her father's search for work. "We told our friends we were traveling by bus or train, but we were really hitchhiking."

Lee Leer, a grocer's son, found home to be no more than "a place of existence." His father's general store at Olive, Oklahoma, failed in the early 1930s. Lee's parents, who had six children, moved to an abandoned cotton farm a few miles outside town. They eked out a living, working to raise the food they ate and a few extra bales of cotton for cash. On a spring morning in 1937, when Lee's mother ordered him to fetch stove wood, he took his savings earned from picking cotton and selling a pig, collected his bedroll, and left to begin life as a hobo: "Little did I realize that life could be worse than on that forty-acre cotton farm, and that I would even become homesick," he recalled later.

While children might have had difficulty comprehending the slow unraveling of home life, a single defining moment could capture it all. Coyle Case's family were "Sooners," who had staked out their claim in the first Oklahoma land rush of 1889. Growing up in the town of Padua, Coyle saw the land literally blown away in the "black blizzards" of the Dust Bowl, which desiccated the western Great Plains in the early 1930s. He watched as friends and neighbors were dispossessed. "They swept and shoveled, planted and prayed, but finally the banks moved in like vultures," Coyle recollects. "My friends left in battered cars and trucks piled high with children and dogs and mattresses and cooking utensils."

His grandfather, Wallace Case, held no debts and owned the land on which he raised cattle. The income from the sale of the cattle and cream kept the family from starving.

"Poppa Case was my hero. A giant tree higher than any other on my childhood landscape. On a day I recall vividly, I met my grandfather at the edge of a canyon, sobbing as though his heart would break," says Coyle. His grandparents had witnessed government agents shoot his cattle herd, a forced stock liquidation in compliance with the Agricultural Adjustment Act aimed at stabilizing prices. "Poppa Case was the rock to which our very existence was anchored. I had never seen him cry before. I knew something was wrong."

Brooklyn teenager Harold Dropkin would never forget February 1, 1933. Around noon that day, he was sitting in the kitchen of his home when there was a knock at the door. A well-dressed young man asked his mother for something to eat. Invited inside, the stranger sat down at the table. Harold's mother asked her son to get a can of tuna fish from the refrigerator. Opening the fridge, Harold saw only one item: the can of tuna fish. His mother spread the tuna on three slices of bread and gave one to their guest. When he finished, the young man thanked them and left. "I walked over

to the refrigerator and looked inside. Nothing. *Nada*, " Harold remembered more than sixty years later.

In September 1932, Duval Edwards was looking forward to his
senior year in high school at Alexandria, Louisiana. He knew
times were tough for his family, though he didn't realize the difficulty his father was having in bringing home enough money for
them to live on.

"Dad was a Texan, a true longhorn born on the Texas frontier
in 1874. He could barely write his own name, but he developed
an exceptional skill. He could look at a steer or cow and figure its
weight with uncanny accuracy. In good times, he made a fair
profit buying and selling cattle," Duval wrote in a personal memoir. Before the Depression, his father owned a slaughterhouse.
He'd been forced to close it in 1930. He used his old Model T to
haul, buy, and sell cattle as an independent, but as the economy
continued to slide, the price of beef on the hoof plummeted to five
cents a pound. Duval remained unaware of his father's struggle
until the roof fell in.

"I overheard Mother ask Dad for grocery money. I saw him
pull out a single wrinkled and torn dollar bill and hand it to her.
He left without saying a word, grim-faced, his battered cowboy
hat on his head. I watched him get into the old truck, set the
hand brake, the spark and gas levers. He climbed out to turn the
crank, then hopped back in and slowly rattled off. For the first
time my eyes opened all the way. The full extent of our situation
dawned on me. It was desperate."

Go Fend for Yourself

The realization that a child's family was flat broke, or just hard
pressed to put food on the table, was the reason many boys decided
to "hit the road." One less mouth to feed would lessen the burden
on their parents, they believed, and in many homes it was true.

In the summer of 1933, Leslie Paul was eighteen years old,
newly graduated from high school in Duluth, Minnesota, the son

and stepson of railroad men. His house was close by a railroad yard, where Paul often played a cat-and-mouse game with the "bulls"—the railroad detectives. Walking through the yard one day that summer, he saw a bundle laying on a pile of switch ties. He picked it up and unfolded it: A hobo's blanket had been sewn together to make a sleeping bag.

"It was the Depression and I could find no work. I was a burden on Mother and Gus, my stepfather. I knew then what I must do," says Paul.

He took the blanket and went home. He said nothing to his mother, only that he was going to the store to buy a box of cigarettes. When he returned home, he announced his departure.

"Mother didn't fight it, but she was sad. She owned no suitcase or tote; she gave me a black satin bag, the size of a pillowcase, to carry my things. I jammed my 'sleeping bag' inside, three or four pairs of socks, shorts, an old sweater. Mother handed me all the money in her purse: seventy-two cents. I gave her a big kiss and a long, tight hug. The tears were streaming down her face. I left with the black satin bag over my shoulder. Had I been brave enough to turn around, I would have been coward enough to go back."

By age eight, Clarence Lee was responsible for caring for a younger brother and sister while his mother washed and ironed clothes for others. Times got so bad for the family that they left Baton Rouge and went into sharecropping. When Clarence Lee was sixteen, his father told him he would have to leave home.

"The landowners put a mortgage on our lives," said Clarence. "We were degraded from people down to merchandise. We were bought and sold over and over again."

Clarence recalls his family's sharecropping slavery as "the dark days." Lying in bed at night in total darkness, getting up in the morning before sunrise and beginning work, working until the sun goes down and never seeing a dollar—to Clarence, even at high noon, it was dark.

"I lived like that until I was sixteen years old. I wanted to stay home and fight the poverty with my family, but my father told me

I had to leave. 'Go fend for yourself,' he said. 'I can't afford to have you around any longer.' It was very hurting, but I had to go."

For Robert Chaney, one of ten children, the parental advice he received at seventeen was just as direct: "If I were a strong, healthy boy like you, I wouldn't hang around here and eat off my old man, I would go to California," he was told. The next evening, Robert left Wadsworth, Ohio, with a friend. His mother had given him fifty cents and a lunch bag filled with fried green tomatoes and peanut butter sandwiches.

Fathers and sons sometimes left home together in search of work. Berkeley "Bill" Hackett started selling newspapers on the streets of Flint, Michigan, at the age of eight. One of six children living with his mother and stepfather on a two-acre plot, all the members of his family pitched in to help put food on the table. One night in summer 1929, when Bill was thirteen, his stepfather came home wide-eyed with excitement. "I've found a job unloading coal cars in Kalamazoo," he said. The pay was twenty-five cents an hour for a ten-hour day. Howard told the family that he was taking Bill to work with him.

With no car and no money, the pair had to ride the rails to Kalamazoo, 150 miles away. Bill remembered his mother taking all the clothes she could find and putting them on him. Then, "in the wee misty hours after midnight, Howard and I made our way to the switchyard to find a train that would take us to that wonderful promise of employment."

Daniel Elliot's father lost the job he'd held for twenty years. At thirteen, Daniel was out of school and helping his Dad, who'd moved to Denver from Kansas. The only work he could find was as a street vendor for the Denver Tamale Company. When his father took work on a ranch at Mountain Home, Wyoming, Daniel went with him, but this job also ended. Father and son walked over the mountains to catch a freight at Laramie, Wyoming, heading for the Idaho potato harvest, the first of many trains Daniel would ride as a young hobo.

* * *

On the road with the young nomads in 1932, Thomas Minehan reported that more than three out of four boys and girls stated that hard times drove them away from home. One Ohio social worker depicted these destitute children: "They have known no financial security, have come from homes broken for that reason, harried, kicked around, and dazed by things beyond their control. Lost, resentful because they have aged too quickly, they cry for something they cannot get from their own group. They are too old and yet too young. They have seen too much and know too much—have thought too little. They may be sixteen to twenty-one in years, but in some things they are thirty, and in others ten."

Gene Wadsworth's father died when he was two years old, his mother when he was eleven, orphaning Gene and his four sisters. The children were farmed out to relatives. Gene landed up in a small Western town with an uncle who had five children of his own. From his first day with his new family, his aunt let him know he was not welcome. The youngest child in the house, Gene had to milk his uncle's cows and feed other livestock. He turned seventeen in 1932 and had just entered his second year in high school when one of his cousins addressed him: "Why do you hang around here where you're not wanted?" That night Gene stuffed his meager possessions in a flour sack and started down the road. Years later, he still remembered his despair: "I was about as low as a kid could get as I walked over the Snake River Bridge. I was thinking of suicide, looking down into the black water, but I kept walking. A freight train was pulling out of a little town. I stopped to let it pass. I'll never know why I reached out and grabbed a rung of a boxcar ladder. I climbed to the catwalk and hung on for dear life. I'd never been on a train before and was scared stiff."

James Pearson's stepfather had three boys and one girl. "They couldn't do anything wrong and I couldn't do anything right," Jim recalls. He ran away from home in Newton, North Carolina, in summer 1931, when he was thirteen. He got as far as El Paso, when he became homesick. He panhandled a penny for a postcard and wrote home. "Mom, I'm coming back. Not because I have to but because I want to. Love, Jim."

When he reached home, peace reigned for a while. Then his stepfather was caught bootlegging whiskey. He was put on a chain gang for two months. Jim went to the welfare office, where he was given a work-relief job for two days a week. He worked nine hours for a $1.80 food allowance at the A&P, plus a twenty-four-pound bag of flour doled out by the government. When his stepfather was released, he showed no gratitude to Jim, who'd been the sole support of his family. Their troubles flared up again.

"This time I hugged my mom and told her I'd keep in touch," said Jim. "I didn't want to leave, but felt I had no choice."

In the early 1930s, Betty Stone served as a caseworker at the Brace Newsboys Home, which opened its shelter to migrants arriving in Manhattan. Ms. Stone observed, "Frequently the boys said they had left home because of a cruel stepmother, and sure enough, frequently social workers would write back that it was true."

Orphanages contributed heavily to the army of wandering boys. In July 1931, nine-year-old Richard Myers' mother, who was gravely ill, signed him over to a Pittsburgh orphanage. The next day Richard was on a train to Iowa, where he had been placed with a farm family.

"They beat me and practically enslaved me," Richard recalled. After a month and a half, he ran away, but was picked up by the police and returned to his guardians. Within two weeks, he fled again, riding the rails back to Pittsburgh. He found his mother out of danger and they were reunited.

John Gojack's mother had perished in the Great Flu Epidemic of 1918. His father, Janos, worked at the Dayton Pipe Company, laboring all day at a fiery drop-forge hammer. Unable to cope with six children, Janos kept his three girls at home and put three boys in the care of the Sisters of the Precious Blood in Dayton. From the age of six, Gojack made repeated efforts to flee, on one occasion after being beaten and having his head shaven for speaking in

Hungarian, his mother tongue. "My runaway attempts failed until age twelve, when I discovered the railroad," Gojack wrote in his memoirs. "It was no trick for a swift, skinny kid to grab the rung of a ladder on a slow-moving freight, then climb up on top or swing into an empty boxcar, going who knows where."

Gy Thomas was pushed out of the McCune Home for Boys near Independence, Missouri, where he spent twelve of his childhood years. In 1937, the home released all boys over seventeen in an attempt to reduce costs. Thomas made his way to Kansas City, where he lived on the streets until he became disgusted with a life of begging. He made his way to the rail yards, where hopping a freight "came almost as second nature."

Scenery Bums

The majority of the youths riding the rails across the United States did so out of desperation and hope, most fleeing abject poverty and want. As the Great Depression wore on, these needy children were joined by increasing numbers of youth out for adventure. Parents often gave their blessing to these "scenery bums," who hit the road in summer to escape forced idleness and boredom at home.

In the summer of 1931, the "five 'boes" of Freeport, Illinois, struck out for the West in an old car bought for twenty-five dollars. The car got a flat tire before they reached the city limits, and finally died on them at Rock Rapids, Iowa. The five hoboes, ages sixteen to eighteen, rode the rails and hitchhiked to the Grand Canyon and other sights of the West. They made it all the way to San Francisco and then back home across the Mojave Desert. The six-week adventure of Robert Schmelzle and his four companions made headlines in the *Freeport Journal-Standard* of August 10, 1931. It told of their return and said, "the boys enjoyed the journey despite the hardships and declared they wouldn't have missed the experience for anything."

When James Carroll graduated from high school in 1932 and couldn't find a job, he took his savings of twenty-four dollars and left to discover the United States. "I rode the locomotive tender out of the Pittsburgh and Lake Erie Railroad station. The moon was full, the sky was clear and the weather was perfect. I had never been more than thirty miles from home, and now I was free, on my own, beginning a wonderful adventure."

However, not every boy adventurer took off with mom or dad's approval. At Fort Worth, Texas, Claude Franklin, thirteen; his brother Charles, sixteen; and their friend Robert Brookshire, also thirteen, planned their trip for three weeks. The night before departing, they put extra clothes in paper sacks, sneaked them out of the house, and buried them under bushes. They set out after lunch on Sunday, May 8, 1938, taking a supply of candy bars and forty cents. "We headed for the Texas and Pacific Railroad yards," said Claude. "We left no note, because we didn't want to be stopped. What a cruel thing to do on Mother's Day!"

In New York City, two days after graduating from high school in 1932, Hank Kaban told his mother that he was going on a picnic with friends. His mother packed a lunch for him. "I got on a subway train and was off to see the United States!" says Hank.

The impulse to wander could come from the experts themselves—veteran hoboes who could cast a spell over a red-blooded boy, as Nels Anderson suggested in his 1923 study of juveniles. At Brewton, Alabama, a small creek a quarter of a mile from the railroad tracks provided the local swimming hole, where Edgar Shanholtzer and his friends spent their summer days. It was also a favorite watering place for hoboes, who would "jungle up" there for weeks. Edgar found the transients energetic and independent. Their stories of faraway places fascinated him. His father was an engineer on the Louisville and Nashville Railroad and made a good wage. Whenever he could, Edgar lugged bags of potatoes and vegetables to the hoboes, a charity his father tried to discourage with a razor strap. "The hoboes thought I was one of them, and in my heart I was," Edgar reminisced. The day school closed in 1937, Edgar, thirteen, hit the road. He asked a friend to take his bike home and tell his father he would back in time for school.

When Harlan Peter was a boy, a hobo came to beg a handout at the kitchen door of his parents' home in Wisconsin. While he waited for food, he sang a ditty about the "lemonade springs in a big rock candy mountain" and an enchanted land to the west. "Just sleep under a tree. In the morning, throw up a rock or two and down comes breakfast," said the old fellow. "Years later I discovered that old bum had a bad habit," said Harlan. "He told lies to little kids."

Partings could be especially poignant for parents strapped for cash and reluctant to let their children ride the rails. This was the only way that Glen Law and his brother, Walt, could travel from their home in Wenatchee, Washington, to college in Indiana, to enroll as freshmen in 1935. On the day of their departure, their mother and father drove them to the Great Northern terminal to the south of Wenatchee. The brothers climbed over the fence and trudged across the tracks to an empty boxcar, where they settled in the doorway. They watched their mother dabbing at her eyes as she spoke to their father, sitting in their old Model A Ford. Their father climbed out and came across the tracks to them. Long after, Glen Law could still hear his father's words: "'Take off those old ragged shoes, Glen. We can't have you starting college in them,' my father said. I started to argue, but a look at Dad's rigid jaw stopped me. Without a word, I exchanged shoes and thanked him."

Boxcar Girls

Ina Máki's father had ridden the rails from Minnesota to the Dakotas for the wheat harvest. She knew boys in her town who had traveled by boxcar. When Ina graduated from high school at Virginia, Minnesota, in 1939, she wanted to see the United States before attending college in the fall. She told her father she was going to ride the freights. "Father always supported my projects," Ina recalled. "'It will be dangerous,' was all he said, and he gave me ten bucks." Before making her way to the rail yards in Duluth, Ina spent most of her money on a permanent wave. On her journey, she would be known as "Curly."

In 1935, Dobie Stadt and a girlfriend were set to strike out from home. Eighteen-year-old Dobie was a waitress and her friend, a theater cashier. They'd heard about the San Diego World's Fair opening that May and decided to hitchhike and ride the rails to that exposition. "We left Miami dressed in skirts and blouses, tan and white saddle shoes and bobby socks, and white tams on our heads," remembered Dobie. "We each carried a small suitcase holding all our possessions."

Vivid images of boxcar girls remain with witnesses who saw them on the freights. Joseph Rieden and his brother Ralph were riding from Chicago to Idaho in 1930 when a man began bothering two young women in the boxcar. The brothers went over and told the man to leave the girls alone. As they approached a town, the girls stood next to the brothers in the boxcar door. Ralph described what happened next: "Suddenly one of the girls took out a gun and shot three of five crows sitting on the telegraph wire. Everyone had respect for them after that."

Clay Nedblake of Ohio was in a boxcar with forty people, including five or six women sitting close to the open door. The women wore boots, and in their boots, all carried stilettos.

A few women rode the rails for love. Seventeen-year-old Violet Perry married at Harrisburg, Illinois, in July 1933. She left on her honeymoon with her twenty-one-year-old husband, Floyd, riding the rails to "moonlit nights on the prairies, deserts, and mountains."

Young wives sometimes traveled cross-country with husbands who where looking for work. Edith Walker was in her teens and married when she found herself living with her husband Bob's family on a farm in Cullman, Alabama, in 1933. Other hard-pressed siblings and their families had sought refuge on the farm. Fifteen people in all sat down at the dinner table there. "There are too many people living on Papa," Bob said to Edith that September. "We are leaving."

Bob had friends who owned a restaurant in California, where he thought he might get work. Edith had an uncle and aunt in Florida. They flipped a coin: Florida it was. They packed their belongings in Edith's suitcase. Edith owned a pair of shoes which she'd bought and not worn. On the way out of Cullman, she returned the shoes to the store for a refund of $1.95. With a bankroll of $6.40, Edith and Bob started for Florida.

In March 1935, eighteen-year-old Norma Darrah's husband, Curly, lost his job in Kenyon, Minnesota. Curly's brother, a carpenter at Casper, Wyoming, offered him an apprenticeship. "We gathered warm clothes, a frying pan, a pot, some knives and forks, our bedding, and my husband's shotgun and shells," wrote Norma. "We had three one-dollar bills for the three of us, which we wanted to last until we reached Casper. What a vain hope that was!"

Harold Kolima's mother was one of many young women and girls forced to take to the road alone. Harold recalls a haunting scene: "A mom, three little boys, ages five, seven, nine, with bed rolls and a large suitcase, and a puppy dog tagging along, walking through the rail yards at Omaha, Nebraska. They are looking for a freight headed west. The year is 1937." The Kolima boys and their mother were fleeing social workers, who sought to remove the children from their mother's custody. For the next four years, they lived a "Grapes of Wrath" existence in hobo jungles and harvest camps, wintering in Sacramento, California, and taking boxcars to and from Nebraska to follow the harvests.

Crushing financial and emotional burdens overwhelmed young couples. Young wives and husbands parted as the men drifted off to seek work in other states. This separation could often become permanent. Naomi Trout was twenty when she gave birth to a son in Seattle in December 1930. Five months later, her husband was laid off. They split up, Naomi and their baby returning to her parents' home in Idaho, her husband going to look for work in Wyoming. It was two years before she received news that her husband was back in Seattle, where he had started a watch repair business. "I sold the baby buggy my Dad and I had made out of scrap for five dollars," Naomi recalled. "I bought rolled oats, cans of milk, spoons, metal cups, and bowls. I put them in an old hatbox and hit the road with Junior." On her journey with the toddler, Naomi would encounter both generosity and harassment from fellow travelers, culminating in her husband's brutal dismissal of her and the baby when she reached Seattle: "He said we were excess baggage and didn't need us anymore."

Lucille Asney was a child when her parents separated in the Depression. "My memories are very bright when I think of my courageous little mother, Mary Elizabeth Anderson," says Lucille. "Mother was a small woman, four feet ten inches, and needed help climbing up into the boxcars." Lucille's mother always carried her cat with her in a box, going from town to town in California with her children, selling crepe-paper roses.

Among the stories of the girls are occasional glimpses of chivalry and concern. Edward Kaufmann and another boxcar boy were swapping off-color yarns when a man came over and told them to stop talking that way. Did they not know that there were women aboard? Edward and his pal obeyed, having not noticed the girls who had their hair tied up beneath their caps and wore coveralls.

In Hempstead, west Texas, nineteen-year-old Bill Aldridge was waiting to board a freight train when a young woman asked him to hold her baby while she jumped into a boxcar. "I took the child in my arms before I realized what she was asking," Aldridge remembers. The woman caught the car in front of him. He caught the next one with one hand, holding the infant with the other. "When I handed the baby to its happy mother, I wondered what I would have done had I not made that train."

Hopping Their First Freight

Whether it was the slow unraveling of their lives that finally bore down on them or it was a snap decision, the hour came when the new nomads stood beside the railroad tracks, hearts pounding as they waited to "catch out" and board their first train.

Bill Hackett remembers his excitement the night he left Flint with his stepfather. Howard hoisted him up into an empty boxcar, where they huddled in a corner: "A switch engine shunted us this way and that. I could see the red and green lights of signal lanterns, but not the men who wielded them. Finally, the train was ready. My heart beat fast and the adrenaline flowed. With a great spurt of steam, the locomotive got under way. Our boxcar creaked and groaned, shivered and shook, rattled and complained. What an incredible adventure! I felt as if I were Tom Sawyer, Huckleberry Finn, and the Swiss Family Robinson combined."

In Seattle, Weaver Dial listened to an older brother's stories about riding side-door Pullmans up and down the coast. When he was twelve, Weaver encouraged a fourteen-year-old friend to ride the rails with him. Weaver's brother showed the pair the way south. "Around eleven, we heard the high ball," said Weaver, referring to the two short blasts from the train whistle that signaled it was leaving. "As the engine made the curve coming toward us, it looked for all the world as big as a house. Before the train picked up speed, my comrade, somewhat taller than myself, leaped through the open door of an empty car, did an about-face, and pulled me in as I ran alongside the track." That Northern Pacific freight hauled him over the Cascade mountains. "I'd never been in the rolling hills east of the Cascades. Picking my first apricot off a tree gave me the feeling that I was in Arabia!"

Decades after the event, many freight train riders still hold their awe at the mighty steam locomotives that carried them across the continent. A Union Pacific "Big Boy" double header, for example, had engines with sixteen ninety-six-inch drivers delivering a million horses to the tracks, making the earth tremble for a mile on either side. Boyhood memories are conjured up, as evocative as the mournful wail of a steam locomotive whistle at night: "A siren song that gets deep into you and pulls you along," reflected René Champion, walking beside the tracks half a century later, with a freight rumbling past. "If I were now on the road, I would have been on that train. I would've gone wherever it led me."

Many former riders look back with undisguised pride on the great adventure of their youth, but almost never do their reminiscences blank out the "bad old days" or the terrible dangers involved in "catching out." Here and there, memories are of well-heeled boys on a summer lark. The majority faced a long, hard road. Even as he "flipped his first freight," many a boy learned just what he was in for.

When Kermit Parker entered the freight yards at Pendleton, Oregon, he was mystified by the maze of tracks. It was 1935, and Kermit had needed to travel to Chicago, where he wanted to enroll in a summer course for trainee electricians. No main line served his hometown Walla Walla, so Kermit hitchhiked to Pendleton, a division point, where freight trains stopped to change engines and crews. "The Pendleton yards were very complicated, with numerous parallel tracks filled with freight cars," recalled Kermit. "I'd no way of telling which string of cars was going to be made up into a train, and which were not." Fortunately, as happened with many novice hoboes, other "passengers" awaiting freight trains took pity on Kermit and showed him how to tell when a train was ready for departure, where to get on, and what part of the train to board.

In some yards, young hoboes were even helped by sympathetic railroad men. A Pere Marquette engineer dismounted from his locomotive and walked over to where Ted Baer and his twenty-year-old wife, Erna, were waiting at a switch. He asked where they were headed and they told him: Grand Haven, Michigan. "That's my train you want," he said. The engineer took the couple down the line and opened a boxcar that was newly cleaned. Ted and Erna never forgot that act of kindness.

On one of Weaver Dial's journeys, he was caught in a rainstorm one night as he stood with a group of hoboes waiting to catch out in the Vancouver, Washington, rail yard. An armed railroad bull challenged the group, making them line up and empty their pockets, but he found nothing more threatening than a pocket knife. The bull demanded to know where the hoboes were going. "Most thought they were going to jail, but with long strides the bull went over and opened an empty boxcar," said Weaver. "He told everyone to climb aboard. When the last person was inside the car, he turned and vanished into the darkness."

Such soft-hearted railroad detectives were a rarity. It was more common for youths caught trespassing on railroad property to be handled brutally or marched off to jail. On a May morning in 1935, Vernon Roudebush was caught by the bulls at Sheridan, Wyoming. As the group he was with was lined up, the chief detective strode up and down the line, wielding a club in one hand, a revolver in the other. "What are you bums doing on *my* train?" he roared. Vernon was a seventeen-year-old runaway from Chicago, roving the country in summer. Whatever answer a hobo gave to the bulls, he was beaten. Vernon was knocked to the ground twice. "My nose was bleeding; my arms were covered with welts from trying to protect my head. I'd befriended a kid with an abscessed tooth. A bull belted him on the side of his swollen jaw. I'll never forget the kid's scream of pure agony."

In 1934, when he was fourteen, Glenand Spencer was pistol-whipped by Texas Slim in the Fort Worth freight yards. Texas Slim, the notorious railroad bull on the Texas and Pacific line between Texarkana and El Paso, was said to boast that he had shot seventeen men. Spencer found railroad bulls from Georgia to Texas to be willing recruiters for local officials who wanted free labor on their farms. The bulls would let hoboes catch out in their yards and then shake down the train at a prearranged spot outside town. Able-bodied men would be arrested by the local sheriff and sentenced to thirty to sixty days on the "cotton farm," which may also have been peanuts, sugarcane, whatever crop needed to be worked. Spencer was caught in two such roundups, but because of his age and small size, discarded like a too-small fish.

On his way west, coal miner's son Arvel Pearson was in Lahotta, Colorado, waiting to catch a freight to Dodge City. Two railroad bulls with sawed-off shotguns stood by to stop hoboes from boarding a leaving train. The fifteen-year-old Arvel saw the last car coming up. "It was now or never. I caught the eye of one of the bulls as I ran to the car, grabbed on and began climbing." The bull started shooting, the buckshot hitting just above Arvel's head. Then he heard a shout, "Swing in here, kid, that guy's trying to kill you." His rescuer was the train conductor, who was standing on the caboose. Arvel swung in between the two cars, the only hobo to make it to Dodge City that day.

Catching out "on the fly," when a train was already under way, was perilous: One misstep could cost a youth his legs, even his life.

After Leslie Paul's tearful farewell with his mother at their home in Duluth, the eighteen-year-old hitchhiked to Carleton to catch a westbound freight, reaching the yards in the fading light of a summer evening.

Leslie heard the blasts of a highball and saw a locomotive a quarter of a mile away at a water tank. Gray and black discs of smoke rose intermittently from the stack. The train began to move toward him, accelerating rapidly. He ran to the side, as the engine roared past. He raced alongside, trying to equalize the speed. He held his mother's black satin bag with his belongings in his right hand, his left hand free. Leslie still relives the moments of terror that followed: "My left hand grabbed the rung of a ladder and held fast. The momentum jerked me off my feet. Suddenly it was dark and like a nightmare. I was grasping for a hold with my right hand, still clutching the bag. I tried to get my feet on a lower rung and missed. I felt the motion of the wheels as my feet brushed them.

"The inside of a hospital flashed into my mind. I saw a young kid lying without his legs, suffering all the agonies of hell. God erased that picture. Out of the dark, a strong hand grabbed me and pulled me into the boxcar."

Leslie's rescuer was an experienced hobo, who lectured him on catching out safely as the boxcar rattled through the Minnesota night. The noise from the wheels rose deafeningly, the car vibrating end to end.

"No further words passed between John and me," Leslie remembered. "His presence was enough to soothe my loneliness. It was my first night away from home and already I wished I was back. Was I leaving little for nothing?"

John Fawcett

———— •◆• ————

1936

*J*ohn Fawcett's journey began on a freezing night in February, *riding the blinds of a passenger train. It was to change the sixteen-year-old's life forever. The son of a prosperous ophthalmologist in Wheeling, West Virginia, Fawcett lit out partly for adventure, partly to rebel against the forced conformity of Linsly College, a boys-only military institute that he attended in Wheeling. His first road trip lasted one weekend. At the school year's end, Fawcett and a friend struck out through the heartland to Texas. His experience among the homeless and poverty-stricken in June and July 1936 made him a lifelong fighter for the underdog and the oppressed.*

I hardly knew there was such a thing as the Great Depression, because we never had it hard. At Christmas my mom would take us kids down to a local settlement house with baskets of food for the poor and their families. My dad would send my older brother to do collections for overdue fees on Saturdays. Other than that, I'd no idea of what was going on in the country. We still had two automobiles. We went on summer vacations to the eastern shore of Maryland. We lived the good life.

I went to public school for four years. Then my dad sent my two brothers and me to military college. That's where he and his brother went. Fawcett boys attended Linsly and that was that. We got to wear a uniform, which was a big thing for the first year.

Afterwards it got to be a bloody nuisance. By the time I reached high school, I hated the discipline.

Mom and Dad were good, loving parents, so I certainly didn't run away because of my home life. Why do boys run away? For adventure, I guess, because it's exciting and dangerous.

I ran away from home three different times. I always left a note on my dad's desk, telling him not to worry. I can only imagine what my mother felt.

At about eleven o'clock that February night, I walked into the waiting room of the B&O passenger station. I walked onto the lighted platform, where people were standing around, and sauntered toward the front of Train Number 77. It originated in Pittsburgh and made a stop at Wheeling, then followed the Ohio River south to Huntington, West Virginia, 180 miles distant. I had a friend who'd moved to Huntington the year before and wanted to visit him. Beyond that, I'd no idea where I would go or what I would do.

I took a quick look at the blind behind the engine tender of Number 77. It would be an easy place to ride, with my back against the baggage car door.

I walked about fifty feet ahead of the engine and ducked behind a small building. I could see the railroad tracks in the glare of the locomotive headlight. I heard a hoot from the engine whistle and saw her big driving wheels begin to turn.

As the huge locomotive chuffed past me, I stepped from my shelter onto the snow-covered roadbed. I caught the grab-iron on the back of the tender with my gloved hand. My foot was in the stirrup and I was on my way!"

John's weekend dash for freedom ended at Huntington, when his friend's parents contacted the Fawcetts and arranged for him to be shipped home "riding the cushions." In June 1936, when John and his friend Mick McKinley, fifteen, ran away, they planned to ride the rails to the Texas Centennial Exposition and afterwards find work as cowboys.

Around midnight our train pulled into the big passenger station in Parkersburg, West Virginia. The train hadn't stopped, and there was a gun and a flashlight in my face. A B&O bull told us to climb down, took us one on each arm, and marched us down the platform, between the people getting on and off the train. I don't ever remember being so humiliated. The bull took us to the Wood County Jail. In ten minutes, we were behind bars.

My first impression was the awful stink of confined humanity and stale urine. I hadn't known what the inside of a jail was like, but sure found out over the next four days. We had a cell mate, Nick, a petty thief who had a good deal of street sense. He warned us to keep our mouths shut and not smart off to anybody. He told us about "the Brute," a prisoner who ran the jail. "He holds the kangaroo court," said our cell mate. The kangaroo court was an informal procedure run by the inmates, the Brute acting as judge. "He'll have you over to his cell tomorrow."

At 7:30 A.M., a guard did the rounds with a kitchen worker, bringing a cart with breakfast. "Dreadful" is the best word I can think of for the food: a bowl of cold oatmeal, a slice of bread, a cup of bitter black fluid, which Nick told us was chicory. At noon, we would be fed lukewarm, tasteless soup; another slice of bread; and a cup of chicory. The evening's fare was a half stew–half soup "slumgullion," as Nick called it.

At ten o'clock that morning, the Brute's henchman came across the bullpen. "You take any money from these kids?" he asked Nick, who replied respectfully, "No, sir." The pug looked at Mick. "He get anything from you guys?" Mick's response was, "We didn't have nuthin' to take." With a surly look at both of us, he said, "We'll see about that. Kangaroo court is on. Come with me."

The Brute was sitting on a wooden chair in his cell. Nick had told us that he was doing a year in jail for killing a man in a barroom brawl.

"How much money did the jailer get from you last night?" the Brute asked. The jailer-judge who admitted us had "fined" us ten dollars or ten days in jail. Mick and I had each produced three dollars and were told we would have to serve out the rest of our fine.

"How much you got left?" asked the Brute.

"Three dollars," I replied.

He asked Mick. "A dollar, maybe more," he said.

"Take off your shoes and let's have it."

What a deflating experience! Mick and I had thought we were so damned clever hiding stuff in our shoes. The kangaroo court took all the money I had left: $3.79. There was yet one brief scene to play out. The Brute told us to strip to prove we had no money belts. Satisfied we had nothing more, they dismissed us and sent us back to our cells.

Sunday evening brought an experience that lowered my spirits even further. About 7:30, the guards admitted eight or ten evangelistic church folk, who sang and prayed and extolled us to salvation before the fires of hell consumed us. I didn't need that. I just wanted something to eat.

Mick and I were in our cell on Tuesday afternoon when we heard the now-familiar clang of jail doors opening and closing. A voice reverberated through the hallway: "Kendall and Murphy coming out!"

We were lying on our bunks in silence, until Mick suddenly yelled, "John, that's us!" We'd agreed on using assumed names on the trip in case we ran into the law.

We identified ourselves and were told we were to be released.

Let out that afternoon, Mick and I both had fair success in knocking at doors and asking for food. Mick was the winner, bringing a chunk of sausage wrapped in a piece of oily newspaper. We went down to the west end of the B&O freight yards. A crossing guard pointed out the next train to Cincinnati. It was a hotshot, a fast freight, which we caught, reclining on the top of a boxcar as the train rumbled over the Ohio River. Mick and I smiled and shook hands, hearing the bark from the exhaust stacks and the wail of the steam whistle. We were free of the confines of Wood County Jail.

* * *

That evening I learned one thing for certain. When you are on the road away from friends and home, it is comforting and reassuring to be acknowledged and recognized by people along the way—strangers though they may be. I saw people wave at us from their fields and from their porches and backyards as we went rattling past. There were so many unemployed and destitute people that I think they felt a kinship.

We arrived at Chillicothe, Ohio, about midnight. At the large freight yard, we saw several figures in the dark, carrying flashlights or lanterns. Mick and I had met two West Virginia lads on the freight. We started running around the cars to avoid getting caught and lost Mick in the dark. The two lads and I spent an hour looking for him. It didn't seem like a good idea to go around calling his name, so we gave up. We found an unlocked caboose on a side track and spent a comfortable night inside, sleeping on the bunks.

The sun was up when we rolled out and started walking up a street away from the yards. We'd gone a couple of blocks when I saw two railroad men coming toward us. Walking beside them, smiling and talking jovially, was old Mick McKinley, who greeted us nonchalantly as you please. The railroad men invited all of us to coffee and pancakes!

We loafed around the Chillicothe yards for a couple of hours before a B&O fast freight came storming out of the yards. We leaped aboard and climbed to the top for a scenic ride in the morning sunshine. Later, we arrived at the Mill Creek marshaling yards at Cincinnati. We'd lucked out again.

We walked to an area close to the yards and spent an hour or two on what would become a never-ending quest for "a little work in exchange for something to eat." You always hoped a woman would answer the door, as women were more sympathetic to someone in bad straits.

It's hard at first for a sixteen-year-old to ask for food, especially coming from the perfectly safe environment that I'd always known. But you learn it in a bloody hurry, when you're hungry and haven't eaten for twenty-four or thirty-six hours. I never learned to panhandle—it was better to offer to work. "Is there something I can do? Got any errands? Chop some wood?" You don't feel that you're getting something for nothing. That's the way I justified it. Probably half the time you made that offer there was no work, but you got something to eat anyway.

Later, we learned how to "put the bum" on restaurants. You walk back and forth in front of a restaurant and look for a man on a stool at a counter. Preferably, two men with an empty stool in between. You buzz right in there, plop down next to them, and speak right up to the waitress. "Have you got any work to do? I haven't eaten since the day before yesterday."

Sometimes a waitress would slip a cup of coffee in front of you. The kicker is that if you get turned down, there's a good chance one of the people beside you will pipe up and say, "It's OK lady, give the man his breakfast. I'll pay for it." And then you're home free. It got easier every time. You knew what to say and not to be crushed if you were refused.

Another way to get food was bumming bakeries for two- or three-day-old dinner rolls or doughnuts called "toppings." You get a sack of toppings and you've got a meal—not a balanced meal, but it lasts you for a few hours.

I never felt I was treated with disgust by people when I put the bum on them. Sympathy, pity maybe, but never "Why don't you go to work?" Everybody in the country knew there was no damn work.

Some nights on the road, we slept in boxcars. It's quick and easy to find an empty boxcar in a railroad yard. Some nights we spent in hobo jungles. There'd often be old jungle buzzards, who lived there for weeks or months at a time. You'd ask permission if you wanted to do something: "Hey, I want to wash my clothes. Is that OK?" And the 'bo would say, "Yeah, well, go downtown and bring us back some cabbage and you can do whatever you want."

I remember sitting around the jungles sometimes all day long. When you missed a train there wasn't another until that night.

Most of the people we saw were in their twenties and thirties, some older than that. There were probably more women than we recognized, because they didn't wear women's clothes. We saw Okie families dispossessed from their farms heading west to California. Some were awful looking, in real terrible condition, and dreadfully near starvation. Many lacked the courage to go up to somebody and ask for something.

Every freight train had dozens, sometimes hundreds of people on the cars. It didn't matter which direction the train was traveling, it would be loaded with guys going east and going west and going south. "No use going back East to Minneapolis. I just came from there and there's nothing," a guy would say in the jungle. When the train came, people would get on and go to Minneapolis anyway. Anything was better than sitting in the jungle, complaining and getting hungry.

People usually referred to us as "kid"—"Hey, kid, get moving there; you're going to get your leg cut off;" "Hey, kid, chop some wood for the fire." They called us kids and that's what we were. It didn't bother us. I think it made it easier, not rougher, because people respond to young children. We took advantage of that.

This is not to romanticize being on the road. Riding the blinds of a speeding passenger train is the quickest way to get killed in the world aside from being a fighter pilot. It is awful and dangerous. I was hungry all the time and I wasn't used to hunger. Sometimes two to three days without anything to eat. When you're active and moving, your hunger hurts physically.

John and Mick rode freight trains from Cincinnati southwest to Gosport, Indiana, where Mick met a young man whose father offered him a few days' work. The same individual told the boys his uncle owned a sawmill in Marshall, Arkansas, where they could find summer jobs. Their plan to attend the Texas Centennial Exposition temporarily shelved, John rode on ahead to Marshall. Only a week after leaving home, he crossed the Mississippi River at Thebes, Illinois. He made his way into Arkansas on the Missouri

Pacific Railroad. He remembered the night he arrived at Little
Rock, Arkansas, the night Joe Louis became heavyweight champion
of the world. The next day, John traveled to Marshall, Arkansas.

Marshall was a small Ozark mountain town with a population
of maybe a thousand. A typical small American country town. A
block away and you're out in the country again.

I checked at the post office, the general store, and the barber-
shop. No one had ever heard of a sawmill near Marshall. There
was nothing for me to do but to wait until Mick arrived.

My next move was to "apply for employment" at the barber-
shop. The barber was a kind old gent who gave me a dime for
sweeping out the place. I spent my wages on a generous bowl of
chili and crackers. After dark, I walked down to the railroad station, where I found an old baggage wagon. I climbed onto it and
curled up for the night.

The romance of adventure was rapidly dwindling. I didn't like
being all alone out in the country. When I was with other people
on the trains or in the jungles, I didn't feel lonely or threatened. I
felt excited at being part of something unique, even frightening,
that was taking place in our country. What I was experiencing was
the human tragedy of the Great Depression, of which I'd learned
practically nothing at home.

The next morning I circled the town to see if I'd missed anything.
What I really needed was to be around people. I spent that hot summer's day hanging around the town square. At any given time,
twenty to forty men, singly or in small groups, sat on their haunches
or stood with their backs against the buildings, quietly talking or
just putting in time. Most wore faded overalls and bore the dry, wiz-
ened look of men who spent their lives on hard-scrabble farms.

I listened to people on the real edge of grievous poverty and unemployment, talking about how tough life was. They weren't
seeking sympathy. They were just talking to each other, sharing
their ideas. There seemed to be a quiet desperation in their concern for the future.

Once or twice during the day, I was included in a conversation. "Where are you from, kid?" When they found out I was wandering around the country, they asked me what things were like on the road. "Are the folks in the cities as bad off as we hear tell?"

I was hearing about conditions in the country from the people themselves, not from the guys disconnected from society like hoboes. These people lived in one place and had homes and children; they were talking about the way things are. This made more impression on me than anything else on that trip.

A man in the square suggested that I go to a camp meeting at a local church—they served cookies and lemonade. The church was a block away and easy to find from the hymn-singing and hallelujahs. I walked in and sat near the back. A girl about my age in a print dress came down the aisle and got right down on her knees facing me. I felt horribly embarrassed and self-conscious and, seeing no tables of food, I left as soon as I could.

It was beginning to rain as I walked down to the railway station. I found shelter on the old baggage wagon, which stood under an overhanging roof. I remember hearing the rain on the roof and being in a quandary of despair that so much was going on in life that I'd never learned about at home or in school.

It was still raining when I woke in the morning and pulled on my shoes, my hat, and my jacket. I stood awhile under the roof with my hands in my pockets, looking down the tracks and feeling sorry for myself. Mick might never come, and it's a cinch I'd starve if I stayed here. I decided I must leave Marshall and go to Texas alone.

Just then I heard a locomotive whistle echoing through the Ozark hills. My transportation was on its way! It seemed ages before the engine finally came chuffing out of the woods. Four cars back, a boxcar moved slowly toward me with a tattered gangly hobo hanging from the ladder, ready to hit the ground. It was none other than young Mick McKinley.

Standing in the rain, it took less than a minute to convince Mick that there was no sawmill and no jobs. This was starvation city and we must get right back on the train and keep moving. And we did.

At Eureka Springs, Arkansas, we caught a westbound freight, climbing into a boxcar with fifteen to twenty people, including an Okie family with a baby that cried all the time. Hours passed before we clanked to a stop in the yards at Seligman, Missouri. A fellow went with the family to try and find a doctor for the child.

The same guy was in our car at 2 A.M., when we caught a freight headed for Fayetteville. The baby had diphtheria and had been taken to a hospital. There was much concern among those of us who'd been in the same boxcar. "Ain't a helluva lot we can do about it now," said the man. We all lay down to sleep as we rattled along in the dark.

When John and Mick reached Dennison, Texas, the two boys went uptown to beg for food. They became separated and wouldn't see each other again until they were back in West Virginia. After looking unsuccessfully for Mick in the Dennison yards, John hopped a passenger train and rode the blinds to Dallas. He arrived at 6:30 on a Sunday morning. He walked out to the centennial fair and climbed a chain-link fence to get inside the grounds.

I remember a feeling of exultation: "By God, I did it!" After three hard weeks of beating the road, I'd reached the fair. Hunger, however, spoiled my visit. I had one hot dog all day, wolfing it down and feeling hungrier than before.

By the time I'd seen the fair, all I wanted to do was to go home and get my feet under the dinner table again. Having witnessed the masses wandering the country, I finally realized that finding jobs as cowboys—or any other kind of work—was an impossible dream.

I sat on a bench at a bus stop in downtown Dallas. I had blank paper and an envelope that a lady had given me in Poteau a few days before. I wrote a letter to my mother telling her I was on my way home.

That evening, I walked over to the freight yards and caught a train to Greenville. I jumped off and got a timetable at the station. The "Katy Flyer" was due out of Greenville in an hour.

I waited at a lighted intersection. The barrier gates came down, with blinking red lights and ringing bell. I could see the engine of the Katy Flyer a hundred yards away. As the locomotive came by, I ran inside the crossing gates. I leaped for the ladder and swung up into the second blind. Homeward bound!

That was the longest ride I would ever have on the blinds of a passenger train: seven hours and 280 miles, as the Katy Flyer made its dash up into northeastern Oklahoma. It wasn't my hunger but the fear of falling asleep and tumbling between the cars that was my biggest problem. I stood up most of that long night in order to stay awake.

I was detected after daylight, just as the train was pulling out of Muskogee, Oklahoma. Suddenly, the door of the baggage car swung wide open. A surprised U.S. Mail agent stood looking down at me. It took him about one-tenth of a second to unlimber his .45 and push it right in my teeth.

"Outta here, 'bo. Hit the dirt. Now!"

I stepped quickly to the corner of the car, grabbed the handrail, and swung down. Minutes later, I was standing on a street in Muskogee. I felt faint from hunger and lack of sleep. I walked aimlessly along, until I saw a pawn shop and went inside.

I took my goggles out of my jacket pocket and laid them on the counter in front of an old man. I made a pitiful appeal, saying that I was trying to get home and hadn't eaten for two days. What would he give me for my goggles? I wore the goggles when riding the tops or in the blinds, but needed food more than protection from cinders.

The pawnbroker took the goggles, turned them over slowly in his hand. "I know times are hard, young man, but I can't give you more than twenty cents."

I could've jumped over the counter and hugged him, but I just said, "Yeah, well, that's OK." I took the two dimes and scurried out the door.

Within minutes, I was in a café spending my twenty cents on ham and eggs, potatoes, toast, and coffee! I can still see half a dozen meals I had on that trip, because of what they meant to me at the time. That breakfast in Muskogee stands above them all because of its life-restoring quality. After eating, I found an empty boxcar just beyond the station, crawled in, and fell asleep as soon as my head touched the floor.

About noon, I awoke to hear two switchmen arguing about the Yankees and Dodgers. An hour later, we were rattling through the Oklahoma countryside, arriving in Parsons, Kansas, about four that afternoon. I walked up the main street and bummed a sit-down meal at a café plus a sack of Bull Durham. Two meals and tobacco in one day. This was more like it!

In another hour, I was on a fast freight bound for Kansas City, where we arrived at one in the morning. At daylight, I walked across the Missouri River bridge to the Argentine yards. I was sitting on a pile of railroad ties, meditating on life, when an old gent came sauntering up to me. He had a bindle on his back and looked the part so I knew he was a brother of the road. We talked awhile, before he said he was going to buy lunch. Did I want to come along? I said that I was "on the nut," meaning that I'd no money.

"That's OK, kid. I'll spring this time."

That afternoon, my generous friend and I caught a freight headed east across central Missouri to Moberly. We arrived at six in the evening and went out on the town. I walked along the streets in a residential area a few blocks from the tracks. Looking in the window of one house, I saw a man sitting in his armchair reading the evening paper, and a couple of kids playing on the floor. I thought of my parents worrying about me.

It was getting dark when I went to look for my traveling partner, but didn't find him. A big locomotive came snorting by, leading a string of boxcars, and I climbed aboard.

The next day, I reached Decatur, where I grabbed a B&O hot shot headed east. It was a long ride but I had the satisfaction of being headed in the right direction. In the Indianapolis yards, the sun was well up when I boarded a Pennsylvania train, but I was kicked off in the little jerkwater town of Bradford, Ohio. I went out on the highway and hitchhiked into Springfield. I'd been twenty-four hours without food and was glad to score dinner at a restaurant. I found a jungle under an overpass east of the freight yards. Three or four guys were lying on the ground with newspapers wrapped around their bodies. I followed their example, and collecting some "Hoover blankets," I managed to get a fair night's sleep.

I was 130 miles from home. I was homesick as hell! I finally leaped up onto a freight train around four o'clock in the afternoon.

On through the night, we charged through the hills of eastern Ohio. No fear of my sleeping that night! At two o'clock in the morning we rumbled slowly across the Ohio River bridge to the Benwood yards at Wheeling.

I got in stride for the seven-mile hike to my home in Woodsdale. When I finally stepped up onto the front porch, I lay down in our squeaky old glider swing and fell asleep.

Mary, a maid who'd been with our family for years, came downstairs to begin her daily routine. That Fourth of July morning in 1936, Mary got one helluva shock. Her yell woke me, as she leaned down to pick up the paper and saw a soot-covered fellow lying on the swing.

Mary went upstairs to Mother. "You'd better come down and see who's here to see you," she said. She told Mother that she didn't recognize me until I smiled.

After my dad got up and shaved, he came to me. He put out his hand and said, "Well, son, you're kinda down to ring weight, aren't you?"

That's all my dad said, and I loved him for it. My parents never gave me hell. Maybe they should have, I don't know, but that wouldn't have changed me.

A phone call to the McKinleys revealed that Mick had gotten back the day before. Fate had been kind to us both.

When I returned to school that fall, my senior year was a troubled one. I was asking questions that embarrassed my teachers. I was hearing them say things that made me want to go up and knock them in the face.

"I'm not here to talk about things like that," one teacher told me. "I'm here to teach you geometry." You couldn't ask a social question or talk about people lying in the street in your hometown.

My parents wanted me to attend college after high school, but I received their permission to go to sea for a year or two. When I finally shipped out in an old tramp steamer, I found going to sea more of a drug than freight trains. You're in it every day, twenty-four hours a day, months on end. I realized I wasn't going off to college to be a doctor or lawyer. I didn't know what I was going to do, but fortunately I didn't have to make the decision right then.

In 1942, John Fawcett enlisted in the Army Air Corps as a private soldier. A year later, the boy who shivered on the blinds of a Baltimore and Ohio express was piloting Spitfires over Tunisia, Sicily, and Italy. He flew 182 missions and was awarded the Distinguished Flying Cross in 1944.

After the war, Fawcett went to the University of Washington under the GI Bill, earning a degree in transportation—a career he followed until 1965. In that year, he resigned from his job and went to Mississippi, where he spent four months organizing voter registration classes. Fawcett participated in the Selma-to-Montgomery march led by Dr. Martin Luther King Jr. In recognition of his volunteer work in Mississippi, he was awarded the Community Brotherhood Award of the National Conference of Christians and Jews.

John returned to a second career at sea, serving for fourteen years aboard Puget Sound ferries until his retirement. His lifelong passion, which was shared by his wife, Ellen, was the human rights struggle. He'd joined the American Civil Liberties Union in 1953. He took part in antiwar activity, women's rights struggles, and gay rights struggles. A Seattle delegate to the World Peace Congress in

Moscow in 1973, Fawcett never wavered in his belief in the working class—a call to arms a boxcar boy once heard on a journey that awakened his conscience.

It isn't an exaggeration to say that my trip on the road in 1936 changed my life and the way I view the world I live in. I had a quick and fast education about how hard life was for millions of homeless and destitute people. I kept asking myself questions. "Is it like this all over?" "Why does it have to be this way when the goddamn guys on Wall Street have millions of dollars?"

I didn't see the suffering until I ran away from home. It would be a cold and unfeeling person who wouldn't be stunned and angered at the squalor of the streets and migrant camps. No one who hadn't been there could possibly know the damage to one's self worth, having to beg for food and work.

I thought that these conditions were a product of the Great Depression, but I learned that they are an integral part of the economic system of our country. A person has to get out into the world to find out how things really are.

How do we change the world? When I was forty years old I thought I had all the answers. I knew exactly what the word "love" meant and how the world was going to be saved. I don't know anymore.

Arvel Pearson

——•——

1930–42

*A*rvel "Sunshine" Pearson's grandfather had living quarters behind the railroad station at Spadra, an Ozarks village five
miles from Clarksville, Arkansas. Arvel's father died before he was
born and his mother moved into the depot, where she gave birth to
her son in 1915. The first sounds the boy heard were the whistles
of freight trains rolling down into Spadra.

Arvel's mother had remarried a coal miner. Working as a waterboy in a strip mine at the age of nine, Arvel had been nicknamed
"Sunshine" by the miners. By 1929, he had already been working
underground for eighteen months. Then the Great Depression hit
and the mine closed. He first rode the rails in 1930 and would continue to hop trains until 1942 as a migrant farm worker in summer
and as an itinerant coal miner in winter. In 1939, when he was
twenty-four, Arvel attended the National Hobo Convention, still
held annually at Britt, Iowa. There he became the youngest hobo to
be elected "King of the Hoboes."

His reign ended with the onset of World War II. After serving in
the Pacific, he returned to civilian life and worked in the construction trades for the next forty years. When Arvel finally retired as a
pipefitter in 1987, he was making $18.75 an hour—as much as he
earned in a week in a good season on the road during the 1930s.

The closing of the mines left twelve hundred miners out of work.
In six months to a year, people who didn't have a place to raise

their own food were practically starving. We were lucky in one respect: My stepfather bought a piece of land and built a house before things got rough.

I was considered a strapping kid, though I weighed around 110 pounds. I heard people talking to my folks and saying things like, "Why should you feed him?" and "Why ain't he out workin'?" I made up my mind I wasn't going to be a burden on anybody, especially my parents.

My mother was apprehensive about my leaving but my stepfather said, "The kid knows his way around. Let him go." He thought I'd come home with my back-end dragging, tired and hungry, but I was determined to make it one way or another.

My first day out, I caught a train at Van Buren, Arkansas. I rode freights all night, and next morning I was in a small town where I had some relatives.

"Any work pickin' strawberries?' I asked them. They said, "There'll be work in a few days."

I worked for fifteen days and made fifty-five cents to two dollars a day, if everything went right. When that job finished, a guy said, "The strawberries will be gettin' ripe in the suburbs of Denver."

A month and a half after I left home, I was in Denver. After Denver, a guy said, "Why don't you try the wheat harvest in Kansas?"

I backtracked a few hundred miles and did some harvesting in Kansas—"You can follow this wheat all the way into the Dakotas, if you want to go with it," I was told. When I finished in Kansas, I caught a train north through Nebraska into Wyoming and the Dakotas.

People advised me to go to California. I'd no desire to go there seeing that 90 percent of the people on the road were headed that way. My greatest ambition was to get to Alaska. I rode the rails to the North. A customs officer came aboard at the border. He asked where I was going. "To Alaska," I said. "You can't get there by train," he told me. A kid from the Ozarks who'd never read much geography didn't know that trains don't go to Alaska. It was twenty-five years before I ever visited Alaska.

* * *

That's the way I started. I picked up a lot from my stepfather, who was an old-time hobo who'd settled down. As I went along I learned from other experienced hoboes. Let me explain how a hobo caught a freight train back in the 1930s:

When you see the train coming, you start running. When it gets level with you, you reach up with your right hand and grab on at the front of a car. Never catch the rear end 'cause it's liable to swing you in and hurt you, maybe run you over and kill you.

It's the same getting off. You don't swing around like a squirrel, but keep one hand holding on tightly. When the train gets to a speed where you can unload, just drop back and hop off. You have to hit the ground running or you could fall and break a leg.

Many times I rode overnight on the top of boxcars. I'd take my belt, pass it under the runner on the catwalk, and hook it through my overalls. With no danger of falling off, I let the train rock me to sleep. I'd also hook myself on with my belt if I was riding on a tanker. It's awful tiresome bouncing up and down all night. You might be holding on with one hand, pretty soon you get sleepy and down you come.

I would never "ride the rods." The old cars had rods under them, where people put boards and lay down. It was dangerous and dusty and once the train gets up speed, you have no way of leaving the rods without rolling off and practically killing yourself. I'd ride the top, I'd ride the engine, I'd even climb onto the caboose. I'd ride anywhere but the rods.

I'd always wait for another train rather than take a chance. I wasn't going to arrive at the harvest fields with one leg off.

Ninety percent of the time I traveled alone. You can travel faster when you don't have to wait on someone else. A couple of times I had a partner but it didn't work out. If you get on a train and your partner doesn't catch it, what are you going to do? If it's not going too fast you can jump off. Otherwise you ride to the next stop and hope that in a day or two he'll get there and you can meet him.

I was a full-fledged hobo in less than two years. I knew enough

about railroads to pass as a brakeman, fireman, or engineer. I knew
what the different hand signals, whistles, and flags indicated. The
old engines had two flags right up front. For example, a red ball on
a white background indicated a fast freight—a "red ball" was what
you wanted to catch if you were traveling a long distance. You
never hopped a local because it stopped everywhere to pick up
things like milk cans—you might make fifty miles in a whole day.

Sometimes I put on a striped jacket and a railroad cap and stuck
an empty lunch pail on my arm. I had dressed like this and was
walking down the tracks at Laramie, Wyoming, when I met a railroad man. "Where ya going?" he asks. "I'm headin' over to Denver," I said. "Come and ride in the caboose with me," he said. All
I had to do was make up a little bit of a story.

One winter, I was traveling with a partner, going from Kansas
City to Joplin, Missouri. At eleven o'clock at night we went down
to the railyards and climbed onto the tender of the Flying Crow, a
passenger train going south. We had gone about forty miles when
the fireman found us. "OK, you so and sos, if you're gonna ride this
train, you're gonna work," he said. We climbed down into the cab.
My partner was a husky guy but he'd no experience on trains. The
tender was rocking from side to side making it difficult to shovel
coal into the firebox. Three shovels full and my partner had coal all
over the cab. The fireman told me to take a turn. I don't think I
missed more than two shovels in ten minutes. "Where did you learn
to shovel coal, son?" the fireman asked. I told him I'd worked in the
coal mines. "I can shovel coal through a ten-inch hole," I said.

There were nights I'd get homesick waiting for a train with nobody to talk to, sitting alone on a pile of ties under a water tank
out in the middle of nowhere. You're only a kid and you get to
dreaming about that warm bed back home and seeing the folks. As
long as I was working, my thinking was that if I go back with fifty
or one hundred dollars, we'll all be in better shape.

I had a hard time getting a job because I still looked so much like
a kid. Matter of fact, I was a kid. I'd walk up to a boss in a coal mine

and ask for a job. He'd look me over and frown. "Kid, what do you think you can do?" I had to put a little brass on my face. "Just anything you got in this coal mine," I'd say. The boss would give me a job to make me prove myself. 'Course I had enough experience that I figured I could handle it. And I figured I didn't have anything to lose if he fired me. Nine times out of ten, I could do what I said.

I'd be working beside a person who was fifty years old. He was getting two dollars a day but because I was a kid they reckoned I wasn't worth more than a dollar. You're working just as hard and feel put down. Whenever possible, I tried to show them that I could do a man's work and get a man's wages.

My first year out on the road, I went as long as forty-five days without a dime in my pocket. Some people felt sorry for you and fed you, but others said, "Get this blasted kid outta here!"

The hardest thing for me was to tell a person that I was broke and hungry and ask for something to eat, but when you go for days without food, you change your mind pretty quickly. Older hoboes gave me advice on what I had to do. For instance, if you ask a lady to mow a lawn for a handout, make sure that it's a small lawn, not an acre and a half. That's going to take you hours and make you miss your train.

On a summer day in a small town in Kansas, I saw a lady sitting in a rocking chair on her porch, fanning herself with a newspaper and trying to keep cool. The train I was riding stopped a short distance away. I hopped off and walked over and asked if I could do a chore for a meal.

"Son, you can chop me some wood," she said. She pointed to a rain barrel that stood out in her yard. "When you've cut it, throw it in the barrel."

That lady's ax was awful dull. I was out there working and sweating, wiping and chopping for twenty minutes and I had about five or six sticks.

I saw the lady was in her kitchen fixing me a meal. When she wasn't looking, I grabbed the barrel and turned it upside down. I took the sticks and laid them crosswise over it.

The lady came outside. "That's enough, son," she said. "Come and eat."

When I took my last mouthful, I said, "Lady, I think I hear the train whistle, I'd better be going." I jumped off her porch and ran down the tracks. I guess she was frowning on the next hobo that came along.

"Let's go to the World's Fair at Chicago," a man says to me in Denver in 1933.

"That's a heck of a long way," I said. "Why should we go there?"

"We can get jobs and see the fair."

He talked me into going to Chicago. Right away I got a job taking care of the elephants with a big shovel and helping to feed and water them. I was paid fifty cents a day and could sleep in the hay.

It was amazing to see people with money to spend, especially families with kids buying ice cream and going on those rides.

"Boy, I sure would like to do that," I said. I had to shovel all that manure and couldn't go out there and play around.

Taking your childhood and going from a very small kid to an adult in a year or two is rough. By this time, I was a teenager, but there I was thinking of the same things as a nine-year-old kid 'cause I'd missed out on all that. Things like that bother you.

I'd worked in the Colorado strawberry harvest and saved forty dollars, when I learned my folks were destitute. I rode a freight train back to Arkansas and persuaded them to move to Colorado.

My parents' old beat-up car broke down. I bought bus tickets for my mother and my sister. My stepfather, my nine-year-old half brother Luther, and I traveled the rest of the way by freight train. I would put Luther on my back to catch a train on the run, my stepfather getting on first to help us aboard.

My stepfather and I found jobs at the mines in western Colorado. We worked through the winter but then my mother got itchy feet to return to Arkansas. My stepfather wanted to stay and work in the fields in spring but my mother refused. They were stuck down in Arkansas for four years before they could get out again.

I'd heard about the King of the Hoboes but had never been to a convention at Britt, Iowa. There were over three hundred candidates in 1939 and my chances were slim, but each day they screened them down. They tested you on your knowledge of different railroads and what the train signals and whistles meant. When it came down to the wire, I was in the top ten. I was competing against experienced hobos of fifty and sixty. When they announced I was king, I almost passed out. I guess you could call it an honor though being king of the hoboes is just a title. It doesn't amount to anything.

I thought the Depression was going to go on forever. For six or seven years, it didn't look as though things were getting better. The people in Washington, D.C., said they were, but ask the man on the road.... He was hungry and his clothes were ragged and he didn't have a job. He didn't think things were picking up.

You leave home with good intentions and tell your folks you're going to come back a millionaire. You return with your head between your arms. You're broke and dirty and they see right away that you didn't make it. I'd stay a day or two and hit the road again.

I was never so desperate that I wanted to commit suicide but I often felt put down. I realized it would take a while to change things. "I'm going to keep going," I said. "I may not end up a millionaire but someday I will be able to face people I used to beg for food." If I hadn't had hope I would have starved to death by the time I was seventeen.

In those days if we got a pound of bologna, we thought we were doing great. When I go to the store today, I pass the bologna and move over to the T-bone steaks. People see me driving a Cadillac and ask, "If you were on the road that long, how did you accumulate this?"

The road taught me that if I made a dollar, I had to save some of it. I used to have a ledger where I put down everything to see how I was progressing. During the sixties and seventies I was saving an average of five thousand dollars a year. That doesn't sound like much today but over the years it mounts up. When you get to where you don't owe anybody a dime, that's the best feeling you'll ever have, if you live to be a hundred years old.

Phoebe Eaton Dehart

1938

"*P*unk," *her brothers called her, a moniker her grandfather ob-jected to. Grandfather Rogers nicknamed her "Peggy," and it stuck. Peggy's parents, Raymond Hannibal Eaton and Ella Frances Rogers, filed a claim on a 320-acre homestead at Sheep Mountain near Glendo, Wyoming, in 1917, five years before she was born. The chalk rock mesa rose fifteen hundred feet above the prairie a mile northwest of the log cabin Raymond built for the family. They ran cattle, kept horses, and raised crops on lands where shots still rang out in range wars. The Eatons and the Covingtons, their neigh-bors, engaged in a long-running battle over fences and strays and anything else that set them to "locking horns."*

Peggy was eight when "the bad years" began with the coming of the drought in 1930. She recalls strings of saddle tramps stopping at the ranch where they would be fed and have their clothes washed before moving on. By 1932, horses were selling for five cents, hogs for sixty cents, and cows and calves from ten to seventy-five cents. In 1934, grasshoppers invaded the prairies and devoured everything in sight, even clothes on the clothesline. Peggy remembers her father filling a washtub with insecticide supplied by the government. She drove a wagon team around the edge of their fields, while her father stood in the back broadcasting the insecticide with his bare hands.

When Peggy started high school in 1936, she rode her horse Babe four miles every day to catch a bus to Glendo. She would leave Babe in a neighbor's barn and ride her back home after school. Through

90

the drought and the dust storms, Peggy's family did not go hungry,
the homestead supplying them with the necessities, but with a farm
income of three hundred dollars a year, they were strapped for cash.
It was especially trying for a young girl in high school. Peggy was on
the basketball team and when she needed forty cents for team ex-
penses, she would have to bring a gallon of cream to sell in town.

One evening in July 1938, when Peggy was fifteen, she was help-
ing her father with the milking. They had words that provoked
Peggy into running away and hitting the road.

I'd snuggled up to old Diamond on my T-shaped stool, tucked the
milk bucket between my legs, and started to milk her. Some
demon-inspired fly bit where it shouldn't have. Old Diamond
swatted me in the eye with her dirty tail. I jumped up and
whopped her with the stool and cussed her out.

I was getting pretty cocky. I thought that as long as I had to
work like a man, I ought to be able to talk like one.

My Daddy came across that aisle like the wind. He hit me up
one side of the face and down the other.

"Don't ever let me hear you talk like that again," he said.

"I'll leave home," I yelled.

"You'll be back before supper."

That was the end of the conversation but it started me thinking
about leaving.

I was skinny, unbecoming, and mad at the world. I'd be a junior in high school in the fall and had no money for clothes. One of
my brothers lived next to a ninety-year-old couple who offered
one dollar a week for help with housekeeping. I took the job.

My friend Irene Willis was boarding with my brother and his
wife. Irene's parents had moved to Issaquah, Washington. She
wanted to see them but had no money to travel and planned to
hitchhike. She didn't want to go alone and asked me to come
along. I thought it was a great idea, considering the conversation
I'd had with my father.

I'd worked for two and a half weeks and collected $2.50. Irene said we could earn money picking fruit in Washington. I wrote my mother a letter telling her not to worry. "Experience is the best teacher," I told Mom.

We left on July 12, 1938, and walked two miles to catch the ferry across the Platte River at Cassa. I wore jeans and a white shirt and had another pair of jeans and a shirt in a roll over my shoulder. Irene carried a tin suitcase. I'd no idea how we'd get to Washington but I wasn't afraid.

We hitchhiked to Wheatland and across the Laramie Mountains to Bosler Junction. Two cowboys came by on a couple of broncos they were trying to break. Up we went behind them, hanging on for dear life, bucking and running all the way into Bosler.

That afternoon we caught a number of rides that took us three hundred miles across the state to Cokeville, near the Idaho border. Arriving late at night, we stayed up until daylight and went back onto the road. We couldn't figure out why no one stopped for us.

We were walking past the Cokeville stockyards where trains watered up, when two hoboes greeted us. "You kids hungry?" they asked. We'd say yes to anybody who asked us if we were hungry.

"Uncle Slim" and "Daddy Joe" introduced themselves: Slim Jack Fuller was thirty-seven and Joe Daniels was sixty. They came from Casper, Wyoming, and were on their way to the harvest in Washington.

We told them that we were going home to Issaqua, Washington, which was half true. The reason we couldn't get a ride, they explained, was because we were too close to the state border. The white slavery law that made it a crime to transport a single woman across a state line was strictly enforced. "If you want to get out of here we can help you catch a freight," they said.

When a train stopped for water, Slim and Daddy Joe found an open boxcar and helped us climb aboard. I sat swinging my legs out of the boxcar door as the train started to move. Slim slapped my shins. "Keep your feet down or you'll be jerked off into eternity," he said, warning that I could be hit by a switch.

We rode that train all day and night and most of the next day. It was a thrill seeing the wonderful scenery as we went along. At night Slim and Daddy Joe showed us how to roll up in the paper that lined the boxcar walls and stay warm.

Late the next afternoon we arrived at Nampa, Idaho. We had to change trains to go northwest. Irene and I waited in the jungle, while our friends went uptown to beg for food. When we'd eaten we went to join other hoboes sitting on a grassy amphitheater opposite the one empty boxcar that was going to Le Grande, Oregon. We were the only women among the group of fifty men.

As darkness came we saw railroad detectives patrolling the track with lanterns and rifles. When the train started and the boxcar rolled forward, the fifty hoboes rose up as one person and rushed to the door.

Somebody grabbed me by the seat of my pants and the nape of my neck and pitched me into the train. Irene was right behind me. I heard Daddy Joe call my name in the dark. They came over and sat protectively in front of us but I didn't sleep much that night.

In the morning, the engine broke down in the hot, barren hills of eastern Oregon. We watched one of the train men climb a telephone pole to call for help.

Sitting in the sweltering heat, I heard a man say something in a low tone. To this day, I don't know what was said but Daddy Joe rose up. "One of these girls is my daughter and the other is my niece, so watch what you say," he said.

There were no further remarks.

A replacement engine pulled us into La Grande. Instead of slowing down, the train speeded up as we entered the yard. "Jump!" Slim shouted. He went first and landed on his feet. I jumped next, rolling head over heels. Irene also took a tumble. Daddy Joe landed as smoothly as Slim.

They wanted to ride the blinds on a passenger train. They would've shown us how to do this safely, but there were too many railroad bulls on duty in the yard. When we said goodbye to Slim and Daddy Joe, they gave us each fifty cents to help us on our way.

* * *

We went back to the highway and hitched a ride with a gasoline truck going to Pasco. Toward sundown, we climbed a pass over the Blue Mountains and topped out on Cabbage Hill above Pendelton. A million little farms, all different colors, lay spread out to the horizon. It seemed as though I was looking down on the whole world.

We got into Pasco after dark and went down to the railroad tracks, looking for someone who could tell us which freight went to Seattle. A man in a pick-up truck told us the train we had to catch wouldn't leave until 7:00 A.M. He took us to a hotel near the tracks, paid one dollar for a room and told the desk clerk to wake us in the morning. We were delighted to clean up and spend the night in bed.

Early the next morning, we jumped up and ran to the rail yard. The only place we could find to ride was on a flatcar crowded with black people. We were afraid and turned away.

An old man in a Model T stopped for us. I sat in the middle and Irene next to the door. We hadn't gone far when the driver reached across and pinched Irene. We made him stop and jumped out before he drove off in a cloud of dust.

We'd been dropped in no-man's land of sagebrush and sand. Then we saw the freight train we'd wanted to catch at a water tower a quarter mile away. We crawled under a barbed wire fence and ran as fast as we could. We avoided the crowded flatcar and climbed a ladder to the catwalk. We put the suitcase between us and lay down scared to death when the train started up. After a while we gained confidence and sat up to enjoy the ride.

Suddenly we saw a man coming toward us along the catwalk. He was a railroad detective and came and sat with us. He was considerate and concerned. "You kids can't go through the tunnels to Seattle. You have to get off at Yakima," he said. When the train pulled into Yakima, the detective helped us climb down.

We hitched a ride over the old road across Snoqualmie Pass to Issaquah, Washington. It had taken us just four days to cover twelve hundred miles.

Issaquah, Wash
July 17, 1938

Dear Mom and Dad,

Well folks I hope this finds you as well as I am.

We got here Saturday 16th. Irene's folks were sure glad to see us. We went to church this morning.

We rode to Wheatland and caught a ride from there to Ferguson Corner. Then we hitched a ride to Bosler Junction. Pretty soon a couple of cowboys riding broncos took us into Bosler and bought our dinner. Their names were Lauren and Red Peden.

Medicine Bow was the next stop. A tourist and touristess picked us up there and took our pictures. They took us to Green River. Next stop was Cokeville. There two guys gave us 50 cents.

In the park at Cokeville a hobo walked up to us and we got to talking. He said he'd hunt up his buddy and they would go with us. His name is Slim Fuller, six feet tall, 37 years old. His buddy (an ex-engineer) Joe (somebody) about 60. We called them Uncle Slim and Daddy Joe. They were sure good to us. All four of us rode freight trains to La Grande, but there was some bad bulls there so we left the boys and hitched a ride to Gibbon, Wash. Caught a freight to Yakima, then hitched to Issaquah.

. . . We are starting back for Idaho, Monday. The law won't let girls work in the orchards here.

Slim gave me a rabbit foot. Sure brought luck too, ha, ha. Take me back to old Wyo., for I'm getting tired of roaming. Take me back to old Wyo, for to stay.

Don't worry. Love and Kisses. Phoebe Eaton.

By August 3, Irene and I had made it back to Nampa, Idaho, where we were arrested for vagrancy. The police fingerprinted us and locked us in a cell infested with bedbugs. In the morning we appeared in front of a judge, who fined us each ten dollars. We didn't have that kind of money. Watching the judge write something on a sheet of paper, we thought we would have to sit it out in jail at a dollar a day. Instead the judge gave us a voucher for a meal.

"When you've had your breakfast get out of town," he said.

On Saturday night we got into Soda Springs. The Henry Stampede was in full swing. We shared a pot of beans with a couple of cowboys who let us sleep in their tent. The next day we saw the rodeo from the chute side, a real excitement for a cowgirl from Wyoming.

That night we had three in the tent. Irene had decided to start a relationship with one of the cowboys. In the morning I confronted Irene. "Let's go," I said, but she told me that she was going with the boys to the next rodeo in Sun Valley. I said I was heading home.

I was frightened to walk out on the highway by myself. My first ride was with a pair of maniacs who drove like crazy on the winding canyon road from Soda Springs to Kemmerer, Wyoming. They had no qualms about taking me across the state line. They drove behind a hotel at Kemmerer, where one of them worked. "You go up to my room and I'll be up after a while," this man said. "OK," I said, and walked round the corner and ran like rabbit down to the railroad tracks. I looked for a freight going east with no luck.

I found an old hotel near the tracks and took a room for seventy-five cents. The next morning the landlady cooked me a big breakfast of bacon and eggs. Her name was Margaret Fitzpatrick, and I sent her a Christmas card every year until she passed away.

I went back on the highway. The first car to stop was the same man who'd brought me from Soda Springs. I didn't want to act afraid, so I climbed in. He immediately made a pass at me. I yelled at him and shoved my hand in my pocket pretending that I had a weapon. He slammed on the brakes and I jumped out.

After that, I got safe rides all the way to Green River. A couple picked me up and drove me to their home in Hot Springs, where they gave me dinner before taking me back to the highway.

I stayed a night at the Salvation Army in Rawlins. I went down the hall to take a bath and while I was gone someone went into my room and went through my belongings. It scared me so I propped a chair under the doorknob. I woke in the middle of the night as someone tried to open the door but couldn't budge the chair.

On the road the next morning, a highway patrol officer picked me up. I thought I was in for it but he only wanted company on his patrol that ended at Medicine Bow. I had relatives not far away at Rock River and thought they would take me home. They couldn't, so I went back on the road. On Monday, August 15, I got a ride across the Laramie Mountains and arrived home in time for supper. I was lovingly greeted and was never scolded.

I'd been gone for five weeks and had traveled over twenty-four hundred miles. I still had fifty cents in my pocket. I'd written three letters and eleven postcards to let my family know where I was. I didn't consider myself a runaway.

In my junior year in Glendo High School in 1938, I wrote the story of my journey. "You have acquired an insight into human nature which few girls your age have," my teacher said.

Peggy DeHart first married at sixteen, served with the army in Alaska in 1943, raised a family, and ran a business. In 1971, Peggy and Dick DeHart lost the nursing home business they had built up over many years. They were living on unemployment when her husband of twenty-seven years had a heart attack and died. "It was hard times again but I knew I could survive," says Peggy. When she retired in 1987, Peggy went on to serve as a missionary in Trinidad. She still hits the road regularly in a converted van and travels throughout the West.

It was easier for a girl than a boy on the road. People bought us meals and gave us the change out of their pockets. I doubt that they would do that as readily for a boy.

When we left home I didn't know that Irene was three months pregnant. It's a miracle that she carried the baby because of the tumbles we took and the way we lived and ate. She went to rodeos all over the Northwest and California. The cowboys finally brought her and the baby back to her Daddy's ranch in Wyoming.

When I returned to school, all I could think about was escaping. I had been away from home and had seen other people and places. I was very dissatisfied, and getting married at sixteen was a way of fleeing the farm and the poverty, but it was still hard times. The reality crashed in real quick.

I would still like to ride a freight train but I know it's not safe. I don't feel any older now than when I was on the road. I look in the mirror and see this old lady and don't recognize me because inside I'm still the same age I was back then.

Hard Travelin'

It was a thrill to ride the top of a boxcar running across the Great Plains or the blinds of a famous flyer like the Twentieth Century Limited. Danger was a constant riding companion and situations could turn deadly in an instant. No matter how nimble or quick, one mistake could cost the life of a rider—and did so with tragic frequency. A thousand miles from home with nothing to identify them, they became the MIAs of the train-hopping era, a lost son or daughter lying dead beside the tracks.

Some young people found camaraderie in the roving army, but many road kids kept to themselves, afraid of older strangers. Some rode the rails with friends, including those labeled as "scenery bums," who were out to see America for free. Even the adventurers faced hair-raising moments when they wondered whether they would ever make it to the next stop.

Black road kids often ran headlong into the most blatant and brutal racism. Sometimes, though, they found common ground with white road kids, their shared privations fostering a better understanding between them.

Eventually, a road kid would have a run-in with the bulls. The railroad detectives' reputations varied from one division to another, but were rarely associated with moderation. For many young people, the bulls made riding the rails an adventure in terror.

Face into the Wind

Van Rance hugged the top of the tender as the long black engine rushed with incredible speed toward Denver. A hail of cinders stung his face. Steam exploded noisily, vaporizing in the night air and streaking down his raw, grimy cheeks.

On this night in 1933, the twenty-year-old Van Rance was traveling west from his home in Cincinnati to Colorado to find work and earn money for college. On his ride from Chicago to Omaha he helped a fireman free a jammed coal chute and in return was hidden from the bulls in the Omaha yards. On the next leg of his journey, Van Rance climbed onto the tender of a Denver-bound passenger train.

The sting of the night wind, steam, and cinders was endless. Water seeped from the tender's hatches and sloshed around him. The engine shook continuously and bounced from side to side as if trying to dislodge him. His ride lasted until dawn, when the sky began to lighten and he saw the rugged outline of the Rocky Mountains. The engine slackened as it approached the Denver depot. Van Rance lifted his numb and aching body and walked toward the ladder at the back of the tender.

"I grew sentimental at the thought of leaving this old friend that had carried me westward for the past twelve hours," he recalled. "I patted its cold side affectionately, threw down my bag, and made a wide leap to the ground. I looked back at the disappearing train. 'Thanks for the lift,' I said."

Riding a passenger train cut days off a journey. On the final leg of their sixteen hundred-mile round trip from Denison, Iowa, to Grand Haven, Michigan, Ted Baer and his wife Erna climbed onto the tender of an express. Ted remembered the sensation: "The engine roared and shook, and with a piercing shriek warned all to beware at every crossing. You feel a vibration and a power surge and at times you seem to float. You expect the train to leave the rails at any moment."

George Rex and a companion slipped aboard the Super Chief at

Gallup, New Mexico. They expected a straight shot to Albuquerque, but they got more than they bargained for. They rode the blinds of the baggage car directly behind the tender as the Super Chief picked up speed, faster and faster until it was hitting eighty miles per hour. The two riders became colder and colder. Looking down at the tracks, George saw an open trough filled with water. The Super Chief was designed to pick up water on the fly: scooping it up and forcing it into the tender's tanks.

Torrents of water cascaded over George and his friend—already numb from the cold and now soaking wet. "Jumping from the train was the only way to escape our misery, and that would have been certain death," Rex recalls.

They hung on until they reached Albuquerque a hundred miles away, where Rex walked straight into the arms of a railroad detective. Taken to the Albuquerque police station, he denied having been on the Super Chief. "Son, take a look at yourself in that mirror," the detective told him. George looked at his smoke-blackened face and admitted his guilt. Next morning George and his friend were taken to the city limits and told to leave town.

Sometimes the deluge that drenched a rider was intentional, as when Ross Crane was riding the blinds in South Dakota: A fireman knew he was hiding there and used his hose to send a jet of water over the tender.

As they flew along at eighty miles an hour, crushed stone used for ballast between the ties sand-blasted faces and tore the clothes of the riders. Hot cinders could penetrate and cut the membranes of their lungs, causing them to spit blood for a day or two. Riding the blinds was fast and thrilling but many boys who took the chance never stole a second ride.

Fellow Travelers

"The railroads were king and like fleas on a dog they carried us with them. Naïve and fearful, overruled by ignorance and bravado, we walked to the nearest siding and caught a freight," wrote Donald Davis, reflecting on the impetus that drove a sixteen-year-old to begin riding the rails.

Sometimes a boxcar journey was launched even more precipitously. One morning in late 1935, L.W. "Red" Barber was on a freight train that blocked an intersection in Salt Lake City. The doors on both sides of the boxcar were open. When an eleven-year-old asked for a lift up, Barber and others in the boxcar thought the boy only wanted a safe way to cross the intersection and get to school. "The boy was still with us when we got to Sacramento, California," said Barber.

There was always the alternative of hitchhiking. Many train-hoppers resorted to thumbing a lift for short distances, particularly when they had to make their way to a main line division point. It was impossible to hitchhike at night, which meant that you had to find a flophouse or sleep in the open. You could ride all night on a train and be a lot farther down the road. Mostly you hitchhiked alone and took chances with the person who picked you up. "On the railroads, you were part of a small army," observed Ralph Shirley, who was a high school junior when he left home in 1936.

It was not unusual for a boy to count five hundred fellow riders on a freight train. Joseph Watters began riding the rails in 1931 at age fifteen and was on the road for the next seven years. He recalls an occasion when he was sixteen and stood in a boxcar door at the rear of a train crossing the Ohio River. "We approached the high bridge over the Ohio on a long curve. I could see the entire train from the engine to the caboose. Literally hundreds of men were in the cars and clinging to the tops. It brought home how vast was the number of men aimlessly wandering around looking for work. Even for a sixteen-year-old, it was a sobering sight."

A boy's first impression of the roving army to which he now belonged often stayed with him long after his last ride. When Leslie Paul had been helped aboard a Minnesota freight by a hobo who probably saved him from serious injury, Leslie settled down in the boxcar with his taciturn rescuer and five other riders. He used his mother's black satin bag for a pillow and was soon fast asleep.

Leslie recalls vividly: "When I awoke a count of noses showed that we had increased our number by three. Two sat in a door and dangled their feet out of the boxcar. One man stood looking out at the rolling countryside. One sat against the wall next to the door. One man was walking back and forth across the length of the car. Three huddled together passing a Bull Durham bag between them. The last occupant was in a far corner, his pants around his ankles as he tried to relieve himself.

"Who we were, why we were there, where we were going made no difference. We talked and laughed as a group. Next to God, nothing was more comforting to the soul."

A boy's first contact with his new traveling companions was not always upbeat. The hoboes that Ralph Shirley met were solitary, stoic individuals who had mostly given up on life itself: "They would stare at one spot for a long time, only occasionally shifting their eyes. I would later see the same expression on the faces of men with battle fatigue in World War II."

The wandering boy sometimes encountered similar despair in his own ranks. Rudy Ursic's first ride was in an open gondola on a train headed west from Fremont, Nebraska. When he climbed in, he found other hoboes sitting along the sides of the car. No one spoke. Some had their heads down on their arms and didn't look up. Ursic took a closer look at the rider nearest him, who could not have been more than ten or twelve years old.

"He was a rough-looking kid with a shaggy head of hair and a mistrusting look in his eye. He had a mouth that hadn't smiled in a long time." Ursic asked the boy where he was from but got no answer. "When the train stopped at Columbus, Nebraska, I got off. The kid remained on the gondola. The harried look in that boy's eye stayed with me for a long time."

Danger Ahead

The first boxcar William Martin and a friend hopped aboard was loaded with clean, fresh Excelsior hay into which the two boys sank for the most comfortable train ride they ever had. The pair were traveling from Michigan to work in the Oregon forests. At St. Louis, Missouri, they caught their second boxcar and had the worst ride of their lives. It was freezing and the boys made a small fire with scraps of wood and paper on the boxcar floor. No sooner had the fire begun to smolder than they realized the last cargo had been sulfur. Smoke and fumes quickly filled the car. Unable to get close enough to extinguish the fire, they rode all night with their heads out of the open door, abandoning the still-smoking car in the Kansas City yards.

Discomfort and danger followed every boy and girl on the rails. Few nights could be passed more miserably than when one landed in a boxcar with a "flat" wheel: These were flat spots on a wheel that set up a pounding vibration as the car picked up speed. "After riding a ways, you feel the vibration will drive you mad. You can walk, stand, lie down, sit, or hang from the roof, but you can't escape," Stan Cole recalled, remembering a ride out of Chicago in winter 1938. "I don't know how many miles I rode that night but every mile was written on my hide. I tried every possible position for the human frame, and some not yet discovered. It only gave that boxcar one more place to pound." Reported another victim of this torture, "It was like sitting on a jackhammer."

Frank Dunn had had no rest for several nights when he climbed into a boxcar that had both doors open. He fell asleep standing up and then started running in his sleep. Fortunately he ran lengthwise instead of out of the doors into oblivion. As it was he ran smack into the end of the car and cut open his face. When he tried to check into the Kansas City YMCA, he was turned away because his appearance suggested that he had a contagious infection.

More common was the danger of being locked in a boxcar as you slept, or by misadventure. Fifteen-year-old Chester Siems and a friend riding from New York to Pittsburgh in a steel boxcar were lulled asleep and didn't hear the door slide shut. They awoke in total darkness and panicked, fearing that they would be shunted into a holding yard and left to die of thirst and starvation.

"My buddy was crying hysterically and beating his fists on the doors," says Siems, remembering the incident of 1935. "We didn't know how long we rode or whether it was dark outside. Now and then the train stopped and we would pound frantically to no avail. Finally the train made a halt and we heard voices. We banged on the doors and screamed and pleaded to be let out. When the door slid open, I remember seeing hoar frost on the ground. To this day, I give thanks but I also suffer from claustrophobia."

Riders trapped in the ice compartments of refrigerator cars, known as reefers, knew a similar terror. Even when the hatch was released it could be difficult to climb out of these compartments, which were ten feet deep with slippery sides. Howard "Bud" Holmes was just fourteen when he hopped a freight in Provo, Utah, headed for Los Angeles. When he climbed onto a reefer, he propped open the hatch door but when the car was hooked onto a train, the hatch slammed shut. "The train started to rumble along the tracks. Yelling and pounding on the walls did no good," said Bud. He rode all night locked inside the reefer. The next morning the train stopped at a switch yard. "No one heard my screams. Suddenly the hatch flew open. A man was just about to drop a three hundred-pound block of ice into the opening when he saw me and stopped."

Manuel Krupin never forgot what he witnessed one morning in 1932. The seventeen-year-old New Yorker climbed out of a reefer when the train he was riding to Los Angeles stopped for water. Walking alongside he noticed red liquid dripping from a car. A rider had been crushed to death when an ice compartment was filled. The car in which Krupin slept was carrying potatoes that did not need to be refrigerated.

Two youths sat on the narrow walkway of a tank car that pulled out of Helena, Montana, bound for Spokane, Washington. Minnesotan Paul Swenson had served a year in the CCC and was bumming around the country in the summer of 1939 before going to college. A fifteen-year-old boy was already seated on the tank car when Swenson climbed aboard and moved closer as the train picked up speed.

"I'd seen the Rocky Mountains in the distance for the last couple of days and had been aware we were gaining altitude. I was totally unprepared for the rapid descent down the range," says Swenson.

"The engine lurched forward, letting out the slack between the couplings with a sudden violent jerk that ran the full length of the segmented monster. When the cars raced forward, the process was reversed and the couplings slammed together. The train thundered down the slope as though it was out of control.

"The kid was scared but I reveled in the ride. We rolled down the mountain and shot across deep river gorges, the wheel flanges grinding against the rails with a shower of sparks, the sound of iron on iron and the rattling of the freight rising deafeningly."

Swenson's hair-raising ride ended at Paradise, a watering stop where the pair of youths switched to a boxcar.

Escaping a ride became a matter of life and death for many novice train riders. Samm Coombs was fourteen when his hobo days began around Easter 1938. Coombs and a friend ran away from Oakland, California, with ambitions of becoming loggers in the Sierras.

They thumbed rides to Oroville, where they caught a Union Pacific freight heading up the Feather River Canyon to Quincy, a town in the mountains. They were sitting on top of the fifth car back from the engine. They didn't ask themselves why thirty or forty other hoboes riding on the train were all bunched up near the caboose.

"We didn't know about the many low-clearance tunnels ahead," says Coombs. "The first tunnel was about a mile long. Live coals and cinders swirled around us. The air was like a thick black soup. The moment we emerged from the tunnel our clothes burst into flames. We somehow managed to beat out the fire.

"Then came another tunnel, the same as before, with choking black smoke and cinders everywhere. We had to move to the back of the train. At no time have I experienced anything as frightening as looking down between those first two cars. I've no idea how many times we sped down the catwalk and leaped over that awful abyss. Our success rate was 100 percent. Anything less would have been 100 percent fatal."

For Verne Smith and his brother Elbert, the battle to stay alive took place on a freezing November night in 1936. Riding on a refrigerated train between Pocatello, Idaho, and Cheyenne, Wyoming, "We jumped from car to car along the length of the train and found every hatch closed," Verne Smith remembered. "We were working our way back up front when the engine blew off steam. It froze instantly on the catwalk. Elbert slipped and fell. He was clinging to a two-inch ridge on the edge of the roof when I crawled over and pulled him up.

"We broke open a seal and climbed down into a compartment. I was trying to remove a cinder in my eye when I noticed my brother had passed out. I had to get him into the fresh air. We had a rope to tie back the reefer hatch so that we wouldn't be locked in. I put this around Elbert's shoulders and pulled him up. He finally came round and opened his eyes." The brothers were going home for Thanksgiving. They reached home safely but didn't tell their parents they had been riding the rails.

When Bill Lawrence climbed into a boxcar at a siding in the mountains of Colorado, he found two other hoboes inside: a boy and girl who were both about sixteen years old. They were lying on a pile of wood shavings and were covered with a thin blanket. The train rode into a blizzard. Around 3 A.M. Lawrence saw the boy trying to get the girl to stand up but she begged him to let her lay still.

"The girl was freezing to death. I told the boy she would die if we didn't get some warmth into her. We rolled her in the blanket with only her head, arms and feet sticking out. The boy got on one side and I the other and we shuck and drug her around until she started walking on her own. When she was all played out, the boy lay down beside her. I emptied my suitcase and piled my clothes on top of them, then lay down on the other side of the girl. We slept until the train stopped at Trinidad, Colorado, at daylight."

Herbert Rand and his friend Frank Hubbs, two sixteen-year-olds out for adventure in winter 1934, were in a gondola in Montana with half a dozen farm hands and a large woman in overalls.

They survived the cold by piling up in a corner with the fleshy female in the middle to provide warmth. In grim contrast, teenager H. T. Roach was traveling through Montana the previous January: At the depot in Glasgow, he saw a small crowd of people standing around a fellow crouched next to a wall. He wasn't sleeping though. They'd found him frozen to death in a boxcar in that position and were waiting for the undertaker.

Reverend Graham Hodges spent the first nineteen years of his life in Wesson, Mississippi, where the tracks of the Illinois Central Railroad ran through the middle of the town of eight hundred souls. At the height of the Depression, Hodges saw numerous men and boys riding the freights. An image that has stayed with him all these years is of a young hobo who had been killed in an accident lying on the floor of the small freight station at Wesson.

"I remember looking at the young man and wondering whose son he was," says Reverend Hodges. "Thousands of men and boys, and females too, were killed far away from home. Many a woman lay awake at night waiting for a husband, brother, or son who never returned. Wesson's citizens took up a collection to pay for a coffin for the young man. He was buried in an unmarked grave like other MIAs of the freight-hopping years."

Oklahoma City teenagers Clifton Fitzgerald, seventeen, and Kenneth Warren, sixteen, rode the freights to visit the Carlsbad Caverns when they opened in 1937. On the return journey they caught a train at Hobbs, New Mexico, climbing onto a hot shot freight high-balling it nonstop to Waco, Texas. Fitzgerald remembers a pudgy kid of thirteen or fourteen sitting in front of them on top of a reefer. The boy wore glasses, which he was trying to clean with a dirty rag. A sudden storm hit the train as they roared through the West Texas night.

"The rain felt like frozen drops of hail fired from a gun," said Fitzgerald. "The boy yelled that he was going to climb down and stand on the ladder at the rear of the boxcar. We watched him start to make his way down the wet rungs. Just as he disappeared from our view the train hit an outside curve and the cars swayed wildly. When we looked for him the boy was gone."

On July 26, 1933, four Boy Scouts climbed into a boxcar that Chester Dusak had boarded at Johnstown, Pennsylvania. The boxcar doors were open on both sides. The four boys sat in one of the doorways dangling out their legs. Dusak was in the opposite doorway, his legs also hanging out, as the train came to a narrow bridge over a river near Lima, Ohio.

"I suddenly found myself in the middle of the boxcar floor. My sneakers were split and my feet were bleeding. The four kids were gone. They'd been thrown off when their feet hooked the bridge," recalls Dusak. In Fort Wayne, Indiana, that night, Dusak read a newspaper report that the four boys had been killed.

Howard Orial White and his friend Bill Smith were both fourteen when they left their homes in Brannock, Nebraska, and began to ride the rails following the harvests from coast to coast. They did this for the next five years, until they took their last journey together in 1934. At New Orleans they caught a train they thought was headed to Florida. They climbed onto a reefer car and went to the ice compartments, one of them at each end. Howard used a stick to wedge open his hatch, but it dropped inside and the hatch slammed shut. He remembered falling asleep and waking several times.

"Next thing I knew someone was pouring hot broth down my throat," said Howard. "I'd no feeling in one leg and my first thought was that I'd lost it in an accident. I could remember little and couldn't talk."

Howard had been found unconscious in the reefer, not on the way to Florida but in the railyards at Chicago. He was suffering from starvation and dehydration and possible toxic poisoning from fumes in the reefer.

"A hospital worker brought a pencil and paper. 'Is my leg cut off?' I wrote. He told me it wasn't. 'Where is my buddy?'" I asked. I was the only one in the boxcar, the man said. No trace of Bill was ever found. East of New Orleans the railroad ran through alligator-infested swamps. I believe Bill never got into the ice compartment but slipped and fell into the bayou."

"The theft of personal effects, food, and money was rampant," said Clemence Ruff, who left the tiny village of Gackle, North Dakota, in June 1933. "To be awakened in a moving, noisy boxcar in total darkness by an unseen thief whose hands were all over your body was a terrifying experience for a seventeen-year-old. The rest of the night was spent huddled against the side in the dark, too afraid to move."

Peter Salzman was on a train headed west out of Minot, North Dakota, packed with hoboes who'd worked at the wheat harvest. Most had fallen asleep when two newcomers leapt aboard. One man had a bright flashlight and the other carried a gun. Recalls Salzman: "They robbed us all, emptied our pockets, even threw out our tobacco sacks looking for money. When the train slowed they jumped out, one on each side of the train, and locked the doors. We figured the two of them got thirty-two dollars. Not bad for a night's work in those days."

Boys had also to watch out for the perverts who rode the rails in search of innocent prey. In southern California, seventeen-year-old William Creed and a friend were welcomed aboard a boxcar by two men. "They gave us candy bars and started calling us 'honey.' We heard enough to know what was going on," said Creed. The two boys grabbed their packs and jumped off the train.

"See America First—Travel by Rail"

"We shed our topcoats and basked in the sunshine on the lumber car. Mount Shasta loomed far in the distance, its perfect inverted cone gleaming white, hovering over us at every turn. Green forests swept down the mountainsides; clear, sparkling streams ran cold and swift. This was the Pacific Northwest, America's new frontier so lavishly pictured on lithographic travel brochures: 'See America First—Travel by Rail.' We were seeing it and all for free."

These ebullient recollections of Virgil Thomsen date back to September 1936 when Thomsen made a lightning tour of the West, five days by freight from Salem, Oregon, to Salt Lake City, through the Royal Gorge on the Arkansas River to Denver and back home.

Though the majority of boy and girl tramps were not "Hoover tourists," as they were sometimes called, riding the rails left all with an indelible view of America.

When Walla Walla high school student Kermit Parker rode freights to attend a course at a summer school in Chicago in 1935, his boxcar view of the Great Plains left a deep impression. "I'd studied the Great Plains in geography but they hadn't looked like this in the pictures," says Parker. "There were no waving fields of grain, no pretty little towns with parks that had lawns and trees. Instead all I saw for miles on end were abandoned farm buildings with dirt piled up on the sides like snowdrifts. I saw few people or animals in a world abandoned by man and beast. I didn't realize that I was witnessing one of the greatest tragedies of American history: the Dust Bowl of the 1930s."

Events such as the Los Angeles Olympics in 1932, Chicago's "Century of Progress" Exposition in 1933, and the San Diego World's Fair of 1935 were magnets for footloose and mostly penniless youth. While some came hoping to find work, others were simply there to take in the sights at no cost save some fancy footwork to outmaneuver the gatekeepers.

Traveling a zigzag route by freight train, Oregon farm boy Willard Berg took three weeks to reach the Chicago World's Fair in late winter 1933. The day he arrived he stood at the main gate, sizing up his chances of getting in without paying. From time to time another road kid would make a run for it only to be caught. Willard and two Texas boys moved off and skirted Soldiers Field, which was part of the fairgrounds. The space below the bleachers was used for storage: At one of the entrances a guard had placed a cart across the opening and lain down for a nap, his legs draped over the cart's handles.

"I sprinted for the entrance, hurdled the cart, and shot

through," Willard remembers. "The Texans were on my heels but as the second boy jumped the cart, a cry went up from the guard."

The two Texas boys were caught but Willard's would-be captors did not see him as he worked his way along the bleacher, crossed Soldiers Field, and mingled with the exposition throng.

"I spent four days and three nights on the grounds. I avoided the Midway except for the hour before closing when I would hit up a hot dog vendor for leftover wieners and stale buns. As the crowd thinned out, I went to the lakefront breakwater where a rock jutting out above a flat slab made an ideal hideaway. In the mornings, I would strip and swim in the lake, dress, and eat any leftovers from the night before, and then go and see the sights. The world was wonderful and life was good!"

Even as the nomads wandered a heartland stricken by drought and depression there were moments that sent their youthful spirits soaring.

"Each time we crossed into another state, I felt like the early explorers. Mountains, rivers, cotton fields, palm trees, people with strange accents—it was an alien world to a boy from a village in the north of Michigan," says George Rex.

For others it was the wonder of a herd of wild horses racing along beside the tracks or seeing the moon rise above the Great Salt Lake. Robert Hamilton never forgot the sight of small shack in a Georgia cotton field with a clean swept yard, a chinaberry tree, and laundry hanging on a barbwire fence.

As he rambled the country from 1930 to 1932, Archie Frost was moved to write poetry:

> Don't grieve for me my bosom friend,
> For I have listened to the wind
> Blow down the canyons in the night
> And chase the shadows in their flight.
> I've looked down from mountain high
> And heard the screaming eagle's cry,

I've searched for gold and hunted bear,
I think I've been most everywhere.

Inevitably, though, the boy or girl tramps' journey brought them back to the reality of what one train-hopper called "an American people fighting to live and help each other." Harry Christian rode the rails in the summer of 1934: "It wasn't the scenery or natural wonders, but the overwhelming abject poverty that I saw in so many places," he says. "I remember a poor farmer in Arkansas who let me have breakfast for helping him put up a fence. The meal consisted of sorghum molasses and a biscuit baked a day earlier. I ate as well as he." Gordon McCarty saw wheat piled up two stories high along a quarter of a mile of tracks. "People were starving and here I saw food rotting. Something was very wrong."

H. J. Heller went from San Francisco to New York in boxcars in 1934 and later became a staff writer for UPI. In an article about his cross-country journey, Heller described his most unforgettable sight from the side-door Pullmans. It was the people in the fields, often just one woman driving a vintage tractor in a field that seemed a mile wide. As the train rushed by, the engineer blew his whistle and waved to the woman from the cab. Wrote Heller: "And just as invariably the woman would turn and wave back and continue waving until the last freight car, with the last hobo also waving, disappeared down the track. The loneliness of the woman was almost tangible and often I was close to tears."

Black Road Kids

Harold Jeffries and five black friends took to the tracks out of Minneapolis, Minnesota, in 1935. "Of course, as black kids from the North we'd heard of racial discrimination but not one of us had actual experience of harsh prejudice. Our first frightening encounter came at the Union Pacific roundhouse in Kansas City. Some of the kids drank from a 'Whites Only' fountain. We were literally run out of the yards," said Harold, who was fifteen at the time. He remembers walking across the bridge from the Kansas side of the city to Missouri to the house of a girl he'd met back home. "We told her family what had happened. They sat us down and gave us a lecture about the ways of the South."

Black experience on the rails was mostly negative, especially when young riders found themselves at the mercy of railroad bulls. On his boxcar journey in 1934, Harry Christian was on a freight stopped by police outside Marshall, Texas. Christian recalls what happened to a black boy of fourteen who was riding with him.

"With no provocation an officer struck the boy with his flashlight, cutting open his face, then demanded to know why the boy was crying. 'Somebody hit me,' was all he said. The police ordered us to run in the direction of their flashlights, telling the black boy to run first. I heard him stumble and fall in a ditch filled with water. The officers laughed." Christian veered off to the right when it was his turn to run, avoiding the ditch, which had a barbed wire fence strung through it.

Because of their shared privations, hoboes were generally tolerant of minorities in their midst. But there were brutal exceptions, as Glen Law discovered when he and his brother Walt left Wenatchee, Washington, to go to college in Indiana in 1935. They rode in a boxcar with twenty whites and one black youth of eighteen. It was dark when a scream came from the back of the car.

"It was the black boy crying for mercy," Glen said. "Walt and I were sitting in the boxcar door. We were too frightened to investigate what was happening. Screams mixed with coarse laughter went on hour after hour. Around dawn the boy suddenly ran from the back of the car, pushed past us, and leaped from the moving train. We never knew if he lived or died nor what indescribable horror he was fleeing."

Young whites often had their first personal contact with black people when they rode the rails in circumstances that would later have a profound influence on their views. Byron Bristol remembers a cold, moonless night in 1933 when he was nineteen, traveling from Kansas to Denver in a boxcar. At a stop in the dark, another rider climbed into the car: "We struck up an animated conversation about our lives and families. It was only at dawn that I discovered my traveling companion was black. It was surprising and enlightening for a boy who had been brought up in a white community."

When Willard Berg was in the Albina yards at Portland to begin his trip to the Chicago World's Fair, he saw three black men among the hoboes waiting there.

"To my misguided eye, they appeared ominous. I fervently hoped they would not be on the same train," said Willard. Late blizzard conditions blanketed the Northwest as Willard's freight rolled through Idaho and Utah. When the train halted at a junction in Colorado for several hours, other hoboes advised Willard to leave the boxcar they were in and seek the warmth of the sandhouse.

"The three black hoboes were already there. After a time I lost interest in the crude conversation of my own hobo cohorts and moved closer to the black men. One was a middleweight fighter going home with his manager. He'd been cheated out of his earnings by a promoter and was broke. The third man held an office job before the Depression. His suit showed the indignity of having been slept in, his white shirt had a frayed collar, his tie had suffered abuse. He'd gone west looking for work but was headed back to his family empty-handed. This was my first encounter with the problems of minorities and began an interest that grew over the years."

Later at a railroad yard in Ohio, Willard fell in step with a black teenage boy. A dirty rag torn from a shirt covered the boy's right forearm. He at first seemed embarrassed by Willard's attempt at conversation and didn't respond.

"Finally he said a few words. He told me his arm had been scalded by steam deliberately spewed out as he was passing a switch engine. I had some Vaseline and cleaned and dressed the burn.

"'I've got an ugly spot on my head too,' the boy announced and doffed his cap. Two square inches of skull was exposed between a matting of hair.

"'How did this happen?' I asked.

"'I was standing on a car looking the wrong way when the train went under an overpass and I didn't duck in time,' the boy said sheepishly."

Willard dressed the second wound too before each of them went on his own way.

When John West, a seventeen-year-old runaway from Texas, reached New Orleans he had fifteen cents in his pocket. He walked along Canal Street wondering how to fill his empty stomach; the bright lights and people enjoying life didn't seem to hold out much hope for a hungry boy. Then he came to a poorly lit section of Canal that had few pedestrians.

"I went into a small café and sat down at the counter. A waiter came over and I told him my story. Could he serve me something for fifteen cents? I asked.

"He told me to sit down at a table. He brought a plate piled high with food, including spicy black-eyed peas. It was the best meal I ever hooked a lip over.

"When I sat back to enjoy the feeling of being well-fed, I saw that I was the only white in the café. Cook, waiter, and customers were all black, something I hadn't noticed in my hunger to eat.

"When I laid my fifteen cents on the counter, I told the waiter the food had been very good.

"'That's what we always serve,' he said. He pushed my fifteen cents back across the counter.

"I had tears in my eyes as I left. I couldn't help wondering what would have happened if a little black boy had showed up in a white café."

The Bulls

The conflict that began when stealing into railroad yards to catch out did not end when the intruders successfully boarded a boxcar. They could be confronted on speeding trains by railroad detectives wielding revolvers and clubs and demanding that they jump off. Thus at Des Moines in December 1933, when a youth was ordered off a moving boxcar by a bull, he slipped on the last rung; his legs slid under the car's steel wheels and were both cut off above the knee.

Margaret Dehn was sixteen years old when she hopped freight trains from Washington State to Nevada: "Riding the rails became an adventure in terror because of the bulls. They beat riders with clubs, rapping their knuckles to make them lose their grip and fall off. We hid in cars carrying animals, manure, garbage, anyplace we could find to escape the bulls."

Wyoming and Texas harbored bulls of renowned determination and ferocity. Few railroad divisions presented more of a challenge to the nomads than Cheyenne, Wyoming—the location of a school for railroad detectives. The Cheyenne yards provided hands-on training for rookies, who frequently let their quarry board without interference only to kick them off the boxcars ten or fifteen miles outside town.

Weaver Dial hopped a freight at Cheyenne, Wyoming, and settled down on the catwalk. As the train began to crawl out of the yards, Weaver saw hoboes scrambling from the cars. One bull walked along the catwalk looking for riders hiding between the cars; two others patrolled the tracks, one on each side of the train, ordering everyone to leave. Nobody rode that freight out of Cheyenne.

Weaver joined other frustrated riders who headed for a steep grade nine miles outside town, where trains slowed down. After a long wait, the hoboes saw a train approaching but uneasiness set in when they noticed that the engine had a helper. The two locomotives roared past in a cloud of dust.

"A fireman showed us a mouthful of teeth and gave the old Wyoming horse laugh," remembers Weaver. Some hoboes threw stones at the jeering fireman but Weaver saved his energy for the long walk back to the Cheyenne yards and another try at catching out. He was with a group who finally boarded a freight under cover of darkness. They rode for several hours before the train pulled into a small town in Nebraska. Weaver tells what happened next:

"The three bulls from Cheyenne had been with us all along.

They rounded us up at gunpoint and herded us all into the railroad station, where we were lined up and told to take off our clothes. While one bull stood guard, the others went through our pockets, the brims of our caps, even detailing our shoes and fingering our belts. They took half of any money they found 'to pay for riding the U.P.' My entire bankroll was four dollars and I was relieved of two dollars. A bindle stiff who had been following the harvest carried eighty dollars, which he was taking home to his family. His boxcar fare was set at forty dollars, a heartless thing to do. My feelings for railroad bulls were never lower."

Gene Wadsworth, who as a seventeen-year-old orphan had never been on a train until he began hopping freights, needed all his wits to outrun a Cheyenne bull. He was headed for Salt Lake City, riding on the top of a boxcar, when he saw the detective coming along the catwalk.

"I saw a crossing ahead with cars waiting for the train to pass. I knew we were traveling too fast to get off safely," said Wadsworth, who had climbed down the boxcar ladder. "I had no choice but to throw myself back as far as I could and jump free. I landed on the edge of the crossing, slid clear across the road on one foot and stepped up on the sidewalk. Cars hooted and people hollered and waved. I gave a little bow and waved back." Wadsworth returned to the yards that night and successfully caught a ride.

Carl Johansen was arrested by the Cheyenne bulls and turned over to the local police. "They walked me one block away from the yards and let me go. 'If you run like hell,' they said, 'you can still catch the train.' While Donald Kopecky personally escaped the Cheyenne bulls, he remained haunted by the memory of a boy of twelve who was clubbed by a detective: The youth's right eye was knocked completely out of its socket and hung down on his cheek. A police car came and took him to the hospital.

The reputation of Texas railroad detectives was just as fierce, especially legendary bulls like "Texas Slim," who was said to have killed seventeen men. Several former riders described how they fled for their lives with Texas Slim's bullets whistling above their heads. Bob Chaney was seventeen, on his way to look for work in California in 1931, when he and five other hoboes ran into this officer at Dalhart, Texas: "We had started to hop a freight when we heard someone shout, 'Hey, you 'bo's!' It was Texas Slim, all six feet seven inches of him, waving two six-guns at us. You never saw six men scatter so fast as when he began shooting those guns."

"Big Red," another raging bull of the Texas rail yards, caught sixteen-year-old John Kercsi as he climbed off a freight at ten o'clock one night. Kercsi tried to bluff his way out, saying he lived nearby, but his Connecticut accent gave him away. "Big Red started to hit me. I fell to the ground and covered my head with my arms. He kept yelling at me and kicking me repeatedly. When I got up, he booted me in the backside. I left the yard crying."

At Amarillo, Texas, teenage train-hopper Thurston Wheeler saw another bull nicknamed "Denver Bob" shoot a man. Attempting to catch out, Wheeler and other hoboes were crouched down in the weeds beside the tracks. "A train approached with Denver Bob riding shotgun on the engine. He jumped off and started firing into the weeds. I saw a young man rise up and make a run for it. Denver Bob shot him as he was climbing a boxcar ladder. When we saw the youth fall, the rest of us scattered."

The railroad bulls' frontier-style justice took all forms, with scant concern for the rule of law. Claude Franklin and his friends, runaway boys ages thirteen to sixteen, were summarily punished by a bull in St. Louis, Missouri. The officer made them bend over a bench and thrashed them with a length of rubber hose.

Harlan Peter encountered what was known as a "dollar division" between Lordsburg and Deming, Texas. The crew stopped the freight he was riding in the desert. With drawn guns and ready clubs, they rousted out the hoboes and assembled them a good distance away from the right-of-way. The order was "Pay up or walk!"

While detectives frequently disguised themselves as laborers to entrap trespassers, the bulls of Portland, Oregon, adopted an ingenious method to round up riders. Ben Fowler was on a freight pulling into Portland when he saw a couple of girls with bedrolls waiting beside the tracks. "Many guys ran for the timber on the opposite side. We decided to hop off next to the ladies," recalls Fowler. "When we did, a bull walked up with a gun in one hand and a blackjack in the other." As the arresting officer prepared to march Fowler and the other hoboes into Portland, they saw the decoy girls pick up their bedrolls, climb into an automobile, and drive away.

The poverty-stricken Dust Bowl family of William Wallace, traveling from Okmulgee, Oklahoma, to work in a California cannery in 1933, received different treatment from the bulls: William, who was twelve at the time, remembers that a squad of detectives stopped the train they were riding when it crossed the Texas border and started throwing off hoboes. But when a bull looked inside their car and saw William, his sister, and his parents, he told them to stay put.

Gordon Golsan was hoboing in Texas in the same year. A bull took the fourteen-year-old Golsan home with him, bought him a pair of shoes, and let him spend the night with his family. A few nights later, Golsan's new shoes were stolen as he lay sleeping in a hobo jungle. A man who witnessed the theft knocked down the thief and returned them.

Jack Jeffrey, a seventeen-year-old hoboing in the summer of 1932, also enjoyed the largess of a yard bull at Havre, Montana, a man whose reputation he had heard of as far away as Roseville, California. Jeffrey was trying to climb onto the blinds of the Empire Builder when he was spotted by a detective and pursued through the Havre yards.

"I could hear his footsteps getting closer as I ducked under a boxcar. The bull ran past me and stopped. He swept the beam of his flashlight back and forth and soon the torch was on me. As he grabbed my feet and pulled me out, I smashed my nose. He seized my shirt front and raised me to tiptoes, shining his light in my face, no doubt to get a sure target for the blow that was coming.

"I was surprised to hear him say, 'I never hit an injured man.' He took me to a shack with cold running water. By the time the bleeding stopped and I was patched up, we were almost friends.

'How long since you ate?' he asked. It was a day since I'd had a meal. That big, rough and tough guy took me to an all-night greasy spoon and bought me a stack of hotcakes and coffee."

Arthur Payne rode the rails as a young harvest tramp from 1929 to 1932. Then he went back to school for an education that would lead to a forty-five-year career as a distinguished trial lawyer in Indiana and the Midwest. Payne never forgot a blazing summer day at Fort Riley, Kansas, when the freight train he was riding was stopped by railroad bulls.

"A group of us young men had filled our pockets with stones from a gondola loaded with ballast. We spread out along the top of the freight cars. We'd no plan, no leader, and no intention of violence, hoping to God that nothing would happen. We had simply decided that we could not get off the train at Fort Riley.

"Armed detectives came down on either side demanding that every man, woman, and child leave the train. No one moved or made a noise. After a considerable time, the confrontation ended when the train whistle blew and we moved on to the West. I have often wondered what would have occurred had the detectives tried to remove us forcibly."

René Champion

———•———

1937–41

"I looked at the hill behind our house and at the
blue sky above. I wanted to reach the other side of
the hill and see what was there."

The impulse that drove René Champion to leave Johnstown,
Pennsylvania, in 1937 at age sixteen kept him on the road for
the next four years. René was born to an unwed mother in Paris in
1921. When he was eight months old, his mother placed him in a
children's home and emigrated to America. He did not see her again
until she sent for him in September 1929. Arriving in the United
States on the eve of the Great Depression, René grew up experi-
encing want and poverty.

I can understand why my mother left me in France. In those days
it was scandalous for a woman to be an unmarried mother. But at
eight and a half years, I never knew what it was like to grow up
with a mother, and my mother didn't know how to raise a child.

I was raised in what would today be called a dysfunctional family. My mother was a high-strung person, strong and demanding.
She never realized her ambition to be a fashion designer, which left
her frustrated. One result was constant warfare between her and
me. I'd never amount to anything, she would say. I was just a
'bum' and a 'no-good.'

My mother let out her anger toward me by hitting me with

whatever she happened to have in her hand, like a pot or a pan. More than once she came at me with a knife but restrained herself. Rare were the times that I went to school without a couple of lumps on my head or black-and-blue marks.

There was no question that the Depression was a big factor. Had we been living in happier times economically, I think things would have been different. My stepfather was twenty-four years older than my mother. He lost his business in the 1929 crash and became a traveling salesman. He later worked on a WPA project. There was very little money coming in, which added to my mother's unhappiness. We went on relief until my father found a ten dollar-a-week job in a department store, hardly enough for us to live on but it was better than nothing.

It was a humiliation for my mother to accept charity. I remember going with my mother to steal coal in the Johnstown rail yards. We nailed a wooden keg onto a sled and pulled this to the tipple, where we filled the keg with lumps of coal. I climbed on top of loaded cars and threw coal down to my mother. I was always afraid my schoolmates would see me at the tipple.

I had to wear hand-me-down clothes given to us by charitable organizations. Kids were not nearly as fashion conscious as they are today, but they could tell a shirt or a pair of pants that was twenty years out of style. I remember being forced to wear girls' shoes because they were the only pair in a package of clothing given to us. The kids at school made fun of me. I told them that the shoes were the latest fashion but they knew I was lying. I got into a couple of fistfights trying to defend myself.

I used to run away for two or three days. The police would pick me up and bring me back. I'd stay home for two or three weeks, then run away again. Eventually I was taken to juvenile court, where a judge decided that I was incorrigible and sent me to the Cambria County Children's Home for two months.

My first day at reform school I was sitting at a long bench table at breakfast. I turned to my neighbor to ask a question. Bingo! Next thing I knew I was lying on the floor with a terrible pain in my side. A guard stood above me holding a long stick, which he used to knock me off the bench. "We don't talk at meals," he said. I had to watch every move I made in the next two months.

One thing I give my mother credit for: She instilled in me a respect for education that made me stick things out until I got my high school diploma. After graduation, I decided to run away for good. It wasn't only my unhappiness at home but a yen for wandering. The horizon has always had an irresistible lure for me. Running away so many times, I learned a lot of street smarts that would be very useful to me as a hobo.

I remember the day I left home. It was sunny and bright. My heart was light and I felt a certain freedom. I was finally getting away.

I was drawn to the West by the cowboy movies I'd seen filled with romantic images of the Great Plains, the mesas and monuments, and the immense vistas of the horizon miles and miles away. Coming from the eastern part of the United States and suddenly emerging on those vast open spaces, I realized this was a world I was in tune with. It filled me with a special joy and made me feel at home.

The first time I tried to hop a freight train outside Johnstown I was lucky not to be injured. The train was going too fast and I didn't grab on tightly enough. My body hit the side of the car and I was thrown headfirst into the cinders. My face and hands were cut up and my clothes torn. I decided to hitchhike. Leaving the railroad tracks, I had to wade through a stream polluted by effluent from a steel mill. When I finally stuck my thumb out on the road, I was such a sight that nobody stopped for me.

I walked fifty or sixty miles before I got a ride with a trucker outside Harrisburg. He was heading for Philadelphia and that's where I went. If he'd been going to New York or Toronto, it would have made no difference. I was ready to go in any direction.

I hitchhiked Route 22, the William Penn Highway, to Chicago and then took Route 66 through Illinois, Missouri, and Oklahoma down to the Texas Panhandle. When I got into Arizona and New

Mexico there were so few cars that I had no choice but to ride freight trains to travel further west.

Experienced hobos taught me how to hop a boxcar safely. Most of the hobos were older: in their mid-twenties and thirties. You'd see twelve or fifteen hoboes sunning themselves on top of a boxcar, sometimes as many as two or three hundred together on a train looking very much like lines of blackbirds on telephone wires. Two trains would frequently cross each other on adjoining tracks, with some hoboes going west, some going east, all looking for jobs.

I worked whenever I could but seldom stayed anywhere very long. I did a lot of migratory farm work. I picked string beans and tomatoes in New Jersey, strawberries in Maryland, oranges and grapefruit in Florida. I cut wheat in Kansas. I pulled peanuts in Texas and broom corn in New Mexico. For a time, I also worked on a cattle ranch in New Mexico, a real live cowboy like my movie heroes.

One of the most moving memories of my days on the road is of a young couple with a baby who rode with us on a Southern Pacific freight. There were probably a hundred hoboes on the train when we pulled into Yuma early in the morning. The train was scheduled to stop for a few hours.

Everyone except the family with the baby got off. The hoboes went uptown to beg for food. They came back with milk, cereal, fruit, and bread, which they gave to the young parents.

It was like a hundred Magi instead of three bringing gifts to the infant.

One Sunday I climbed off a boxcar in San Jon, a small town in New Mexico. At the local general store, where I offered to work for some food, I learned that Pearl Rasnick, an old widow who lived ten miles down the road, was looking for a farmhand. I walked out to her ranch and got the job. She couldn't afford to pay me but would give me food and a roof over my head.

Pearl Rasnick was a devoutly religious woman whose one

pleasure besides reading the Bible was to attend revival meetings. San Jon was literally a wide place in the road, Route 66 its main street, with seven churches in town.

Pearl had an old Model T in which I drove her to a revival meeting at the Methodist church. This was the biggest church in San Jon and had the largest congregation. The revivals were conducted by itinerant evangelists, Elmer Gantry types who could be very persuasive.

I was listening to the evangelist's harangue when all of a sudden I felt a surge of electricity go through my body. I felt a force lift me out of my seat and drive me up to the altar. I had tears running down my eyes. The evangelist saw how moved I was and didn't stop me from addressing his audience. I appealed to the congregation to rededicate themselves to Christ. Usually half a dozen people would go up to the altar but that night practically everybody came forward.

The congregation knew that I was a young hobo who had hopped off a freight train a few weeks before. When the evangelist left, they asked the regular minister, Reverend Tossel, if he would let me preach to them. He was responsible for three churches and needed help so he agreed.

At seventeen, I became a lay preacher and spoke in one of the churches each Sunday. I felt at peace with myself, even believing that this was what I was seeking in my life as a vagabond.

But I was also a person who needs a rational explanation for things. I started asking myself how I could preach the existence of an all-knowing, all-powerful, all-beneficent God? What proof did I have of His existence? I didn't realize it but that question was the first crack in my faith.

I told Reverend Tossel that I'd begun to feel insincere. "It's the devil testing you," he said. "It happens to all of us. Fight it. Don't let it get the best of you."

I was losing the battle. More and more I asked myself questions that I couldn't answer, until I could no longer live with my doubts. I woke up one night in the middle of the night, packed my few belongings, and walked out of San Jon, ending my brief career as a preacher.

I knew hunger and cold, nights in jail for vagrancy, and beatings by railroad bulls, but most people realized I wasn't a hardened hobo. I looked young and was polite and well-spoken. People took pity on me, more than they would with older men. Women on the farms where I worked felt maternal toward me.

My experiences on the road gave me a great appreciation for this country—both for its physical beauty and for many of the people I met: honest, hard-working people with a good sense of values, who were kind and generous to me on the road.

I remember getting off a train outside Tucumcari with another hobo. The Tucumcari railroad bull had a reputation of being a killer. Neither of us knew whether this was true or false but we weren't taking any chances. We left the freight two miles out of town and walked the rest of the way. The first building we saw on the outskirts of Tucumcari was a diner.

The owner stood in the doorway wearing a white apron that came down below his knees. He called us over.

"I've been watching you walk up that road," he said. "You have a hungry walk about you."

My boxcar partner and I had come from Los Angeles and hadn't eaten for a long time. As we rode together we'd been telling each other what we would buy if we had a dollar. I wanted a deep-dish apple pie or a half a dozen hamburgers.

The owner of the diner had set out food for us. We offered to work for our meal, but he said no. "I know what it's like to be hungry. I'm glad to help you," he said. It was heartwarming to know that a total stranger cared for you.

I would go back to Johnstown periodically and spend a month or so at home. Johnstown lay in a hollow surrounded by hills blackened by soot and slag from the coal mines and mills. It wasn't long before I'd begin to think of the great open spaces

and the sunlit Western ranges that I'd traveled. The wanderlust
seized me again.

Hoboing is a lonely business. You're far from the town that you
grew up in. You're removed from the people and friends that you
knew. You're among strangers, each of them going his own way.

The wide open spaces of the West enhance the feeling of loneliness. When I was hitchhiking in Texas and New Mexico, I would
sometimes be picked up on the highway and given a ride that
ended five or six miles down a dirt road. "Here's where I turn off
to my place," I'd be told. I'd be stranded there all night.

I could characterize my social life while I was riding the rails in
one word: nonexistent. You're constantly on the move and don't
establish relationships, certainly not with women. Firstly, there
weren't many women riding freight trains. And secondly, women
in the villages and towns where we passed didn't want to have
anything to do with us. We were hoboes willing to work, but we
were viewed as bums. We dressed like bums, we looked like bums,
we smelled like bums.

I have often been asked, "What kept you going? What kept you
alive?" What kept me going was the freedom of it—and my cu-
riosity to see what lay on the other side of the mountain or beyond
the next horizon.

*In 1940, while hitchhiking in New Mexico, nineteen-year-old René
Champion was picked up by a dean of the University of New Mexico, who convinced him to attend the college. He tutored French to
pay for his tuition and worked in the dining hall for his meals. The
year he spent at the University of New Mexico sparked an interest
in anthropology, which would later be his chosen career.*

*In August 1941, Champion's wandering days ended when he
heard General Charles de Gaulle's call to arms and joined the Free
French Forces. He signed up in New York and sailed for Europe,
where he was assigned to the famed 2nd French Armored Division,
serving first as gunner and later as tank commander. On August 25,*

1944, in the liberation of Paris, his tank (dubbed "Mort-Homme," for the name of a World War I battle) was set ablaze as he stormed the German headquarters. Oblivious of his wounds, Champion fought to extinguish the fire and drive the tank to safety. He had a second tank blown up under him before coming back to the United States as a decorated war hero. In 1994, the French government bestowed the Légion d'Honneur on Champion.

On his return in 1946, Champion went back to school and earned his Ph.D. in anthropology from Columbia University. After a ten-year academic career, he joined a Rand Corporation think tank, doing research for the U.S. Air Force. He later worked as a strategic planner for several corporations, including Johns-Manville in Denver. Retiring in 1990, he went back to teaching, as a part-time professor of anthropology at two Denver universities.

The memories of a lonely runaway in 1937 have never faded. On a day more than half a century later, Champion walks down a country road outside Denver, the train tracks just a stone's throw away. The aging boxcar philosopher retraces his steps on a rite of passage from youth to maturity.

If I had to do it over and choose between going on the road or going to college after high school, there's no question I would do exactly as I did. My experience on the road gave me self-confidence. I overcame a profound shyness and saw that I could shift for myself. I could survive and be respected by people. Without that experience I don't know what kind of person I would've become because I was so beaten down psychologically and emotionally as a child.

As Champion watches a long freight come into view and roll across the Colorado landscape, his memories move him to tears.

The sight of that train, the smell and sound of it makes me cry. It reminds me of the freedom of the road. It is such a sharp contrast to the life I lead now, which is completely organized every moment and hour of the day. On the road, I would have been on that train. I would have gone wherever it led me, its whistle a siren song that reaches deep down and pulls you along.

Watching that train pass, I sense that I am saying goodbye to an innermost longing for that old freedom I knew. It makes no sense. It's no way to live, certainly not now.

Clarence Lee

—◆—

1929–31

Clarence Lee was born in Baton Rouge, Louisiana, in July 1913. There were four brothers and one sister in his family. At the age of eight, Clarence was given the responsibility of caring for his sister and younger brother while his mother washed and ironed clothes for people. She received five cents for every child's garment laundered, ten cents for adult clothing. Times got so bad for the Lees that they were forced to leave Baton Rouge and go into sharecropping.

When Clarence was sixteen, his father could no longer support him, and sent him out on the road. For eighteen months, Clarence hoboed throughout Louisiana, riding freight trains up and down the state in what was essentially a search for food to save him from starving. In 1931, he found work on a dairy farm at a wage of ten cents an hour. With his earnings he was eventually able to buy his parents out of sharecropping servitude for an amount he remembers precisely: $111.40.

My childhood ended the day we became sharecroppers. We worked the land of a man who owned a dairy. We had to milk his cows as well as plant crops. I had pain in the ligaments of my knees and couldn't walk. My father woke me in the darkness at 3 A.M., put me on his back, and carried me to the dairy to help with the milking. For three solid months, we worked without pity or mercy.

There was no time to play like other children. I wasn't allowed

131

to go to school. To this day I've no book learning. The kind of cropping we did was with strawberries, sweet peppers, cucumbers, and stuff like that. I was always loaded up with something.

Sharecropping was selling yourself to the devil. A Negro sharecropper had no farm equipment or farm animals. A white sharecropper often had both so that a farmer received only a third of the crop. You go in with nothing and the farmer is going to get more than a third of what you grow. To begin with, you owe money for board. If your mother wanted a little sugar or coffee, she had to go to the landowner to get it. He charged interest on every nickel.

The farmers put a mortgage on our lives. You get deeper and deeper into debt. When you can't stand one landlord any longer, you make a deal with another. He comes and pays what you owe and takes you to his place. One man sold you and another bought you like a slave. This happened over and over again. You were degraded from people down to merchandise.

You lie in bed at night on the farm, no light whatsoever, everything in total darkness. Next morning you beat the sun up and start to work. You work until the sun goes down. You are always at the mercy of someone else. Oh, yes, it was dark days—dark even at twelve noon.

I could see my parents' sadness. I remember my father saying to me, "Someday we'll see the end of the tunnel," and I replied, "Yes, and we'll have to be careful, there might be a train." My father had to laugh at that, but there was nothing to look forward to.

I'd never seen a dollar. I never knew a dollar had a face on it. I wanted to make a little money so my father let me plant a nickel bean crop. I planted twelve long rows of beans. The plants came up loaded with tender green beans. When it was time to harvest my crop, Mr. Summers, the landowner, took the beans away from me.

"Why did you take my crop, Mr. Summers?" I asked.

Mr. Summers came up to me, put his finger in my chest, and said: "Boy, this is not your bean crop, this is my bean crop. You're on my land. You use my animals. You sleep in my farmhouse. Your ma and pa are nothing on my land. And you are nothing and can't be more than I let you be."

After Mr. Summers told me that, I always thought I was going to prove something to myself. Someday I was going to have a piece of land of my own.

I wanted to stay home and fight the poverty with my family. I didn't have it in my mind to leave until my father told me, "Go fend for yourself. I cannot afford to have you around any longer." Until today it hurts when I think about it but there was nothing I could do. It was eighteen months before I saw my parents again.

We were mostly boys riding the freight trains at harvest time. You'd see some older boys with their little brothers but no fathers. Most of the time it was boys of fifteen or sixteen, teenagers like myself whose parents had put them out to make their own way. Sometimes two or three of us rode together but never a gang of youths. One or two could go and ask for help and a man might let you work in his fields. If he saw a gang of you, he didn't want you around.

It was dangerous riding the freights. You had to be careful not to stumble and fall under the wheels when you climbed on the cars. You had to jump off at the right time too 'cause once the train picked up speed you had a hard time getting off. Sometimes you slept in a boxcar in a rail yard; next morning when you woke up the train would be taking off with you. It was scary and dangerous but you had to do it to survive.

You never knew who was going to be on the train with you. If you hopped on a freight train with white people, you'd sit together in the boxcars. When they hit the ground they went their way and you'd go yours.

What I remember most is the "clunk" sound of the wheels hitting the joints in the track. It was a good sound and a good feeling too. "Clunk, clunk, clunk, clunk..." After a while you hear the whistle blow and other noises. "I'm doing OK," I'd say. "I've got a ride, I don't have to walk." You are not wandering without a purpose but going from point A to point B. You felt good 'cause you knew you were gonna get there. You were gonna try to better yourself.

I came right off sharecropping into the Great Depression. On the farms I always had something to eat. Now I had nothing. There came a time when a piece of bread meant a lot to eat. There was no waste like I see today, throwing away a sandwich and so on. Many times we didn't know one day from another whether we would have food or not.

Being on the road was a destructive experience for me. When I was riding the freight trains I didn't feel like an American citizen. I felt like an outcast.

I wasn't treated like a human being. I was nothing but dirt as far as whites were concerned. If you walked into a place to get a soft drink they'd kick you out. If you asked for something to eat, some would give you a piece of bread at the back door and tell you to get off the premises. Some would sic the dogs on you. It was hurtful to be treated like that. I felt very, very down.

When you went to people's houses to ask for food, if the color of your skin was white you fared better. If it was black you didn't fare too well. They might let a white man stay in the house with them, but me, I could sleep in a barn with the mules and hay.

One evening I got off a freight train and asked a farmer for work. His name was Mr. Ree. He told me I could sleep in his barn that night and he would give me something to do in the morning. So I slept in his barn and worked for him the next day.

"OK, boy, here's your pay, take it and be on your way,' he said when the day was over.

And I said, "Thank you, Mr. Ree, for letting me sleep with your mules in the hay. Thank you for letting me work twelve long hours for one dollar's pay."

That's what the Depression meant to me: riding freight trains from place to place looking for something to eat. You didn't panhandle and ask for a handout but offered to work. You didn't go around stealing anything.

Once we went to a place where people were selling chickens and they gave us one. There we were, three boys with a chicken like Mr. Hoover said, but no pot! We picked off the feathers, pulled the intestines out, and stuffed it with mud. We dug a hole, put the chicken in the ground and made a fire above it. When the fire burned down, all we had to do was remove the dirt and we had ourselves a chicken dinner.

You wanted to buy a pair of pants or some shoes but you had nothing. I found a shoe and a boot and I wore them so long others nicknamed me "Shoeboot." You could buy second-hand shoes for forty cents, but where are you going to get the money from? You are working twelve hours a day for one dollar just to survive.

My worst fear was being shot by a farmer who didn't want me on his land. If dark hits and you were on their property, they might just shoot you. If you got to their place before dark, they might let you sleep in their barn or just tell you to keep on down the road.

I saw too many hungry people to believe that it was just me. Poverty existed all over Louisiana. Nobody had anything much. Practically everybody I met was hungry. I saw little children with bloated stomachs like those you see over in Africa.

I'd see trains coming in and going out of Baton Rouge. People were sticking on the sides or sitting in the boxcar doors with their legs hanging out. People from the country coming to the city, people from the city going to the country to look for work. Passing each other on the tracks and finding nothing when they got to their destination.

I thought the Depression would never end. I saw it was bad all over. All I could do was stay in Louisiana and try to survive doing farm work. It was the same as the sharecropping that I grew up with, only now I was getting a little pay.

I was on a train from Baton Rouge to Denham Springs, Louisiana, going to look for work in the fields. I rode in a boxcar behind the coaches. The train was stopped at a small station along the route. I saw some people climb aboard to talk to the conductor.

After a time they left the coaches and came to the boxcar, where they looked me over real good.

"He'll have to get off," I heard the conductor say.

I asked why they wanted me off the train.

They told me that a white woman had been raped near Denham Springs. They said I fit the description, my color, my height, the way I was dressed. But they figured that I was innocent. I was in the boxcar traveling from Baton Rouge when the woman was raped. I couldn't be going and coming back at the same time.

At Denham Springs they would've ignored this. They would've taken me and lynched me.

I got homesick many nights as I lay in the total darkness of a big empty barn. Sometimes I lay crying, but then I would see myself and say, "I will go on."

I was motivated by poverty. I wanted to overcome it and do better in life. I had no education, no money, no home but I had common sense. I never reached for something that was too high for me nor did I stoop to something that was so low it would drag me down.

That's what kept me going—I wanted to do better so that I could go back and help my parents and my little sister and brother.

I was doing a man's labor, not a child's labor. The work didn't get too hard and the day didn't get too long. I figured I was a man and started to think of going back home. I would be helping to put something on the table before I put my feet under the table.

Clarence Lee's life as an itinerant farm laborer ended in 1933, when he took a job with a 7-Up bottling plant in New Orleans. In World War II, he worked on troop trains run by the Florida Central Railroad. Afterwards he was with the Jackson Brewing Company for thirty years before moving to California in 1974. In his sixties, Clarence became groundskeeper at St. David's School in Richmond, outside of San Francisco.

Clarence never forgot his vow on the day in 1928 when Farmer Summers seized the twelve rows of snap beans he'd planted. He came to own two properties in New Orleans and bought a house in California, where he and his wife raised their two daughters.

In his late eighties, Clarence was still working energetically on the grounds of St. David's School, a beloved figure to teachers and young pupils alike.

I like working with the earth and beautifying things. That's what gardening is: beautification. I find it good for the mind. You don't have to worry about anything else. I get out and work with the flowers and they depend on me and I enjoy it.

When I first started to work here I used to have nightmares thinking I would lose this job 'cause I was uneducated. My wife and I had sold everything we had in New Orleans when we moved out here. As time went on, things grew better and I wasn't afraid. I've been here over twenty years now, and in all that time I've used only one sick leave day.

I think I've done pretty well. Never stole anything. Never spent a day in jail. The children at St. David's ask me how I would like to be remembered. I tell them, "As someone with love in my heart, faith in God, and confidence in myself."

I have fought four battles in my life—war on poverty, share-cropping slavery, the Great Depression, and the civil rights struggle. I've been in all four and lived to tell it.

Tiny Boland

———•———

1934

C. R. "Tiny" Boland comes from South Dakota pioneer stock. His grandfather, John Edmund Boland, was a riverman on the Missouri who got his first job on a steamboat in 1868 at the age of thirteen. In 1876, John Boland worked on the Far West, a boat carrying supplies for General George Custer's cavalry on the Little Big Horn River. He subsequently served with government vessels that took part in the capture of Chief Sitting Bull's followers.

When Tiny Boland's father was a boy he cleaned pool tables in a saloon run by John Boland at Brule City, a South Dakota backwater below Chamberlain that was notorious for poker and drinking. At twelve, Tiny's father was a working cowboy roping and rescuing strays for a cattle company. But his early introduction to gambling led to his becoming a professional gambler on riverboats and trains.

Tiny Boland was ten at the beginning of the Great Depression and saw his family fortunes decline drastically over the next five years. By 1934, Tiny and a younger brother were living with their parents on a sharecropping farm at Jackson, nine miles outside South Sioux City, Nebraska. With no money for gambling, his father sold off his farm equipment piece by piece until his wife and children were left destitute. In May 1934, when he was not quite fifteen, Tiny left home to seek harvest work on the West Coast.

My last meal at home consisted of boiled potatoes for supper, no

138

gravy, no bread. It was the only meal that day. I hugged my Mom and said goodbye and then left.

My only possession was a new Gruen wristwatch, which I had bought for a dollar down and fifty cents a week. I went to the grocer and asked him if I could pawn it for five bucks. He said four dollars was all he could spare, so I took it.

Three friends and I arranged to travel together to the West Coast. I met them at the rail yards across the Missouri at North Riverside on the edge of Sioux City, Iowa, where we found a train going north to Aberdeen, South Dakota.

None of us knew anything about riding freight trains. You simply did it. You went down to the yards, climbed on a boxcar, and went wherever that train took you.

It is four hundred miles from Aberdeen, South Dakota, to Miles City, Montana. In twelve hours we had one drink of water and no food. Immediately after we pulled into town, I went into a bakery and lucked out. The baker gave me a bag of day-old rolls without even asking that I wash his pans or sweep the floor. One of my buddies was given coffee grounds. At a hobo jungle beside the tracks we built a fire, hooked a Number 10 can on a crotch stick, and tossed in the coffee grounds. That was probably the best cup of coffee I remember.

When we crossed the Great Divide around the middle of May, the weather was still very cold. One of my buddies had a fever and looked as though he was coming down with pneumonia. I gave him my bedroll to keep warm.

I was riding in an open gondola car loaded with reinforced steel. When the freight stopped at a siding to let a passenger train pass, I was shaking so badly that I caused that rebar to vibrate. A fellow stood up and took me by the shoulders.

"Son, you're going to freeze to death. You wanna come and get in my bedroll with me?"

It was night and I couldn't see who was talking to me in the dark. "Sure," I said. Anything was better than freezing. I climbed in with the stranger.

The following morning my three buddies expressed shock to see me asleep in a bedroll with a black man.

"Are you all right?" they asked.

"I sure am," I said. "Thanks to this gentleman here."

We sat talking with my rescuer, who was one of the most knowledgeable men I came across in all my days as a hobo. He knew when every train was going to make up and when and where it was going to leave.

We'd left because there wasn't a prayer of getting a job in our home town and we heard that we could earn money picking fruit on the coast. Four nights and three days later we arrived at Spokane, Washington. The depot had an unloading dock four city blocks long, where they stripped the boxcars and loaded the freight onto trucks. We were told that there were over two thousand hoboes sleeping on the dock that night.

I still had three of my four dollars left. We went to an eatery on Skid Row. For fifteen cents we got a pork chop with hash brown potatoes and peas and a cup of coffee.

There was absolutely nothing for us in Spokane. We rode a freight out the next morning taking the advice of hoboes who told us to go south toward Oregon. At Pasco, Washington, we were offered jobs picking strawberries. You're bent over all day long and if you worked your brains out, you couldn't make a dollar at the price they gave us per basket. One day of that and we quit.

We wound up in The Dalles, Oregon, where a farmer hired the four of us to harvest peas, pods and all, for a penny a pound. Each time you filled a basket, they would punch out a ticket with the number of pounds you had. If you worked real hard you made three dollars a day.

We spent the summer at The Dalles. At the end of each week, we went into town and sent a money order to ourselves general delivery. When I got home I had around forty dollars waiting for me. I bought my first car, a Chevy '26. In those days if you took a sixteen-year-old and cut his head open, you'd find a set of wheels. It was every young man's dream.

I returned to the same situation that I'd left. Dakota County, Nebraska, probably didn't have fifteen hundred families, of whom seven hundred were on direct relief. My father had a bad back and claimed that he couldn't work. I found employment on a WPA project that paid forty dollars for a forty-hour week. We cleaned drainage ditches and creeks and built a three-mile-long storm sewer in South Sioux City. I was working on that project in the middle of winter with the temperature at ten degrees below zero.

My family received two checks, one for $20.80 and one for $19.20. We'd compare the sales bills from local grocery stores. We'd see six boxes of wooden matches selling for a quarter at one store, three cans of canned milk going for a quarter at another store, and so on. We'd look for the lowest prices of every item to get the most out of every dollar.

We didn't have much in the way of meat. Out of one check we might buy three pounds of pork neck bones for ten cents. If we were really lucky, we'd get a bacon square from the jowls of a hog at eight cents a pound.

The Depression tore my family apart. What hurt my parents most was knowing that they did not have food to give us. I remember an occasion when a milk company put coupons on the back of their canned milk. I walked up and down the streets and alleys until I collected the ten coupons needed for a free can of milk. When I handed the can to my mother, she stood in our kitchen and cried. I would pick up rags and metal to sell for scrap and earn a few pennies for bread. To think that a little kid would have the moxie to know that his family's survival was all that mattered.

I was taken out of school in the early part of the eighth grade, when my father broke his arm while cranking our Model T Ford truck. I had to drive the truck and help my father peddle vegetables we raised on a garden plot. I repeated the eighth grade the next year, by which time we had moved to the sharecropping farm near Jackson. I had to hitchhike nine miles to school every day. Two months into the ninth grade, my formal education ended when my family fell apart.

After twenty-one years of marriage my parents broke up. My mother couldn't stand the poverty any longer and left. I did not see her for six years, until we moved to Topeka, Kansas, where she was living. She never spoke about abandoning us, only that she'd had no choice if she wanted to survive those tough times.

My father started drinking and left me to support my little brother. When he'd been flush, he was a real dandy who wore brocaded vests and carried a big moose tooth on a gold chain. I used to watch him practice the sleeve "holdout" and other sleights of hand hour after hour. He would go out and win a thousand dollars and then come back to Sioux City and lose it all on a crap table. He'd have a big story to tell but in the meantime we were at home without a loaf of bread on the table.

I resent my father for what he did to our family—how he took away from it when he should have added to it.

In 1935, my friend Dusty Mustain and I decided to ride the rails to the fruit harvest in California, taking the southern route down through Kansas.

I remember coming into Canadian, a division on the Santa Fe Railroad in Texas. When we stopped we saw railroad bulls shaking down the train. We were in a gondola car and crouched down, hoping we wouldn't be seen.

All of a sudden a flashlight shone in our faces. "Come on up out of there with your hands in the air," a detective ordered.

We got down on the gravel and stood with our hands up over our heads.

"Where do you think you're going?" he asked.

"To California," Dusty said.

"You ain't gonna go to California,' said the bull. "You can't get into California unless you've got one hundred dollars in cash. I don't think you've got one hundred cents."

He told us to wait beside the tracks until he finished searching the train. Then he was going to lock us up in jail for the night.

"When I let you out in the morning, I'm going to kick your little butts and head you back east."

He left us standing beside the tracks. When he got up by the engine, about three-quarters of a city block away from us, I told Dusty to make a run for it. We took off across the prairie.

In the hobo jungle the next morning, we learned that four riders had been beaten by the bulls.

We didn't go back to the Canadian yards but headed for the road and stuck out our thumbs.

Unable to enter California, Tiny Boland returned to Nebraska, continuing to work at menial jobs until he found a position as a meat cutter. Except for a stint in the navy in World War II, he made the meat trade a lifelong profession, eventually becoming a meat inspector. Tiny never forgot the pork neck bones and hog jowls served on his parents' table nor the lessons he learned in the Great Depression. Recalling those days, he visited the rail yards at Tempe, Arizona, where he retired, coming upon a present-day hobo jungle that stirred old memories.

This is very indicative of the way life was back in the thirties. It is a place to be in the shade, to cook something, and to go to bed.

Look around and you can see there's adult shoes and smaller ones too. Over by that tree, a child's stuffed toy. There's pots and pans, a cooker they could use if they had some charcoal or wood. Somebody probably slept in that old chair.

This is what you do when you're destitute and have to make do with whatever is at hand.

We're not in a depression, but people are still in desperate straits. It makes me sick to my stomach that we tolerate this today. Everybody has a right to life and the pursuit of happiness but you can't find much happiness here.

About the Photographs

> "The good photograph is not the object, the consequences of the photograph are the objects. So that no one would say, how did you do it, where did you find it, but they would say that such things could be."
> —Dorothea Lange

The core selection of the historical photographs in this photo gallery comes from the Farm Security Administration collection in the Library of Congress. In 1935, Roy Emerson Stryker, a Columbia University economics instructor was appointed head of a special photographic section of the Resettlement Administration, a New Deal agency set up to aid farmers impoverished by drought, soil erosion, and the effects of the Great Depression. This agency later became known as the Farm Security Administration (FSA).

From 1935 to 1942, Stryker and the photographers employed by him created 77,000 black-and-white documentary still photographs, capturing an unmatched portrait of the land and people of the United States in a period of profound change. Stryker's mission was to document the human catastrophe in the heartland to underscore the urgency of the FSA's work and still the voices of the agency's enemies.

Stryker's genius lay in tapping a team of photographers with soul—men and women who could translate thoughts and feelings into pictures. Some of those who worked for him, notably Dorothea Lange, Walker Evans, Carl Mydans, Gordon Parks, and Ben Shahn, would achieve great renown.

The FSA photographers were sent out on assignment throughout the United States and Puerto Rico, often on the road for several months. Given specific subjects and geographic areas to cover, before beginning their task they would make a detailed study of the region they were bound for. They went into the field with an educated, understanding, and compassionate view of their subject.

The result of their work, an unprecedented collaboration between government and the arts, is an enduring legacy of life in America without which we would all be poorer.

A child's-eye view from the other side of the tracks in Minneapolis, Minnesota. *Courtesy of the Library of Congress; photographer: John Vachon.*

A boy sprints for a boxcar in the railyard at Dubuque, Iowa. *Courtesy of the Library of Congress; photographer: John Vachon.*

Leonard McMilian rode the rails from Missouri to the California harvest in 1936. When his image appeared on the poster for the *Riding the Rails* documentary in 1997, he was identified by his family. "That's just the way I remember him," said his widow, Ethel Mae. *Courtesy of the National Archives; photographer unknown.*

"Naïve and fearful, overruled by ignorance and bravado, we walked to the nearest siding and caught a freight." —Donald Davis, age 16 when he rode in 1933. *Courtesy of the National Archives; subjects unknown; photographer unknown.*

Climbing to the catwalk. *Courtesy of the National Archives; photographer unknown.*

Hopping aboard a boxcar on the fly was perilous. In 1932, the Interstate Commerce Commission reported 425 fatalities and 1,344 injuries getting on or off cars or locomotives. *Courtesy of the National Archives; photographer unknown.*

Two youths ignore a cardinal safety rule, riding on top of a load of pipes that could shift in an instant. *Courtesy of the National Archives; photographer unknown.*

An Arthur Rothstein photograph shows the perplexity of a boy sitting on the drifting sands that encroach upon his Kansas plains home. *Courtesy of the Library of Congress; photographer: Arthur Rothstein.*

The family of a sharecropper in the Ozarks of Arkansas. Ben Shahn's lens reveals what 16-year-old John Fawcett discovered in the small town of Marshall, Arkansas—"People on the real edge of grievous poverty, with a quiet desperation for the future." *Courtesy of the Library of Congress; subject unknown; photographer: Ben Shahn.*

For African-American youths like this Florida boy, the beckoning rails seldom held any promise. *Courtesy of the Library of Congress; photographer: Gordon Parks.*

Families, often just kids themselves, landed, penniless, on the road. Dorothea Lange encountered this young mother, 17, father, 24, and child hitchhiking on U.S. Highway 99 in California. They came from West Salem, North Carolina. Their baby was born early in 1935 in the Imperial Valley, where they were working as field laborers. *Courtesy of the Library of Congress; photographer: Dorothea Lange.*

Above and right: Dorothea Lange's album of anonymous family despair beside the tracks at Toppenish in the Yakima Valley, Washington. *Courtesy of the Library of Congress; photographer: Dorothea Lange.*

Roving boys sometimes enjoyed a sense of camaraderie in the army of
wanderers. "Who we were, why we were there, where we were going
made no difference. We talked and laughed as a group. Next to God,
nothing was more comforting to the soul," says Leslie Paul, who rode
the rails in the summer of 1933. *Courtesy of the National Archives;
subjects unknown; photographer unknown.*

"What I remember most is the clunk sound of the wheels hitting the joints in the track. 'Clunk, clunk, clunk, clunk . . .' You felt good 'cause you knew you were going from point A to point B. You were gonna try to better yourself." —Clarence Lee, who left his Louisiana home to look for work in 1930. *Courtesy of the National Archives; subject unknown; photographer unknown.*

Every state, city, town, and village threw up its defenses against "unsettled persons" arriving on their doorstep. *Courtesy of the National Archives; photographer unknown.*

John Vachon shot these pictures of railroad bulls and guards in Michigan (top) and on a bridge in Tulsa, Oklahoma (bottom). *Courtesy of the Library of Congress; photographer: John Vachon.*

Young mother, age 18, stranded in Imperial Valley, California. *Courtesy of the Library of Congress; photographer: Dorothea Lange.*

An Oklahoma farming family forced from their farm by the drought of 1936, on the highway between Blythe and Indio, California. Their car had broken down and was abandoned. *Courtesy of the Library of Congress; photographer: Dorothea Lange.*

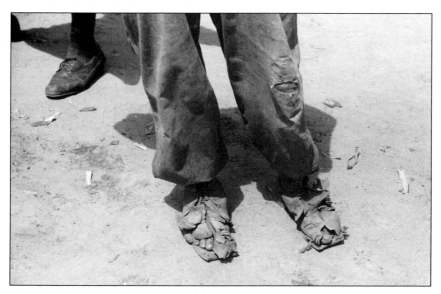

The shoes of a tenant farmer, photographed by Marion Post Wolcott in Columbia, South Carolina. *Courtesy of the Library of Congress; photographer: Marion Post Wolcott.*

Waiting for a ride in Halifax County, Virginia. *Courtesy of the Library of Congress; photographer: John Vachon.*

Carl Mydans found this mother and baby of a family of nine on U.S. Highway 70 in Tennessee, near the Tennessee River. They were living in a one-room hut built on an old Ford truck chassis. *Courtesy of the Library of Congress; photographer: Carl Mydans.*

Unemployed youth, Washington, D.C. *Courtesy of the Library of Congress; photographer: John Vachon.*

Boys in front of a drugstore in Dover, Delaware. *Courtesy of the Library of Congress; photographer: John Vachon.*

Asleep in the park in the Gateway district of Minneapolis, Minnesota. *Courtesy of the Library of Congress; photographer: Russell Lee.*

Storefront gospel mission in Minneapolis. *Courtesy of the Library of Congress; photographer: Roy Stryker.*

Young boy waiting to get a place to sleep for the night at the city mission in Dubuque, Iowa. *Courtesy of the Library of Congress; photographer: John Vachon.*

A harvest tramp in a camp in Harlingen, Texas. *Courtesy of the Library of Congress; photographer: Russell Lee.*

Preparing supper in a field in Belcross, North Carolina. *Courtesy of the Library of Congress; photographer: Jack Delano.*

"Some hoboes would sit and stare at one spot, only occasionally shifting their eyes. It was the same expression we later saw on the faces of men who'd seen too much combat in war." —Ralph Shirley, 17 years old when he rode in 1936. *Courtesy of the Library of Congress; subject unknown; photographer: Russell Lee.*

"Sometimes you'd find a mirror hanging up in the branches of a tree so you could take a shave." —Robert "Guitar Whitey" Symmonds. *Courtesy of the Library of Congress; subject unknown; photographer unknown.*

Shoeshine boy on 47th Street, Chicago's main African-American business district. *Courtesy of the Library of Congress; photographer: Edwin Rosskam.*

Two boys working as bootblacks in the market square in Waco, Texas. *Courtesy of the Library of Congress; photographer: Russell Lee.*

A young harvester photographed by Walker Evans in the fields of Westmoreland County, Pennsylvania. *Courtesy of the Library of Congress; photographer: Walker Evans.*

On the pea farm in Nampa, Idaho. *Courtesy of the Library of Congress; photographer: Russell Lee.*

"I was doing a man's labor, not a child's labor."—Clarence Lee. *Courtesy of the Library of Congress; subject unknown; photographer unknown.*

Cotton picking was backbreaking work at starvation wages for young migrants. *Courtesy of the Library of Congress; photographer unknown.*

A boy worker at Eleven Mile Corner, Arizona. *Courtesy of the Library of Congress; photographer: Russell Lee.*

Food! An army of hungry boys had their bellies filled and their broken lives mended in the CCC, the Civilian Conservation Corps. *Courtesy of the National Archives; photographer unknown.*

Hope! In the barracks at Camp Watersheet in Michigan, a CCC boy's expression beams with the promise of a new beginning. *Courtesy of Chester Siems; photographer unknown.*

On the road toward Los Angeles . . . "Despite all the horrors of the Depression, we didn't live in terror but looked ahead. We knew that down the road things were going to get better." —Jim Mitchell, who ran away from home in 1933. *Courtesy of the Library of Congress; subjects unknown; photographer unknown.*

John Fawcett.
Photographer: Lexy Lovell.

Arvel Pearson.
Photographer: Sam Henriques.

Phoebe Eaton DeHart.
Photographer: Lexy Lovell.

René Champion.
Photographer: Lexy Lovell.

Clarence Lee.
Photographer: Lexy Lovell.

Tiny Boland.
Photographer: Lexy Lovell.

James San Jule.
Photographer: Lexy Lovell.

Jan van Heé.
Photographer: Lexy Lovell.

Clydia Williams.
Photographer: Lexy Lovell.

Charley Bull.
Photographer: Lexy Lovell.

Jim Mitchell.
Photographer: Lexy Lovell.

Left to right: Michael Uys, Robert "Guitar Whitey" Symmonds, and Lexy Lovell. *Photographer: Sam Henriques.*

Hitting the Stem

Romantic ideas of life on the road vanished when a young hobo felt the first pangs of hunger. Pride and shame led many to go without eating for days, raiding garbage cans, picking up crusts of bread in the street, pilfering food. Finally they gave in and begged for a handout or a "lump," which they typically received in a sack. Sometimes they enjoyed a "knee-shaker," eating a meal on a back porch, and occasionally, a "sit-down," where they were invited inside the homes of sympathetic folks. In the lingo of old-timers, novice hoboes were also taught how best to "bum" a house or "put the arm on" passersby in the street.

The majority of homeowners and storekeepers helped the hard-luck kids. Sixty years later, the simplest acts of kindness were remembered by those who'd been half-starved and utterly dejected when they knocked at a stranger's door. Other kids, too, recalled seeing mothers and fathers help hoboes who came to ask for food. It was a lesson in giving that was never forgotten.

There were mean streets where young nomads were driven away without a crumb and towns where they were subjected to frontier-style justice. As young as sixteen, they were sentenced to work on chain gangs or labor on the "pea farms," and other fields where corrupt law officials supplied local growers with cost-free workers.

Destitute youths drifted from one shelter to another, paying for a bed at the YMCA when they had money, staying at the Salvation Army or other missions when they were broke. Some landed on "Skid Row," or in the newer "Hoovervilles" that proliferated in

American cities. Government transient shelters eventually provided wider relief, but still could not accommodate the human flood moving over the land.

The one place where the road kids were welcome was the "jungles," the hobo camps near the tracks—especially if they could "hit the stem" (Main Street) and scrounge scraps for a Mulligan stew. A boxcar boy, and girl—mostly they were in disguise—could eat their fill and then sit by the fire to hear the stories of old jungle buzzards, who had also been young a long time ago.

Hoover's Prodigal Children

On San Francisco's Nob Hill, William Csondor stood begging on a street corner in the damp and drizzle. Passersby in the wealthy neighborhood took pity on a small boy shivering in the cold in his shirt and shorts. In less than an hour, William netted two dollars that paid for a cheap room, where he showered before going for a meal and taking in an all-night movie. This went on for three months before the police finally got wise to him and he skipped town one step ahead of the Black Maria.

William Csondor was fifteen when he ran away from home in 1929 because of an abusive stepmother. He rode the rails for the next four years, making thirteen round trips from California to New York in a single year. Wherever he landed, he hit the stem and begged for money that came easily because he was so young.

On Miami Beach, an old couple gave William twenty-five cents. They followed him and saw him go into a café and sit down at the counter. He asked if he could buy something to eat for a quarter. Before William could order any food, the couple called him out of the café. They gave him another two dollars.

He recalled another occasion when he had a boil on his heel. A railroad brakeman took him to his home and summoned a doctor to treat him.

"The brakeman and his wife had no children," Csondor remembers. "They gave me a bath, clothes, and socks and begged me to stay. They wanted to adopt me and said they would send me to college but I said no. By then I was enjoying being a bum!"

Clay Nedblake's mother died when he was a boy, and he spent a decade in foster care in Nebraska and Colorado. In 1931 at age fifteen, tired of life in foster homes, Nedblake struck out on his own to explore the country and look for work. He rode the rails for the next four years, taking his first lessons in survival from old hoboes who had been on the bum since the early 1900s.

"I walked up to a group of hoboes cooking stew. They asked if I was hungry and I guess I was but I was too timid to share their food. One old 'bo looked across the tracks, indicating toward an old lady sitting on her porch. 'Go to her, tip your hat and smile, and tell her you'd like something to eat,' he said. 'Say that you will mow her lawn or do whatever she asks.'

"I went over and asked for food. The old lady gave me sandwiches, an apple, and an orange and put fifty cents in my hand. I didn't have to work for my first handout.

"I remember thinking, 'Boy, it's going to be a great life.'"

After his first experience, Nedblake felt no shame in begging. He knew that he could always get a little money, even if it was only a nickel that would buy him a cheese sandwich and a pint of milk. Panhandling the big cities, he ran into people who said, "Get outta here, you bum."

"I wasn't angry when they called me a bum. Why should I be angry? Hell, I was a bum. They were probably more frustrated trying to make a living with a wife and kids at home."

Not every young hobo was able to master the art of begging. Archie Lawson, a South Dakota farm boy, and his friend Jack Arney were on the road to California. At two o'clock on Thanksgiving Day 1932, they had left the rails and were hitchhiking when they came to a small Kansas town. They saw a family who had finished dinner gathered on their porch. Archie wanted to ask for leftovers but could not persuade Jack to go with him. A few days later, with their meager money exhausted, Archie was forced to beg food for both of them.

In his memoir, *Freight Trains West*, Lawson describes his feelings: "I went into a store to ask for something to eat. My face was red and I was practically crying. I could never remember what the storekeeper gave me. I went out of there like a dog with his tail between his legs. I made up my mind that was the last time I would go begging."

Ben Fowler fled a ravaged Dustbowl farm in Oklahoma in 1936 when he was seventeen to begin a five-year stint as a harvest tramp, sometimes finding a few weeks' work, sometimes forced to hit the stem: "Being on the bum is the worst thing in the world. You don't know anyone and have no one to turn to. First thing you know your clothing is run down. You walk into a place and they throw you out. You feel like a second- or third-class citizen, or not like a citizen at all."

In summer 1933, Ross Reager hitchhiked and hopped freight trains between California and Missouri. His solitary hitchhiking left him feeling reduced in the eyes of strangers. "I was nothing to most people. When they gave me a ride in their car I was like a piece of paper that they picked up, read, and then dropped on the roadside."

Sometimes a novice hobo was too young to comprehend what society thought of him. So it went with thirteen-year-old Harold Hoopes, bumming around Colorado in 1930 with two other boys not much older. When his companions landed day jobs at Limon, Colorado, Harold headed for a park bench and stretched out in the sun. A man and woman walked by and he heard them say, "There's one of Hoover's prodigal children." Harold, a runaway, did not know the meaning of 'prodigal child' but decided to get up and move on anyway.

When Norma Darrah, her husband Curly, and his nephew Harry rode the rails from Minnesota to Curly's new job in Casper, Wyoming, Norma found adventure on the road but Curly felt like a failure when they were compelled to beg for food. On a bleak wintry day in March 1938, the trio were waiting beside the tracks in Crawford, Nebraska, with no money for a meal. Norma knocked on the back door of a house close to the rail yard.

"A woman came to the door with a child in her arms. I was

shamefully aware of the dust and dirt on my imitation karakul coat and muddy snow boots. I wanted to run but my hunger was stronger than my shame." The woman fixed two scrambled egg–and-bacon sandwiches, which Norma took back to her husband and his nephew. "Curly wouldn't accept a sandwich. 'If I can't go for my own food, I shouldn't eat yours,' he said. No matter how Harry and I tried to change his mind, Curly would not eat."

On Peter Pultorak's second day on the road in 1931, he met an old tramp and asked him how to get by without money. "Put your pride in your pocket, your hat in your hand, and tell them like it is," his mentor advised. The lesson served Pultorak well riding the rails for the next eight years from his Detroit home to the blueberry harvests in northern Michigan.

"Being broke never bothered me," said Sol Tucker. While Tucker was standing on a street corner passing the time, a car pulled up in front of him with a flat tire. He offered to fix it for fifty cents. He spent twenty-five cents on a meal, fifteen cents for cigarettes, and ten cents for a movie. "I was back to square one. I never worried that something would turn up."

H. B. "Doc" Harmon was down to his last three cents. Walking along Route 66 in Gallup, New Mexico, he found a purse on the shoulder of the road with over two dollars in coins. With nothing to identify the owner and no one there to claim the purse, seventeen-year-old Harmon went to enjoy his best meal in weeks.

Hungry Times

Hunger conquered the pride of young hoboes. The roving horde was constantly hungry, living for days on stale buns and bread or "toppings" and frequently going without food at all. Recalled Clifford St. Martin, who was on the bum from 1931 to 1938: "When I woke in the morning I worried about something to eat. After breakfast I worried about where to go. In the afternoon, I'd more worry about getting food. When it started to get dark, it was time to worry about a place to sleep."

Robert Engle remembered picking up a crust of bread that looked as though a dog had peed on it. He was so hungry he ate it anyway but could not keep it down. He went into an orchard and ate a dozen apples that made him violently ill. For Jery Basham, who had gone three and a half days without food, a plate of cold beans looked like "manna from heaven."

William Hendricks graduated from the De Queens, Arkansas, high school in the spring of 1932 and began riding freight trains in search of a job. On his way to the apple harvest in Washington, he saw a sign in a grocer's shop at Bismarck, North Dakota, offering six one-pound cans of pork and beans for twenty-five cents. He used his last two dollars to buy forty-eight cans and ate them over the next four days on the ride to Wenatchee, Washington. Though the apple trees were loaded with fruit, the previous year's crop had sold for less than what the crates cost growers to buy. In 1932 there was no harvest, the apples left to fall on the ground and rot. At Portland, seasoned "knights of the road" advised William to press on to Klamath Falls to look for a job. It would take twenty-four hours to get there and he needed food for the trip.

"I asked a woman if I could split some logs in her backyard for something to eat. I worked for two hours and she came and said dinner was ready. I asked for a sack so that I could take the food with me but she refused. I sat down and ate until I was full. I went to another house and offered to rake leaves. After an hour's work, I was called inside to eat. The woman also refused to give me a sack. I went to a third house, was put to work and again had to sit down to a meal. I was in misery when I left and vomited before I reached the freight yard. By the time I reached Klamath Falls, I was starving."

Burland Webster and three road buddies set out from Long Beach, California, in the summer of 1934 to see the Chicago World's Fair. Within two days of leaving home, the boys were learning the meaning of life on the bum, as excerpts from Webster's diary indicate:

July 4, 1934: We spent most of the day going over the mountains in Idaho and Montana. About 6 P.M. we arrived in Missoula, where the train stopped for fifteen minutes. I rushed up town to get a loaf of bread but found the stores closed. I went back empty-handed and empty-stomached. To improve our mood we opened Hammond's can of horse meat, as we called it.

July 5, 1934: We had a marvelous breakfast of figs. Dinner consisted of part of a loaf of bread and a can of beans. Supper is the most delightful meal: a hunk of bread broken off rather than sliced.

Just as the beautiful Montana sun was sinking over the hills, I saw two figures dash across the front of the sun. It was a man and a girl. We watched them melt together in a lover's embrace; then they disappeared over the hill. We all sighed. Hammond and Clyde just looked kinda sad. Jack said "doggone" and looked forlorn. I felt lonesome.

Harold Kolima was six, his brothers five and nine, when they rode with their mother and puppy dog to follow the fruit harvests in California over four years from 1937 to 1940. Harold remembers standing in line at soup kitchens run by churches and the Salvation Army. "We begged food at groceries and were given bread, crackers, beans, and canned sardines. We'd invite ourselves to share meals of hobo stew." One day hunger drove Harold's mom to kick out the door window of a grocery store at Yuma, Arizona. "We were caught and expected to go to jail. Instead the Yuma sheriff paid our bus fare to California."

Overcoming his reluctance to bum a meal, seventeen-year-old Fred Hess approached a house in a small Kentucky town. He had lost his job in Champaign, Illinois, and was beating his way south to Texas, where his parents lived. Invited in by the woman of the house, Hess sat down to a feast of roast beef and mashed potatoes finished off with chocolate cake and a glass of milk. All the while, though, the new bum was worried to death: "I had loose change in my pocket and was scared the woman would hear the coins rattling."

Peter Chelmeldos never forgot the first time he plucked up courage to ask for a handout. The California-born Chelmeldos was sixteen when he began riding freight trains partly to escape strife at home and partly because he wanted to go to sea. He recalled his first days on the road in his memoir, *Peter, the Odyssey of a Merchant Mariner*. Arriving in Lafayette, Louisiana, after a week's journeying from Tucson, Arizona, he had had little to eat for days.

"I climbed off at Lafayette with an older hobo who'd joined me at Houston. The hobo told me to take one side of the street while he covered the other. I was to call him when I saw a family at dinner. I spotted a couple sitting down at their table. The hobo made me sit by a lamppost and watch until they finished. Chances were that the man would take his newspaper onto the porch while his wife cleared the table. When she did I was to knock on the back door and ask for any leftovers.

"When the woman heard my story she told me to wait on the porch. Her husband was settling down in his rocker as I came up the steps. His wife brought me a washbasin-sized dish of rice and beef stew, a loaf of French bread, and a dipper of water. To this day I remember watching the sun set over Lafayette, Louisiana, as I ate that banquet."

"Hallelujah, I'm a Bum"

Experienced hoboes were willing to pass on the refinements of the vagabond's life to the young beggars.

"Son, you don't ever have to go hungry," an old hobo said to Giles Wilkins. The hobo told Wilkins to look for a slice of bread in garbage cans. "Walk up to the nearest house, drop the bread on the steps, and ring the bell. When someone comes to the door, tell them that you are hungry. Ask if you can have the slice of bread. It will get you a meal every time."

Harry Fisher learned an equally effective ploy: When the woman of the house came to the door, if she looked sixty-five or seventy, you asked if her mother was at home. Hoboes taught Fisher never to bum a frame house for cast-off clothes as the occupants were generally renters with nothing to spare. A brick house was a better prospect, though the best place for clothes was the undertaker, who always had unwanted garments.

One of the techniques Edward Warr perfected on the bum was to hover at the window of a restaurant and watch for people who were about to go leaving food on their plates. "I would slide into the restaurant and sit down before the table was cleared. I got many a good meal of leftovers that way." Nine years old when he first rode the rails from his home in the Bronx in 1933, Warr was an accomplished hobo by thirteen.

Ed Shanholtzer's fare was more Spartan; the thirteen-year-old summer tramp would go into cafés where he would tell a waitress he was waiting for someone. "Almost all cafés brought you a glass of water. The tables had ketchup and crackers. I'd drink some water, pour ketchup in the glass, and mix in the crackers. It helped when it was your only meal of the day." In Kansas, when Shanholtzer had only nickels to his name, a hobo told him to buy a bag of sugar. "I made it last several days eating a little at two-hour intervals to kill the hunger pains."

Sometimes ploys used in hitting the stem were not so innocent. In 1938, Geneva Fuqua was sixteen and married, riding the freights with her husband from Oklahoma to Oregon. They hooked up with an older man and boy of twelve. Recalled Fuqua: "The man took the boy and me into town every evening. We stood outside bar doors with the light shining on us while he went inside. He told everyone he was trying to get us home to be with our mother who was dying of cancer. That's how we got money for food."

Paul Gould ran away from his Brady, Texas, home at ten because he did not want to attend school. He drifted down to the local hobo jungle where he saw an elderly man sitting alone at a fire. He gathered wood and laid it down beside the hobo who invited him to share his food. The pair went on to roam the country together until the following spring; for Paul it was the introduction to ten years' hoboing that lasted until 1936. Among the lessons that the boy learned from his first road partner was the work of chicken thief: "The old man's name was Ed, that was all he told me. He taught me how to steal chickens so they would not squawk or flop around and raise the devil. I would walk up to a chicken roost and put my elbow over a bird, at the same time grasping it with my hand. I would steal two chickens, one under each arm. Ed said he sent me because farmers wouldn't shoot a kid."

That first winter on the bum with Ed, Paul was in a boxcar with his partner one bitter winter night. The old 'bo asked him if he knew what day it was.

"I didn't. All I knew was that it was ten or twenty below zero and I was about to freeze to death. Ed told me it was the day before Christmas. 'You ought to be with your mother, kid,' he said."

Another pint-sized plunderer, James Overby, was on the road from 1928 until 1935 after taking off from a foster home in Rogers, Arkansas, at age twelve. One day Overby and a black boy were with a group riding a freight into Fort Smith, Arkansas. One rider knew of a watermelon patch just outside town. Overby, the black youth, and several others jumped off and raided the field.

"We had no more than kicked open the first watermelon when a shotgun started blasting at us. There was a cornfield at the end of the watermelon patch, the corn higher than our heads, and stands of Johnson grass higher still. I was going full bore when the black boy passed me like I was backing up. I can still see the Johnson grass seed flying like a jet stream as he went by. I never saw him again."

When Overby and the others climbed out of the field on the edge of town, they were arrested by the sheriff and taken to jail. "Being a youngster they didn't do too good a job searching me. They didn't find a .38 pistol I had under my belt. We were told to get out of town."

"I raided garbage cans but they were a poor source of food," said Donald Kopecky, a harvest tramp for nine years from 1931. "As a farm boy I knew by instinct where farm gardens were likely to be and looked for them as we rode into town. I would go back to the place after dark. You could usually find vegetables, melons, corn, and so on."

Waiting for a harvest job to begin at Phoenix, Arizona, Kopecky lived for three weeks in an orange orchard. "I found a bakery and saw that delivery trucks brought in day-old goods from their routes in the evenings. They dumped this into a bin to be picked up by a hog farmer. I loosened a board in the yard fence and replenished my supply every night. Milk was delivered by horse wagon. I waited at a dark, little-traveled intersection as the milkman went on his rounds. After a suitable time, I would go up to a house and retrieve his delivery. Sometimes the *Arizona Republic* or the *Phoenix Gazette* were also available."

Kopecky lived for three weeks on milk, cream, butter, eggs, bread, and oranges. Too hot to stay in the orchard during the day, he watched a murder trial in the local courthouse.

"I didn't like the life I was leading. I had to do it to survive," says Kopecky.

This was so for the vast majority of young nomads driven by hunger to pilfer food. To this day many are contrite recalling their desperate misdemeanors. When the Canadian freight they were riding stopped for water, Louis Vincent and a friend climbed into the cook car of a passenger train and swiped fourteen raisin pies. "We climbed back onto the roof of our boxcar and invited others to share our booty. We sat eating those pies and skimming the empty plates off into the night like Frisbees. I often wonder how mad that cook was in the morning."

On a stop in Colorado, C. D. White and his friends went into a café and ordered the most expensive meal with pie for dessert: "When we'd eaten, I asked the owner if he would sell us a pie. He disappeared into the back of the café to fetch it. May the Lord forgive me! When he returned, we were on a train heading east."

The Kindness of Strangers

A majority of people were sympathetic to the boy and girl tramps who came to ask for food. Dirty and hungry and far from family and friends, the young migrants were buoyed by numerous acts of kindness. William Aldridge retained a lifelong memory of a pretty girl who opened her door to him. "I asked for a glass of water, which she brought me," Aldridge recalls simply. In southern California, as Aldridge walked beside the tracks, a brakeman tossed him a quarter. "Go get yourself a meal, kid," the man said.

Paul Booker was sixteen when he decided to go on the road in June 1931. He hitchhiked and rode freight trains from Bedford, Indiana, south to Texas and Arizona and then back north to Seattle. Riding from San Francisco to Seattle at night, he fell between two boxcars when the train lurched. Only because they were moving slowly could he grab a steel bar and pull himself back up. In Texas, he was shot at by Texas Slim as he fled the Longview yards; in the northern states, vigilantes threatened to shoot him if he tried to climb off a train.

"I thought I was tough but changed my mind finding myself suddenly thrust into the buzz saw of life," said Booker. "I arrived in Milwaukee weak from hunger, my lips in scabs from sunburn and thirst. My only goal was to get home as soon as possible." A fast mail train was getting ready to pull out of Milwaukee's Union Station. It carried no passengers except one: Booker grabbed the back of the engine and climbed onto the water tank. In a short time, he was in Chicago.

"An angel in the form of an eighty-year-old woman touched my hand in downtown Chicago. She asked if I needed help. When I told her my story she pressed a dollar bill in my hand. 'God bless you, son,' she said." Booker hitchhiked the remaining 275 miles to his Indiana home. "In two months I'd gone to hell and back. It was good to be home again."

Since he was thirteen, Daniel Elliot had been traveling with his father, who had lost his job of twenty years. The pair accepted whatever work they could find from selling tamales in Denver's streets to building fences in Wyoming. In Idaho, father and son were forced to take different farm jobs and separated. Daniel roamed around the country on his own, landing up in Nebraska in a bitter winter. Homesick and penniless, he wanted to return to his mother in Minnesota.

"A cattle train came into the yards at Grand Island, Nebraska.

The cattlemen traveled in a passenger car behind the caboose. I was so cold I just walked in and sat down. The brakeman wanted to throw me off the train but the cattlemen stopped him. They gave me sandwiches and coffee and let me sleep. I had to get off the train at Omaha. The cattlemen had held a collection and gave me twenty dollars. I felt like a millionaire."

Edward Palasz was panhandling in Boston in late April 1932 when he wound up at the 4th Precinct station on Washington Street. Two weeks earlier Palasz's foster parents had put him out of their Pennsylvania home. Hauled into the police station expecting the worst, he met Sergeant Johnny Hourihan, who took pity on the homeless fifteen-year-old. Sergeant Hourihan gave Edward a blue work shirt and paid $2.50 for his bus fare to New York. Six years later Palasz had joined the merchant marine and was on a ship that docked in Boston. "I found Sergeant Hourihan and paid my debt with interest for a memorable day in 1932," said Palasz.

Alvin Svalstad, a young teacher from Sissenton, South Dakota, was equally grateful for the generosity shown him on the road. Svalstad was returning from the Chicago World's Fair with $2.75 in his pocket and eight hundred miles to get home. Hitchhiking outside Springfield, Wisconsin, he was picked up by three people in a car. Before they dropped off Svalstad, a young woman asked how much money he had. "When I told her she gave me fifty cents. 'When you have some money, pass it on to another needy person,' she said. You can't imagine the number of times I have passed on that fifty cents."

Seventeen-year-old John Gojack had been hoboing for a year when he left Houston with a friend in February 1934 to go to Mardi Gras at New Orleans. Finding the city swarming with transients, they decided to return to their home in Dayton, Ohio. Three days later they were on a slow-crawling freight rumbling through Mississippi.

The son of Hungarian immigrants whose mother had died in the Great Flu Epidemic of 1918, Gojack ran away from a Catholic orphanage in Dayton and began riding the rails when he was twelve. He recalled his train-hopping experiences in a family memoir, *A Long Way from Hungary*.

In the three days after leaving New Orleans, Gojack and his companion had had little to eat. When the train stopped at a siding outside Hattiesburg, Mississippi, Gojack ran over to a shack two hundred yards away at the end of a cotton field: "A wrinkled old man with white hair sat in front of a tiny cabin with clapboard windows and no glass. His rickety chair appeared to be ready to fall apart and he looked the same. I told him I hadn't eaten in three days and asked if I could buy some food. The old man pulled himself out of his chair and walked over to the cabin door.

"'Mandy, this white boy says he is hungry.'

"'We've got the pot likker from last night's supper,' his wife replied.

"A gray-haired lady stepped out of the cabin. She looked even older than her husband and had trouble carrying a blackened kettle. The bottom held the congealed remains of a butter-bean stew. It didn't look appetizing but it smelled delicious.

"The old couple smiled and watched as I scraped the pot clean. In the cabin's dim light I could see how poverty-stricken they were. I marveled at how well they maintained their pride and dignity. It was a pleasure to slip two quarters under the kettle."

Oklahoman Edgar Bledsoe had believed a newsboy's cry of "Stock Market Collapses" in October 1929 referred to a disaster at a cattle auction barn. By 1932, Bledsoe had been riding the rails for two years, picking cotton and doing menial work that rarely provided a living for the eighteen-year-old and two cousins who traveled with him. That summer the trio were returning to southern California, where Edgar's cousins lived with their widowed mother.

Climbing off a freight in Oklahoma City, they had gone to a soup kitchen where they found a long line of people waiting with half-gallon buckets in their hands. The boys were told that they had to bring their own containers for soup. While they were scrounging around for these, the kitchen ran out of food and closed. They went to a baker who gave them a loaf of day-old bread.

"We walked away from that depressing area to the edge of a residential district and sat on the curb to eat the bread," said Bledsoe. "We found it dry going and were choking it down when a squeaky-clean kid of junior high school age came along. He stared at us and then quickly walked on down the street. Pretty soon he came back with a quart of milk and half a dozen slices of bologna. He handed it to me and then turned and ran like the devil was after him."

Bledsoe and his cousins rode a freight to Comanche, Oklahoma, from where they had to hitchhike to his cousins' home on a drilled-out oil field. They had to walk the last thirteen miles, taking a shortcut through the woods.

"We ran across a log cabin deep in the blackjack oaks. It had a well in the backyard with a rope and a pulley. A man who must have been close to ninety years old came out of the cabin. We asked if we could have a bucket of water.

"'When did you boys last eat?' he asked.

"When we told him, he asked his wife to bring us food.

"She set out a gallon crock that was half full of milk, a pone of cornbread, and a bucket of sorghum molasses. The milk was beginning to turn sour—'blinky' we called it—and the molasses was full of tiny ants. We were hungry beyond being picky and we lit on the food. Besides, I still remember we couldn't fault the old lady's cornbread."

"Being Jewish didn't hurt at all. When we arrived in town we headed for the nearest synagogue. They would give us two vouchers, one for lodging and one for food. Sometimes we would bring a gentile friend along and he would get vouchers too," Brooklyn-born Harry Kaban remembered. Kaban left home at seventeen and traveled the United States for a year. In Kansas City in 1933, Kaban and a road partner went to watch Barney Ross train at a local gym. When the boxer asked where they came from, they told him they were on the road.

"Barney Ross could have ignored us but was most generous. He told us to meet him at his hotel, where he took us into a fine restaurant and asked the waiter to serve whatever we wanted.

When we finished dinner, Ross came over to our table, paid the bill, and gave us each five dollars."

Sidney Kaufman, who bummed around the East in 1933, also found that Jewish boys could often make out better than most by passing on information about the "soft touches" among Jewish businessmen. There was a drawback in some towns with a small Jewish community: The wandering boys often were plied with food and offered jobs by fathers eager to marry off a homely daughter.

Help could come from totally unexpected quarters. Watching from the window of a passenger coach at Minot, North Dakota, a traveler witnessed Myron Overland being thrown off a boxcar by a bull. The good Samaritan called Myron over to the train, paid his fare to his destination, and took him to the dining car. Myron could not believe his luck as he tucked into a plate of fresh poached salmon.

On one of Ben Fowler's first outings as a hobo in 1935, the seventeen-year-old harvest tramp threw his bundle of belongings onto a flatcar in Ogden, Utah. When he tried to catch the train, it was traveling too fast to jump aboard. He was left with nothing but the clothes on his back.

Four days later in Portland, Fowler knocked at a door to ask for food. He told a woman he had lost all his possessions and offered to weed her backyard for a handout. "While I was busy she collected clothing from neighbors. She not only fed me, but sent me on my way with a bundle of jackets, shirts, and trousers," said Fowler.

When Otto Oliger and two other youths walked past an ice cream parlor at Flagstaff, Arizona, the owner asked if they had gotten off a freight train that had just pulled in. When they said they had, he invited them into his store: "He sat us down at a table and asked when last we had written to our mothers. Not for several weeks, we admitted. He brought paper, pens, and stamped envelopes for us to write home. When we finished, he rewarded us with chocolate ice cream sundaes."

Russell Morrison, sixteen, and his friend, Art Louch, set out to conquer the West from Staples, Minnesota, in July 1936. They had a dollar's worth of groceries that Russell had charged to his father's account. On their two-week trip to Oregon, they were stranded in a small town in North Dakota.

For an hour, the boys stood outside the only grocery store trying to get up the nerve to ask for food but gave up and headed back to the railroad tracks. On the way they passed a house with an apple tree in the yard. They filled their pockets with unripe fruit and took off as fast as they could.

Several hours later they were still trying to catch out but the trains rushed through too fast to board. They decided to hitch a ride to a larger center where the freights stopped.

"We had to pass the house with the apple tree," recalled Russell. "A woman came out and called us over. Now we're in for it, we thought. All the woman had to say was: 'You boys must be very hungry to eat those green apples.' She prepared us a delicious brown bag lunch."

Channing Smith was also sixteen and on the bum in the summer of 1935. Riding the rails in the dry country of eastern Washington he made the mistake of not carrying a canteen. His thirst increased as the train started its long climb into the Cascade Mountains. Looking out of the boxcar door he saw a shack on the side of a hill five hundred feet from the tracks. He figured he could run up and get a drink. He jumped off the train and was about halfway to the shack when a man stepped out. Smith recalls: "He gave me a drink of water and then went back inside for two loaves of bread that he shoved into my hands. I have often thought of his sheer generosity. A man living in that isolated spot and probably owning little more than the clothes on his back feeding a dumb kid with no better sense than to ride freight trains."

Have Pity on the Boy

In the Omaha rail yards, twenty-year-old Van Rance climbed down from the crack passenger express he had ridden from Chicago in late summer 1933. A decade later he would make the same journey in style riding the cushions as a member of the Metropolitan Opera

Company. Now he slipped into the station restroom, washed off the soot and cinders as best he could, and went in search of food. At a lunch counter near the yards, a waitress studied him attentively.

"'You look weary,' she said. 'Have you been riding the freights?'"

Van Rance told the waitress he had ridden on the tender of an express.

When she brought his food, there was much more than he had ordered. She gave him several refills of coffee.

"I finished and she reached over and held my hand. 'This is on me,' she said. 'Take care around those trains.'"

Several former riders recalled the openheartedness of waitresses. Max Sarnoff praised the "Harvey girls" who served at restaurants along the Atchison, Topeka, and Santa Fe line. When you appeared at the back door of a Harvey House restaurant you would always get soup and a sandwich if you were willing to do some "pearl diving," or dishwashing.

Dorothy Gavin, a waitress in Oshkosh, Wisconsin, in 1937, saw many young men down on their luck riding the rails to find work. One particular Wednesday night a young man came in and sat down at her counter.

"He wore a droopy hat and was dressed in jeans and a khaki jacket. He looked at a stale breakfast roll in a glass case and asked how much it was.

"'Ten cents,' I told him.

"'How much for a cup of coffee?'

"'Five cents,' I said.

"He sighed and set a dime on the counter. 'I'll take the roll and a glass of water, please.'

"I knew he only had a dime. 'I guess we could sell that roll for a nickel,' I said. I served him and went over to two young women who were beckoning me from their booth. They both spoke at once. 'Give us that boy's check.'

"I gave the boy back his dime. The night cook had been watching through the window in the kitchen door. When I told him the story, he made me send the boy to him. Mystified, the boy went to the kitchen. The cook dished up a meal of meat and potatoes, corn, bread and butter, and a slice of pie. The boy was happily stuffing himself when our proprietor came in. After hearing the boy's story, he personally took him to a shelter where he could find a place to sleep.

"This happened frequently during the Depression. 'That could be me,' we all knew. We saw boys like that and also thought of their mothers and how they were worrying about their sons."

Eighteen-year-old Wallace Horton joined the Dustbowl diaspora from his home state in Nebraska in 1935 when he was eighteen. He picked peaches in central Washington and cut cordwood in the forests of western Oregon. He had worked for a couple of months felling and splitting hundred-foot trees when he began to have severe pains in his side. Realizing that he was seriously ill, Wallace decided to go home to his mother.

In Kemmerer, Wyoming, a bull forced him to jump off a boxcar as the train was picking up speed. Catching his foot in a switch rail, he fell, bruising his arms and legs and ripping his clothes. The bull jumped down and caught him. Given the choice of buying a rail ticket to the next town or going to jail, Wallace handed over his last $1.50 for a ticket to Green River.

"I arrived cold, tired, and bruised and desperately wanted a place to sleep. I came to a sign: 'Rooms Upstairs.' I thought I would ask for a room in exchange for an offer to work the next day. When I rang the bell, a young lady came to the door. I told her I was looking for a room.

"'Honey, men don't come here to sleep,' she said. I started to leave but she stopped me. 'You look as though you've been through a lot.' I told her my story. 'I won't be needing my room tonight,' she said. 'You can stay here.'

"I couldn't believe this was happening to me. I washed and went to bed. In the morning the lady took me to breakfast with the other girls. It taught me there are good people in every profession."

Wallace Horton reached his Nebraska home and had an emer-

gency operation to remove his appendix. A day later and it would
have ruptured, a doctor told him.

When Charles Doty left Oklahoma for California, his mother
advised him to go the "hustling class" should he ever find himself down and out. Prostitutes and pool hall hustlers were more
likely to help him, his mother said, since to them money was easy
come, easy go.

There were exceptions, as Chuck Bishop and Jimmy Nugent
discovered when they tried to bum the red light district in
Winona, Minnesota. They were traveling with an experienced
hobo who showed them how to hit the stem for food. They were
sitting on the curb eating stale rolls and cheese when Nugent
asked a passerby for a cigarette. The man gave him a cigar. As
they started back to the station, Jimmy lit the cigar and strutted
out in front of his companions. Chuck Bishop recalled that pan-
demonium broke loose: "Girls rapped on windows and called to
Jimmy. One of them stepped out and led him into a house. Moments later he was tossed back on the street.

"'I told them I was hungry and asked if they had anything to
eat. They kicked me out,' Jimmy said."

Arriving in Little Rock, Arkansas, with fifty cents in his pocket,
sixteen-year-old Parley Jensen looked for a twenty-five-cent room.
The only accommodation he could find was in a house of prostitution, where the Madam had a son of the same age. The boys hit
it off right away and the mother let Jensen move in and share her
son's room while he looked for work. "I lived for a month in a
whorehouse and left, so help me, still a virgin," declared Jensen.

On his second cross-country trip in 1933, James Pearson ran
down into Mobile, Tennessee, with a road partner. At fifteen, Pearson had been on the road for two years, after leaving Newton, North
Carolina, to escape a hell-raising stepfather. On the way to Mobile,
he and his companion had several hours' layover in Memphis.

"We knocked at the back door of a two-story house. We got the
surprise of our lives when a beautiful woman answered the door
wearing a see-through gown, garter belts, and high heels.

"We asked if we could work for food. She said her cinder driveway had low spots and when it rained her shoes got wet. Could we fix the driveway?

"'Yes, ma'am,' we said. She told us we'd find tools in her garage. She had a new Cadillac, a mile long, parked in there.

"We made a project of the driveway. She called us to eat and we went inside the house. What a meal and what a floor show: a steady stream of women dressed for action and men coming and going from the front door. It was a sight to remember."

A Good Place for a Handout

The young hoboes never forgot those who reached out to them in their time of need. For their benefactors, too, the ragged bands who knocked at their doors were remembered, especially by the boys and girls of the house. Many were deeply touched by seeing their parents' compassion toward total strangers.

In the 1930s, Albert Tackis' family lived in the small West Virginia town of Colliers, where their house backed onto the Burgettstown Grade. Two-engined freight trains stopped at a water tank behind the house before starting the thirty-mile haul to Burgettstown. In summer, Albert would see sixty or seventy hoboes climb off the cars to stretch their legs, every train delivering as many as eight hoboes who came to the Tackis' home to ask for food.

"We were five people in our family: Mother, Father, Grandpap, my sister, and me. Grandpap grew all our fruit and vegetables in his garden. In season, Mother canned vegetables and made jellies. Every week, she baked twenty-one loaves of bread.

"When Grandpap saw the hoboes coming to our house, he alerted Mother, who would start making egg sandwiches and packing bags with carrots, tomatoes, apples, and peaches. Grandpap always had something for the hoboes to do. There would be wood to chop, cans to pick bugs and insects in his garden, buckets to fetch water from a spring. The hoboes worked for about twenty minutes and then hopped back on the train with a good meal in hand."

The Pennsylvania Railroad moved a tremendous amount of coal on the Burgettstown Grade. When the double-headers stopped at the water tank, lumps of coal dislodged from heaped-up cars. The kids of the area had the chore of filling gunnysacks to restock their families' coal bins. Once a week the Brooke County sheriff sent a bull from Wellsburg to patrol the stop. While the engines took on water, the bull walked up one side of the tracks for a hundred yards and then back on the opposite side, sometimes with five or six hoboes in tow.

Albert Tackis recalled that when the bull came to the water tank, he made the children empty their gunnysacks and chased them off railroad property.

"In retaliation, we ran down the tracks shouting, 'Bull is coming! Bull is coming!' Hoboes jumped off the cars by the dozens, crossed Colliers Creek, and waited until the train started moving before climbing back aboard. They were thankful that we had warned them. Whenever they could, they helped us fill our sacks with coal. Never once did we experience an unpleasant incident, the hoboes who came to our house were always polite and gracious. I also remember there was no happy-go-lucky mood about them. They were riding the freights through tough times until a better day came for all of us."

Las Cruces, New Mexico, was an important crossroads on the southern route to California, where the Santa Fe railroad passed through town linking Albuquerque and El Paso del Norte with the Southern Pacific line. Manuel Chavez was ten when the *trampas* first began to come to the Chavez house two blocks from the center of Las Cruces.

"My mother, Margarita Bombach Chavez, never turned down anyone. She would prepare a delicious chili from the Mesilla Valley, a big pot of pinto beans, and hot tortillas. She put a table under the shade of a mulberry tree where the hoboes could enjoy their meal with a little dignity. I would hear them say, 'Thank You,' and see them leave with a smile on their faces.

"Mother had a younger brother who hopped a freight from Albuquerque to Las Cruces around 1917. He slipped while trying to board and was killed. Maybe this is why mother had such a soft heart for the *trampas*."

At Cottonwood, Idaho, William Loft—a local dentist's son—would watch the freight trains pull in with tired hoboes riding on the top "sitting with their heads slumped down and looking more like sacks of grain." One day William saw one of the men put a mark on their fence. He ran out and asked why he did this. The hobo explained: "Son, when you're starving and on your last legs, this means there's a hot meal and friendly people you can trust."

The mark on the Loft's fence was one of many signs hoboes traditionally used to alert each other to houses where they could get a handout, what approach might work best, and what houses were best avoided.

〒	SIT DOWN MEAL	⬭	ONLY BREAD GIVEN HERE
⊗	GOOD PLACE FOR A HANDOUT	8 ▲▲▲	KIND WOMAN
†	RELIGIOUS PEOPLE	⌇ o x o	GOOD WATER
⚲	SLEEP IN BARN	o ⬿ o	SAFE CAMP
⅀	SOMEONE HOME	⑃	NO ONE HOME
⌣⌣	BARKING DOGS	///	UNSAFE AREA
▭	DANGER	⌁	HALT
⊘	GOOD ROAD TO FOLLOW	⌒⊙	BEWARE AUTHORITIES

The houses in Patricia Schreiner's neighborhood in Ypsilanti, Michigan, were just blocks from the railroad yards. Schreiner recalls a hobo coming to their door one cold, below-zero day. "Mother had just heated up tomato soup to go with our sandwiches. She grabbed another bowl and filled it for the hobo, telling him to step inside and warm up. He looked half frozen but refused to come in and stood outside the door as he ate. 'May God bless you, ma'am,' he said when he finished, and left quietly. Mom had tears in her eyes as she watched him walk down an alley to the tracks."

A friend who was a policeman told Pat O'Connell's father that his house number was written on a fence in the hobo jungle at Billings, Montana. O'Connell's father was a cattle buyer and frequently shipped animals by rail. He would pay hoboes to help sort and load animals and would employ some on his holding ranch. "At home mother always gave 'askers' a sandwich and a cup of coffee when they arrived," said O'Connell. "After they'd washed up, she fed them a full meal on the steps of our back porch. When they left, she gave each a quarter. It was a damn difficult time—a humiliating time for many."

Glenna Emlenger and her six brothers and sisters lived in a small town half a block from the Pennsylvania Railroad tracks, where their mother's kindness toward hoboes led them to "mark" their house. In the depths of the Depression, Glenna's father lost his job.

"My father walked the streets looking for any kind of work to no avail. One day a young man came to our door to ask for food. All we had in the house was a little chicory coffee and some bread. My mother felt bad having to tell him that she had only enough for us kids.

"'Save it for the children,' the man said, and left our house.

"Later we would find food on our porch, sometimes a slab of bacon, sometimes a sack of cornmeal. We knew it came from the hoboes."

As a child, Vivian Holland helped her widowed mother in her restaurant near the railroad yards in Chattanooga, Tennessee. She remembers feeding many transients and giving them leftovers for the road. "When they got on their feet again, some sent money to pay for the food they had eaten. The deadbeats we encountered were not hoboes but men who had white-collar jobs with oil companies or owned their own businesses. They brought their families for three meals a day and ate on credit. They ran up debts of as much as twenty to forty dollars before they skipped town—or went bust."

Betty Glover's folks lived in a coal mining camp in Hartwell, West Virginia, in the 1930s. Their house was on top of a cut over-looking the railroad. Betty's mother never denied food to hoboes who asked for a handout, though once she came close to cutting off the supply. "Mom left clothes hanging on a line on the hill. Daddy's long johns disappeared, along with some bacon from our smoke-house," Vivian said. "Mom was very mad. She said she wasn't going to give out any more food. I am sure she didn't hold to that."

Whenever Father Roger La Charite of the Edmundite Missions in Selma, Alabama, eats a bologna sandwich, he remembers the hoboes who came to his mother's door. They lived on a dead-end street in a small town in Vermont, and word had gotten out that people could get help from his mother. Father Roger recalled one summer evening when two men trudged up to their door and knocked timidly.

"Mother listened silently as they stammered out their plea for help. Even as a child I could tell that they were deeply embarrassed by the fact that they were jobless and had to beg for food. These desperate men always left our house with something to eat and drink. At that time of year, the sandwiches were made with bologna and homegrown tomatoes and lettuce from my father's garden. Sometimes I'd get in on it too. Mother made me half a sandwich as a snack, which I would eat sitting up in the pear tree in our backyard."

Baptist minister Jack Kidwell first rode the rails out of high school in 1934, traveling from drought-stricken northeast Okla-homa to look for work. For the next three years Reverend Kidwell followed the harvests in the West and South in summer. In winter he returned home and worked as a trapper, earning enough to get him started on the road in spring. Said Reverend Kidwell: "Most of the boys riding the rails were not criminals, just good, honest boys wanting a chance to make a living."

Reverend Kidwell later served for three decades as pastor of a bilingual Baptist church at Mirando City, Texas, thirty miles from the Mexican border, where he came across a new generation of train-hoppers among illegal immigrants: "It is far too late for me to repay those who helped me when I was on the road, but I can pass it on to the Mexican boys who are trying to make it now. I feed the hungry, give a little cough syrup or aspirin to the sick. I have some barns and sheds along the tracks where they stay when the weather is bad."

Alexander Gretes's family owned the Brooke Avenue Confectionery one block from the railroad terminal in Norfolk, Virginia. In the Depression, Alexander worked in the store after school and would do his homework on the counter. One evening he was reading an assignment on Shakespeare when a hobo came in and asked for something to eat.

"I gave him a sandwich and a cup of hot chocolate. He asked which of Shakespeare's plays I was studying. *Macbeth*, I told him.

"'Tell me the act, scene, and line you are reading.'

"He quoted the passage from memory. He asked that I do the same at random and again correctly quoted the section. To this day, I wonder who he was. A former Shakespearean actor or a professor of English? He didn't say and I was too astonished to ask."

Mary Coulter's parents were southerners who had moved to Collins, Iowa, where they were farming in the 1930s. A railroad ran through their property bringing a steady stream of boxcar riders to the Coulter's door. Mary remembers a day when a black man came to their house at lunchtime.

"He'd been riding the freights but had changed into a black suit, white shirt, and tie. Mom asked him to wait on the porch and brought him a plate of food and a cup of coffee. Years later my mother still worried about whether it was right to make him eat outside. White hobos dirty as could be sat down at table with us but she'd made that black man sit on the porch with the flies. My mother's concern taught me a lesson that changed my attitude toward black people."

Ann Walko was deeply moved by her mother's compassion for the downtrodden who came to their home at Wall, Pennsylvania, where freight trains were broken up and rerouted.

"One day a man came to our door asking for food. Mother invited him in but he stood in silence for a moment. 'I have a family with me,' he said. Mother said she would feed them too. He brought his wife and three children. They still refused to come inside so mother spread two rugs on the ground for them. They ate her homemade bread and baked beans and couldn't thank us enough. In a way what a beautiful time it was."

Mean Streets

Not every footloose youth received benevolent treatment. They would be met at the lot line by an owner's dogs and forced to keep moving. They would have doors slammed in their faces. They were shouted at and driven off—"Get outta here, you dirty bum!" Sometimes a heartless owner could be downright cruel to a child tramp.

Everett Childers, one of seven children, quit his home in Marshfield, Oregon, in December 1931 to alleviate the burden on his parents. The fifteen-year-old was also heartbroken over the recent death of a favorite sister. Everett buddied up with a youth from Montana and rode the rails through sixteen states over the next two and a half years. He never forgot a time when he had been without food for three days and offered to mow a woman's lawn in exchange for a meal.

"I worked two hours with a push mower and finished the lawn. When I asked for my food, the lady said I had to cut the backyard as well. I was so weak with hunger I couldn't do it. I just went up the road crying."

Even meaner was the Arizona housewife approached by fourteen-year-old Freddie Pate. Freddie ran away from his family farm at Versailles, Illinois, to escape his chores and was on the road from August to September 1932. Arriving in Phoenix, he climbed to the town that was high on a bluff and went to bum a residential area. A woman opened her door and he asked for a few slices of bread.

"'You're hungry? I'll fix you some big meat sandwiches,' she says. 'Two or three pieces of plain bread be plenty,' I say. She was gone a long time. I didn't like it one bit. Sure enough, a patrol car came with two officers. They asked if I was begging. I told them I just wanted a couple of pieces of bread. 'You'll have to come with us,' they said. As I was getting into the police car, the woman came to the door. 'Kitty, Kitty,' she called. Four or five fat cats that matched her size came running. She was feeding them the sandwiches she'd made as we drew away."

The police told Freddie the woman did the same to every hobo who knocked at her door. They took Freddie back to the rail yard and ordered him to leave town.

Iowa-born Ulan Miller remembered knocking at a door in Des Moines with a friend who followed the harvest with him. "A lady told Lyle and me to wait on the porch. She came back with two slices of dry bread. 'Now, boys, I'm not giving this for your sake or my sake, I'm giving it to you for the Lord's sake.' Lyle asked in a forlorn way: 'Please, lady, for the Lord's sake would you go and put a little butter or jam on this bread?'"

When Ernest Blevins and his road partner bummed a grocer near the tracks at Mobile, Alabama, the man gave them two green bananas, saying they would probably kill them. "I guess he'd had his bellyful of bums," said Blevins. "We laughed and ate the bananas anyway." Casimir Brzeczek hitchhiked and rode freights from Philadelphia to Hastings, Nebraska. A truck driver offered him a ride if he would help unload fifteen tons of crushed marble. "When we finished, the trucker ate fried chicken and ice cream. He bought me a hot dog." Edward Palasz approached a man in the street in Great Falls, Montana, and asked if he could spare a dime for a cup of coffee. "For ten minutes I had to listen to a lecture on the economy and how much food we were wasting in the

U.S. I was awarded a ten-cent piece by the man, who had more money in his bulging pocketbook than I would make in a year."

In the Jailhouse

In the South especially, a vagrant boy jumping off a train or just wandering into a strange town often met a rude welcome. Local sheriffs subjected road kids to frontier-style justice, rounding them up in cahoots with farmers needing harvest hands or town boards seeking free labor.

Colorado teenagers Vernon Chadwick and Buster Cook were picked up by the police in Hutchinson, Kansas. Chadwick remembered being taken to a farm with a large compound, barracks, and mess hall, somewhat like a military base. The boys were deloused, given a meal and sent to bed.

"We asked how long we had to stay there. 'Until the peas are all picked,' they told us. We could pick peas or go to jail," said Chadwick. The boys did neither, slipping out of the barracks the next morning and making a run for the rail yards, where they hopped on an Oklahoma-bound train.

Carl Boden narrowly escaped forced labor on the El Paso airport that was under construction in 1932. Climbing off a freight, Boden found a line of hoboes waiting for a ride. One warned him to get back on the train and leave. "The hobo pulled up his pants' leg and showed me the marks of a ball and chain. The El Paso police seized a group of hoboes every ten days to work on the airport. The only tools were shovels, rakes, sledgehammers, and picks. The men ate and slept where they worked, strapped with a ball and chain at night. When the El Paso authorities needed a fresh crew the police marched the hoboes down to the rail yard and cornered a new gang."

On a day in October 1934, Jack Butler heard a judge in Savannah, Georgia, pronounce sentence on him: "Butler—thirty Brown." Born and raised in Philadelphia, nineteen-year-old Butler had been riding the rails for two years, making four trips to California and

Florida before his arrest by railroad bulls in Georgia. He was sentenced to serve thirty days on a work gang at Brown County Farm.

"You didn't want to be arrested in Georgia in the spring or fall when they did road repairs," said Butler. "Things were rough at Brown Farm. You slept on a straw mat infested with every bug you could think of. The shower room had six inches of urine on the floor. You stood in it while you washed. At breakfast you got grits and grease and a cup of chicory."

Butler was given a "banjo," a primitive weed whacker. By the end of the second day, his hands were a mass of blisters. It made no difference, and next morning he returned to swinging the banjo.

"Every six prisoners had an armed guard to watch over them. If you tried to make a break and were caught, they automatically doubled your sentence." Butler recalled a particular moment when his gang was working near the railroad tracks: "A freight came by real slow. The guard stood with his rifle ready. 'Here's your train, boys,' he said. 'Let's see who can make it.' We just stood there and watched the train roll past."

Eventually Butler's thirty days were up and he left Brown County Farm. His one fear was that he would be rearrested. Local sheriffs would notify the sheriff in the next county that a newly released prisoner was on the way. Butler escaped a second arrest but the experience ended his days on the road.

At sixteen, Herbert Ganger was sentenced to six months on a Georgia chain gang for vagrancy. He had hoboed through forty-seven states and was on his way to Florida when he was caught.

"'Chain gang' was now added to my vocabulary, along with words and expressions such as 'stripes,' 'screws,' 'wire city,' 'water soup,' 'hard tack,' and 'man on the hill.' I also learned some poetry. Every morning, rain or shine, the same screw recited the same chant:

> Rise and shine, you sons of bitches
> Get your ass out and dig them ditches
> It ain't near daybreak but it's half past two
> I don't want you but the boss man do.

* * *

Dominick Grella grew up on the streets of Brooklyn's tough East New York section. In January 1934 he left for Florida with two friends. His companions dropped out and he reached Jacksonville alone. He spent the winter in Florida at camps run by the Transient Relief Bureau and headed back north in May. At Rockingham, North Carolina, a railroad bull caught him as he climbed off a freight train. A justice of the peace fined him six dollars. He told the judge he was broke and was going home to Brooklyn.

"'Do I wire your folks for money?' asks the judge.

"'Hell, no,' I say.

"'OK, then, thirty days on the chain gang.'"

His head shaven and outfitted in prison garb, Grella worked from 7 A.M. to 6 P.M. his first day, digging ditches along the North Carolina roads.

"I knew right off ten hours a day was for the birds. On the second day a car pulled up with a VIP tag. I dropped my shovel and ambled over to the car.

"'Where do you think you're going, Brooklyn?' hollered a guard.

"'Come on over, kid,' the man in the car said.

"I gave a crying spiel that I could not take the work. The man asked my age. I told him I was sixteen. He asked why I was on the chain gang. 'Riding a freight,' I told him.

"'Let the kid carry the sign,' the man said. The guards gave me a 'Men Working' sign, which I had to hold one hundred feet up the road. I liked my new job that gave me first crack at the 'clinchers,' cigarette and cigar butts tossed out by motorists."

'Brooklyn' was later made a trusty and given light duties in the prison mess hall.

"That was some uplift. Clarence, the cook, was a real down to earth human being. After we prepared the men's lunches, we'd have the afternoon to ourselves. 'Go pick a mess of blueberries, Brooklyn,' Clarence would say. He'd make blueberry pie for us."

Freed after twenty-four days, Grella grabbed a freight on the Seaborne Air Line. "Don't you know that I got pulled off in Henderson, North Carolina. I cried and told the railroad dick I'd just got out of a chain gang and was going home. He pointed me in the direction of the highway. 'Stick to the road until you get to New York,' he said, and let me go."

The holiday season of 1938 became memorable for Charles Samz: He spent Thanksgiving Day in a boodle jail in New Orleans; Christmas Day in jail in Valdosta, Georgia; and New Year's Day locked up in Tampa, Florida. Samz had started his hobo days after graduating from high school in 1933 and leaving his parents' struggling farm in northern Wisconsin. The next four years he roamed the country working at any job he could find. By 1937 he had saved $250 and enrolled at the University of Wisconsin but the following year he was broke again and returned to the road.

"While being in jail was not remarkable given the attitude of the time that to be homeless and penniless was criminal, my failure to evade the railroad bulls on those three days was unusual," Samz concedes.

Roy Taylor and his friends Bob Wallen and Leland Brown shared the misfortune of being caught by railroad bulls on Christmas Eve in the San Diego rail yards. They were taken to the San Diego police station, booked as vagrants, and herded into a holding tank with thirty other prisoners. At 6 A.M. on Christmas morning, they were fed "two slices of stale bread and a cup of black water." Two hours later the tank was emptied of all its occupants, including Leland Brown, the oldest of the trio. Taylor and Wallen heard they would have to stay in jail until the following day because they were juveniles. Recalled Taylor: "A couple of hours later they drove us by police car to city hall, where we were taken before a judge. He complained that we had interrupted his Christmas celebration but after a sermon about the sins of being jobless and broke, he released us."

The pair met up with Leland Brown and reached the seaside town of San Clemente on Christmas night. At the fire station that also served as a jail they asked for a place to sleep and were again locked up for the night. The next morning the jailer sent them to the Salvation Army, where they had their first meal since their Christmas breakfast of stale bread and coffee.

While it was more common for destitute youths to be running from the law, local police stations frequently provided the only place of refuge for wandering boys. Werner Wirth and a high school pal ran away from San Francisco's Bay area in 1937 hoping to become lumberjacks in the north. One day luck turned its back on them: Caught in a rainstorm, drenched and hungry, they came into Manhattan, Kansas, just before nightfall. They went to the local jail and asked for accommodation.

"A hospitable jailer showed us to a cell. He said we could bunk on the cots and told us to hang our clothes near a steam pipe so they could dry. He gave each of us a blanket to keep warm," said Wirth. "In the morning we swept out the jail and were ready to leave when the jailer asked if we wanted something to eat. When we said yes, he reached under the counter and placed several different sizes of sledgehammer in front of us. 'You'll find a rock pile out back,' he said. 'Work for an hour and I'll give you a meal ticket.'

"We did our time on the rock pile and each got a ticket for breakfast. It was a wonderful meal but it barely filled one rib cage. We had a decision to make. Should we go back and break more rocks or should we move on? Move on, we decided."

When fourteen-year-old King Henderson applied to the town marshal of Heber, Utah, for help he did not expect the royal treatment he and another hobo received. Every evening the marshal played cards with them. When he left for home, he gave them the keys to the jail so they could lock up if they went into town. A snowstorm forced Henderson and the other hobo to stay at Heber for a week. The marshal brought them food from his house every day.

When Arvo Niemi sought shelter at a police station in a small Illinois town, he found his stay unexpectedly prolonged: "A policeman took me to some cells in a field behind the station. He said they rarely used them and locked me in for the night. Next morning when I woke up it was very quiet. I shouted but no one came. I stayed all that day and the next night with no food or water. The next morning I hollered until someone heard me and let me out. They plain forgot I was there."

Bughouse Hotel

Young nomads seeking shelter at transient centers established by the federal government in 1933 found that the condition of the refuges varied drastically. Steve Hargas stayed for a week in a center at Denver, Colorado: "I went to put out the lone bulb hanging from the ceiling. Men hollered for me to leave the light on so the cockroaches wouldn't crawl over our faces."

In Madison, Wisconsin, Alvin Svalstad checked into the transient center in a one hundred-year-old building that had been a livery barn. "I could smell the odor of horses past. A sallow-faced man behind a desk said that I had to leave any money or valuables with him. I lied and said I had nothing. I wouldn't have trusted him with a penny, to say nothing of the $11.25 in my billfold." The man gave Svalstad two blankets and led him upstairs to a loft with a hundred cots, nearly all occupied. "A tough-looking two hundred-pound man sat on the cot to my left. Another man with a scar on his face stood on my right. 'What's in your case?' he asked. The sound of his voice and the sweaty odor of all those men made me think twice. I grabbed my suitcase and fled onto the street. I decided that forty cents was little to pay for a room and privacy at the YMCA."

Wisconsin-born farm boy Fred Schatz was nineteen when he went on the road with his friend Leo Elder. They lived the migrant's life for two years, working in harvest fields in the Dakotas and Minnesota and joining railroad extra gangs as laborers. Few jobs lasted more than a couple of months or provided adequate money for accommodation. Schatz became acquainted with the best and worst of the transient shelters and flophouses.

"When we checked into the Billings, Montana, shelter, for example, after filling in a questionnaire we took a bath. While we washed, they took our clothes and fumigated them—after a while your clothing started to disintegrate from all the fumigation. When you had your bath, you were checked over by a doctor, the larger centers having dispensaries. Some places let you stay up to three days but most had a twenty-four-hour limit, as we found at Billings."

In Oakdale, California, Schatz and Elder had stayed the night in the shelter and were eating breakfast when a group of women came there. They had organized a program to can fruit for families on relief. They asked for volunteers to spend the day peeling pears.

"Leo and I volunteered. The room we worked in had a stage up front. The women put on plays and held a sing-a-long to help pass the time. At noon we ate sandwiches and coffee; at supper we had a sit-down meal, all you could eat and apple pie for dessert. It was one of the good days."

When Leo Elder found work in San Francisco, Schatz traveled on alone, hopping trains and continuing to do odd jobs. Finally he landed on Chicago's Skid Row, the biggest in the country, extending twelve blocks south along Halstead Street.

"The Transient Bureau gave you a card good for four nights at a flophouse hotel. Another card entitled you to three meals at a Skid Row restaurant. If you didn't find employment in four days, you were supposed to move on to another town. Of course, they knew there was no work, especially for transients."

The floors of the flophouse where Schatz stayed were partitioned into rows of tiny rooms big enough for a single bed and a metal locker. A light dangled from chicken wire stretched over the top of the partition. The cubicles cost twenty-five cents a night. Dinner in a Skid Row restaurant cost the same. There were taverns and bookie joints on every corner, the bookie joints crowded with men trying to get rich making ten-cent bets.

Some evenings, Schatz would go to listen to the soapbox orators in "Bughouse Square." Sometimes there would be a speaker from the International Workers of the World, or the "Wobblies." After the speeches the audience would join in IWW songs, one particularly meaningful to Schatz:

> If you all shut your trap I will tell you about a chap
>> That was broke and up against it for fair
> He was not the kind to shirk, he was looking for work
>> But he heard the same old story everywhere
> Tramp, tramp, tramp, keep on tramping
>> Nothing doing for you here.

The song struck a chord with Schatz. "I didn't want to spend the rest of my life on Skid Row picking up a few dollars passing out flyers and then betting it on the horses," he said. "One morning I took the streetcar out to the Milwaukee Railroad and caught a freight going north. At Waukesha, Wisconsin, I switched to the Soo Line and rode to Spencer, where I hopped a passenger train back home to Glidden. It was the end of my journey to nowhere."

Beginning in 1934, George Nelles spent four summers riding the rails and found transient camps ideal rest stops on his adventures. "The camps were at railroad divisions about four hundred miles apart. After a rough day on the road we would sign in around 4 P.M., take a shower, and eat supper at 5. They expected you to go on a work detail in the morning. We'd take a little walk before going to bed. And just keep on walking toward California."

When Gene Wadsworth began stopping at transient camps, he fretted over the fact that his name began with "W." "When we checked in or stood in line for chow, we had to do so in alphabetical order. I was always way back in line so I changed my name to Ed Bebb. I didn't want to be first like 'Abbot' or 'Anderson.' I wanted to have an idea of what was going on in front of me and have my answers ready, so 'Ed Bebb' I became."

The Jungle

The one place where the young hobo was assured a welcome was the "jungle," as the hobo camps were called. These were generally not far from the tracks, some nothing more than a clearing for a camp fire, some well-established sites overseen by old jungle buzzards who set up home there.

Bill Hackett, who was bumming his way around the country as a fourteen-year-old in 1930, recalls the jungle at Sandusky, Ohio, located beside a brook populated by red and gold carp.

"Sandusky jungle was a mecca for weary hoboes who came to the camp tired, dirty, ragged, and whiskery. The stew pot was on, water from the brook was boiling. The 'bos would empty their pockets in preparation for a stew. One might have an onion pinched from a fruit market, another brought potatoes and an ear of corn leased from a farmer's field.

"Edible greens are gathered and added to the pottage: dandelions and sourdock, wild leeks and pigweed. A handful of navy beans carried in a pocket for a month are thrown in along with a smattering of lint and tobacco. Scraps of meat bummed from the local butcher.

"Dig in with your cans, men! We eat heartily and with bellies full take our ease and drowse. In the night, we sit around the glowing coals and swap tall tales of the road. Many talk of home and loved ones and jobs they held before the collapse of their world."

Between stops at transient camps, Gene Wadsworth—"Ed Bebb"—dropped into hobo jungles. He found permanent denizens of the camps living in shacks made of flattened tin cans, boards, railroad ties, anything that could be scavenged to build a shelter. When a freight train rolled by and hoboes started arriving, the old buzzard would issue instructions: "Hey, you, Whitey, go up to the meat market and ask for scraps;" "Red, you go get carrots;" "You, skinny, go find spuds."

"I've seen stuff go into a stew pot that I wouldn't feed to a hog," recalled Wadsworth. "We'd take a tin can and the old 'bo would fill it. If he liked your looks, he'd dip down deeper for meat and vegetables; others got mostly soup."

Even where there were no permanent residents, crude equipment would be left for the next visitor. Gene Tenold, who hoboed for three summers from 1938, would look for a Number 10–size can set in a sheltered place with a board and a rock on top of it for a cover: "It would contain coffee grounds, how many times used no one knew. You gave it one more boiling and if you got the flavor of coffee, you enjoyed a cup or two and left the grounds as you found them. If the flavor was gone, you emptied the can and pitied the next guy who came along."

An innocent-looking road kid was always welcome as a forager more likely to appeal to a store owner than a weary old tramp. Kermit Parker, who made a twenty-five hundred-mile journey from Walla Walla, Washington, to Chicago in 1935, recalled his introduction to the jungle at Pocatello, Idaho. He had climbed off a freight with a group of older hoboes.

"'Anyone got the makings?' asked one.

"'I've got spuds and onions,' another replied.

"'Some bacon and half a loaf of bread,' chimed in a third.

"'What do you have, kid?'"

A hobo directed the question at Kermit, who had nothing to contribute to the stew.

"'Got any money?'"

Kermit said he had fifty cents.

"'OK, kid, find a store and buy some stew meat.'"

First, the hoboes showed Kermit where the jungle was, half a mile from the outskirts of Pocatello. He carried a small suitcase with his belongings. They promised to look after it while he went to buy meat, which he agreed to with somewhat less than peace of mind. He walked several blocks before finding a butcher, who sold him scraps from a box next to the butcher's block. When he arrived back at the jungle, he first checked that his suitcase was where he had left it.

"'You did good, kid. There's enough meat to make us a fine Mulligan.'" The hobo inspected Kermit's package of scraps, cutting up the largest chunks and discarding some bones before adding the meat to a container of boiling water.

"'The kid doesn't have any tools,' one of the men said when the stew was ready."

The hoboes lent Kermit a dish and a spoon.

"Soon I was comfortably seated on a large rock with a bowl of hot stew. What more could one ask for?

"'Kid, would you like some bread?'"

Kermit received a hunk of bread.

A hobo asked where he was headed. "Chicago," he replied. Was he taking the Union Pacific line through Green River or the Denver and Rio Grande Western route through Salt Lake City? Kermit's mother had friends in Provo so he opted for the southern route. The hobo was catching out for Ogden in two hours and offered to show Kermit where to board:

"'Good luck, kid,' came a chorus of good-byes as I left Pocatello jungle. It felt heartwarming to have so many total strangers wish me well."

Fredrick Watson knew the same jungle from a different perspective. His father worked in the Union Pacific yards at Pocatello. Watson recalled that the jungle was on the west side of town near the Portneuf River.

"There was always a population of 100 to 150 people, including entire families with kids. They weren't bums but good citizens who were flat out of work and trying to get by."

Watson and his young friends would go to the jungle and eat lunch or dinner with the hoboes. "We would take our share, mostly coffee that we purloined from our homes. Mom and Dad probably knew about it but didn't say anything."

Tennys Tennyson had been on a freight train for three days when it pulled into Havre, Montana. The fifteen-year-old Tennyson and four hoboes scoured the town for food. Two hours later Tennyson and three others had collected an assortment of items, including bread, fruit, and vegetables. The fifth hobo, who had been assigned to get meat, showed up half an hour later with two live turkeys. An equally enterprising and more legal way of trapping a stew was taught to thirteen-year-old Robert Foster at Seaside, Oregon. A group of hoboes made Foster and another teenager climb into an empty grain car in the rail yard. When pigeons flew in to eat the spilled grain, the boys slammed the doors shut. They caught a dozen or so birds for the stew pot.

For many youngsters, some just out for adventure, the despair met with in the jungles left profoundly disturbing impressions of ruined lives. Howard Kemp was nineteen when he worked as an itinerant harvester on the northern prairies. He described one occasion when he was in a jungle with a group of migrants who had failed to find jobs: "They were in their thirties, married, and hungry. They'd hit the stem and were cooking up. They'd counted on jobs for winter money for their families. One of the men blamed the combines for taking away the need for separator crews. 'I've been putting end-gate rods in the swaths. Let the bastards thresh those things,' he said. I felt bad that he should do such a thing but I didn't dare let it show."

Observed Murray Simkins, who rode the rails in the Midwest in 1932: "Have you seen grown men cry? We saw them in the jungles, both young and old, healthy and sick. They were crying for just enough work to keep body and soul together until something came along to fill their spiritless days."

Donald Davis was one of numerous teenagers who hoboed to the Chicago World's Fair. He had left home with a friend, taking thirteen dollars between them, most of which went early. Commented Davis: "It takes time to learn such a haphazard trade as hoboing. We sacrificed many inhibitions and Sunday school precepts but our morals were never seriously threatened and we never really suffered. One summer was not time for sickness and certainly not enough to become discouraged. The difference between us and so many others on the road was that we could go home."

James San Jule

———•⊳———

1930-32

*J*ames San Jule's world disintegrated when the crash of 1929
ruined his father's oil land leasing business in Tulsa, Oklahoma.
San Jule had enrolled at Amherst College and planned to go on to
Harvard Law School. Instead the ex-millionaire's son rode the rails
for two and a half years, gaining an education radically different
from that which he had anticipated.

He ran away from home in 1930, partly because he did not want
to be a burden on parents reeling from a crushing financial blow.
Like other boys of his generation, he had read the books of Richard
Halliburton, a young globe-trotting adventurer "bumming" his way
around the world. In the long, dark winter of 1929–30, Halliburton's exotic ideas captivated San Jule:

> Delhi was a sort of terminus, a relay station where one re-ori-
> ented oneself and began again with new destinations. New
> enthusiasms! What was to come? Whither would the road to
> romance lead me? To Kabul—as I hoped—or to Argentina?

San Jule left home wanting to ship out and see the world. Reality came quickly to a "happy-go-lucky kid living the spoiled life," as
he crossed the country at the onset of the Great Depression.

I was six years old when my mother and father moved from New
York to Oklahoma in 1919. Father had been vice president of the
Buick Motor Car Corporation in New York City, a man about

185

town in the early days of the automobile industry. I remember him taking me down to the old Waldorf Astoria hotel when I was very young, and introducing me to the head chef.

My father became infatuated with the idea of getting into the oil business so we moved to Tulsa. Mother was an English woman who liked New York and was never happy in Oklahoma. Father became very successful in the oil business and I guess that by 1929 he was a millionaire. I graduated from Tulsa Central High that year, just an ordinary rich kid with a life that wasn't particularly spectacular.

The first thing my father lost was the house we lived in. We moved to a smaller rental house he owned. Because of all the turmoil, it seemed to me the best thing to do was leave. Why didn't I stick around and try to help? I was seventeen years old and my big adventurous mind said, "I want to ship out." I'd read books by Richard Halliburton, Ross Simpson, and others who'd done that. I thought I would run away from whatever trouble there was. I don't recall the precise day I left, but I remember I was crying. It seemed like the end of everything.

I first wound up in the east Texas oil fields outside a little town called Arp. I got a job with the Amerada Petroleum Company working as a roustabout—digging ditches and doing other menial work. The Depression had sent the price of oil down to twenty cents a barrel but it was still a boom field frantic with activity. I'll never forget lying in bed at night and feeling the house where I stayed rock on its foundation. The entire land vibrated with the force of seventy-five thousand barrels of oil gushing over the top of the derrick every day.

It was dirty work and I hated it, but there was also a certain excitement. It was one of the contradictory things about this period of my life. While part of it was terrible, part of it was exciting and filled with discovery.

I was a kid, literally, and what's a kid to do? You are thrown out of the life you had before. No worries about anything, lots of money, going to Amherst, going to Harvard. All of a sudden I am in the east Texas oil fields digging ditches. You were hungry all the time, you were afraid, you didn't have any friends.

Sometimes I'd get homesick. My mother sent me a birthday cake. It was my eighteenth birthday. The cake was kinda squashed from being in the mail. I'll never forget sitting on a hillside in the oil field, eating that cake and crying my eyes out.

I was angry half the time and when I wasn't angry I was sad. Why was this happening to me? It was more than a lack of understanding. It was an aimless, discombobulated feeling, as though the world had disappeared. The same feeling you have during an earthquake that's beyond your control. You were searching for something and didn't even know what the hell you were looking for. So, you did the best you could just to survive.

I rode my first flatcar down to Houston, getting a thrill as I saw the city rise in front of me. I tried to ship out, but nobody had a place for a kid. I went to New Orleans, where I stayed for three months in the Cabildo, the old Spanish jail that had been opened for homeless people. You slept on stone shelves in cells that had open ducts of running water as toilets. Every morning we went down to the docks where the Central American banana boats unloaded. Ripe bananas were thrown on one side. That's what I mostly ate in New Orleans. Bananas. I still like 'em.

I begged for dimes on the streets of the French Quarter. It was terrible to beg with a background like mine. A displaced prince asking for a handout on the street? I looked young and desperate and people were generous. I don't remember anybody ever making fun of me or showing anger because I was poor and on the road.

I couldn't ship out of New Orleans and started riding freight trains across the South. I remember sleeping several nights in Chattanooga, Tennessee, under a clump of bushes next to a church. In Rolling Oak, Virginia, I must have been a pitiful sight when I went begging at the back of a house. The woman invited me in and washed my clothes. At Baltimore I tried to find a ship but couldn't so I hitchhiked to New York.

I lived for three months in what was the Washington Market

area. I slept behind a pile of construction material in a subway kiosk. Around four or five every morning, I'd go into the market and steal my food for the day, including loaves of bread and bottles of milk.

I called on a friend of my father who had some influence in the Port of New York. He gave me an introduction to the U.S. Lines. I went down to the docks, where I had to pass a guard to get into their offices. He was a black man. Coming from Oklahoma, I wasn't going to be stopped by him. "Get out of my way," I said, and called him a bad name. He phoned the man I was to see. I got one hell of a lecture about racial prejudice and was told that under no circumstances would I be hired.

I left New York somewhat bewildered, not really knowing where I was going. I rode across Pennsylvania and part of Indiana. One evening I was walking along the Wabash River beside the railroad right-of-way and came to a trestle bridge. There was a valley filled with fireflies. A train went through but I didn't try to catch it. I sat there for an hour just watching those fireflies.

I went back to Tulsa. My mother was very emotional when she saw me. I surprised my father as he was coming into the driveway. I startled him so badly that his first reaction was one of anger. It was a bitter, bitter time. I stayed home for a while but didn't make much of an attempt to get a job. All I was thinking about was getting on the road again.

I finally left and instead of going east this time I rode the rails west. This was in 1932, and there were hundreds of people riding freight trains. You were always with people on the trains but there wasn't much camaraderie. Everyone had his or her problem and seemed to be turned inward. Everyone on the road was lonely.

You talked about practical things, how to get your next meal or whether there's going to be a job in the next town. You would hear about work but most was just rumor. Once I was told about a job in a St. Louis quarry. I worked for a week pounding rocks. It was like being on a chain gang.

You met disappointments all the time. It was the latter part of the Hoover administration. Twenty-five percent of the work force was unemployed. There was no parachute in those days. No welfare, no unemployment insurance, nothing that would've helped you along. There were poorhouses but those were places were old people went. Everybody I ran into hated Herbert Hoover. They didn't know precisely why, but they blamed Hoover for the Depression.

Young people were 100 percent on their own. You'd no help from any source except begging. That wasn't a normal thing for a young guy to be doing. You learned about society's underbelly and about existing. Something about a society that forces people to beg for food causes a person to be very thoughtful. It's a better education in basic economics than going to college.

It wasn't "us" versus "them." Our thinking was that we're not part of society. We're off to one side and have separate problems. We have a problem of getting on a freight train, for example. Normal people don't have that problem. We have a problem getting our next meal. We're dirty, we haven't had a shave. We're not like normal people. We're different. We're "us."

The thought that something was wrong must've crossed my mind but those days I didn't think of it in political terms. I spent so goddamn much time just staying alive.

We were thrown off a freight train that stopped for water at Lubbock, Texas. The police took us all to jail. They made us work on a road crew for a week. Then they took us back to the rail yard and put us on a train headed west. I always thought that was a tricky way of getting street work done.

Riding out of Lubbock, I climbed into a reefer compartment. There was a black man inside. In the middle of the night a couple of guys climbed down and started to rifle through my clothes looking for money. The black man tackled them and drove them out. He didn't know me from Adam and I didn't know him. We were just two guys in a reefer and he was protecting me. A black man who came to my rescue. It was a revelation to me.

James San Jule saw the lessons learned as a hobo as a "primary school." His advanced education came on the San Francisco waterfront, when he stopped riding the rails and found work as a stevedore in 1932. He became a radical union organizer under Harry Bridges, leader of the San Francisco longshoremen, and participated in the bloody strike of 1934. In 1937, San Jule cowrote a pamphlet with John Steinbeck to bring attention to the plight of migrant workers in California.

Forty or fifty of us would be on the docks at six o'clock in the morning for the "shake up." A straw boss would come out. "You and you and you," he would say. You paid him off to get a job on the docks. The work was more dangerous than any other I knew.

I was in the 1934 strike that led to the formation of the International Longshoremen's Union. We weren't striking for wages, although that was part of it. Working people were subjected to the most terrible labor policies by their employers. We wanted democracy in hiring.

We were bitterly opposed. Martial law was declared. There were tanks on the waterfront and National Guardsmen with bayonets. Two of our members were killed. Most of us younger men were gung ho to have a socialist state of some kind. We thought that "the Revolution" was next Tuesday.

They finally settled the matter by arbitration and we became part of the body politic. The whole atmosphere changed under Roosevelt. It wasn't just his welfare programs like the WPA and the CCC, but a new democratic society that reestablished hope in the minds of the American people.

Being on the road made me a totally different person. Can you imagine a guy about to go to Amherst and Harvard and destined to work for a law firm on Wall Street becoming a radical union man? I can't think of anything more different. I'm glad of what I became and proud of the things I've done. I'm not sure I would be that proud as a retired Wall Street lawyer in Westchester County.

Jan van Heé

———— •◆• ————

1937–38

*J*an van Heé was sixteen when he ran away from his parents' farm in the Montana buttes in 1937. "I left a note between the salt and pepper shakers: 'I'll be back when I have money and a car.'" He promised to repay five dollars he snitched from his folks.

Born in Holland, where he spent his first ten years with his grandfather, Jan was a city boy when he came to the isolated community near Marysville, Montana. "Farm animals scared me, especially the pigs that looked about ready to eat me. Dad soon changed that. Within a few years, I was doing the work of a man around the farm, working seven days a week during harvest time."

An outsider in a community populated by the descendants of pioneers who arrived in covered wagons, Jan was plagued with problems throughout his school years. Three months before he was due to graduate in 1937, his principal gave him his diploma and sent him home.

Already living close to the belt and forced to slaughter half their herd of a thousand sheep, his father told him he had no paying work for him on the farm. His mother and he didn't get along. When his parents went to bed that night, Jan stuffed his things into a pillowcase and left.

He hiked to the train station at Marysville, Montana, where he heaved his belongings into an open boxcar. "Welcome," he heard a voice say from a dark corner.

191

A hefty Scotsman greeted me. I told "Scotty" I'd run away to look for work. He tried to talk me out of leaving home but I wouldn't go back.

I got my first lessons in hoboing from Scotty. He laughed when he saw my big pillowcase stuffed with all the world's goods. He took my blanket and showed me how to roll my things into a tight, trim bundle I could carry on my back—my first hobo bindle.

There were many things I wasn't prepared for when I rode my first freight train. The noise as the locomotive took up slack— Crash! Crash! Crash!—you could hear it coming closer. A huge bang from the boxcar coupling and I fell flat on my face. Until you became accustomed to it, the noise was frightening, all the banging and rattling and the clatter of the wheels. As you picked up speed, the wind blasted through the slats in the wooden boxcar.

You try to sit on the floor but four-fifths of the time you're airborne. So you stand until your feet start hurting. You try sitting on your bindle but the vibration and the jolts just keep coming.

You worry about how you are going to climb off. No matter how good you get, there are things you're not going to see, like a hidden rock or a signal standard. I saw one guy who smashed into a signal and wiped out his face.

Are you gonna wait until you roll into the train station? Maybe have the mayor greet you? Are you going to get your head bashed in by some guy with a pickax handle?

You're uncertain about the people out there. What kind are they? How are you gonna get along with them?

Scotty dubbed me "Dutch," after I said I was born in Holland. He told me to use my moniker and never give my real name. "Don't trust anybody," Scotty said.

Scotty and I traveled together to Stockton, California, where we checked into a flophouse. I remember sitting on a double-tiered bunk, Scotty on the bed below me. As I looked around it seemed I was in a black-and-white movie. It was a strange feeling. I'd survived my first freight train ride and had gotten off safely.

I'd found a friend who was showing me the ropes. In that huge crowded room, with strangers hacking and coughing around me, I suddenly felt a great despair.

"I'm going to survive," I told myself. "One way or another, I will survive."

The next day we went to a Skid Row restaurant for breakfast. A waitress asked if we were looking for work. She told us that a farmer came once a week looking for hands. That evening, the farmer hired Scotty. He thought I was Scotty's son and told me to climb in his pickup with Scotty.

I also got a job on the farm. The farmer took me to his wife. I was her birthday gift. Didn't have a bow on me but her husband said, "This is your birthday gift—he's gonna help you make a garden."

It turned out that the couple had lost their seventeen-year-old son the year before. The woman missed her child, and little by little she began talking about me living with them. One night I heard her and her husband discussing me. "He's a lovely boy. He's going to stay and be our son," she said.

It took me half an hour to get my stuff together in the middle of the night and pussyfoot out into the world. I'd had every intention of sticking to Scotty like a bird to a sheep's hide but I had to leave him behind.

I sometimes walked for twenty-five miles along the railroad tracks. It was usually shorter to follow the tracks in a straight line than take the road. Stepping on each railroad tie, you'd be taking small steps; every other one you'd need giant steps. So what do you do? You put one foot on the tie and the other between: Step, crunch, step, crunch, mile after mile. When one foot becomes tired, you change over: Crunch, step, crunch, step.

In summertime you'd be aware of the smells, maybe a dead skunk, the smell of dry grass, the sweat of your body. You feel the gravel and rocks under your feet. The rope around your bindle chafes your shoulders.

You see a farm way out in the distance. You go over and ask for a job or just a drink of water.

Your mood depends on how much work you have had recently. You can feel pretty good with just twenty-five cents in your pocket.

The miles seem endless. You look behind and the place you left is fading out of sight. You look ahead but can't see your destination.

"What in hell am I doing here anyway?" you say. And maybe you think, why couldn't I have rich parents?

I survived by charm, guts, and cons. Every kid on the road had something that he specialized in. Mine was looking sweet and innocent and taking off my hat and going, "Oh, shucks, lady." The type of thing that appealed to the woman of the house. I also pulled some scams, stole some chickens, sang, and begged on the streets.

My grandfather with whom I lived in Holland despised beggars. When Scotty told me about knocking on back doors to ask for food, I was shocked. "Never be too proud for begging. When you've tried everything else and you are weak for lack of food, lad, then beg," Scotty said.

I remember the first time I sidled up to this fellow and said, "Mister, can you spare some money?" The guy said something encouraging to me like, "Why the hell don't you go back to your parents?"

I tried not begging but when your backbone and your stomach are fighting to see who gets the last nut, your pride goes.

I learned to knock on doors and know the signs that told you something about the people living there. You looked at clotheslines, for example. If you saw only women's clothes chances were her man was away and you'd get nothing. If there were men and women's clothes and toys in the yard, that told you something. Because she had a child, the woman was likely to have pity on this poor little boy coming to her back door.

When she opens the door, you watch carefully. How does she speak? How does she stand? Anything to find out where she's coming from. You smell good food: "Gee, sure seems like you're a wonderful cook, ma'am!"

Maybe she looks stern, so you say, "I haven't always been on the road. I had to get out because my mom and dad lost every-thing." Sometimes you talk about your dad who is traveling with you. He's so tired and ill, you had to leave him back by the tracks. You might get an extra lunch for your would-be father.

Sometimes you jolly them along, and suddenly you say something that makes them upset and angry. Then you gotta withdraw fast.

When you're hitting the stem you learn to read people. For one thing, I found that you don't stop a woman over forty because you're not going to get a red cent. People from the Dustbowl states were usually generous. They knew what it was like to go without.

The drunks were always good but you had to get them talking and laughing. I remember a drunk who was just about falling down. "Let's go into a restaurant and have some chili, It will burn out the alcohol," I said.

I ordered for both of us. When the waitress came with the bill, I said my friend would pay. Just then the drunk had the good grace to fall with his face in the chili. I got out his wallet and took enough money to pay for the food. He had a bundle of cash. "Now's the time you've gotta be honest," I told myself. I didn't roll him, but I bet others did after I left.

I'd see a woman and her husband or boyfriend having a big spat in the street. She'd look over at me and say, "Hey, kid, what do you think of this?" You gotta think very fast. Who's gonna give you the money? She or he? I would usually go with the woman.

When I was singing, I hit the stem with a harmonica player. I had a good voice and knew cowboy songs, railroad songs, and love songs. You had to keep an eye out for the police. Most had uniforms on and you could spot them a mile away.

One of the ways to get away from the cops, especially the bulls, was to look for a family with kids. You'd ease over and become part of the family. I remember more than once looking up at mom and dad and making some friendly remark. "Oh, shucks, mom . . ."

In retrospect, that was funny—but it wasn't so at the time. You thought only of the next second or two, not even the next two minutes. That's what kept us going: knowing that we were alive and OK at that moment and never thinking about tomorrow.

One time I was riding on top of a boxcar when a man came up and asked if he could sit with me. He put his arm around me and began fumbling with my belt. I stalled for time. There was a flatcar behind the boxcar. "Let's go down there," I said. We made our way down the boxcar ladder. The man started loosening the buttons on his pants. I pretended I wanted to help him and pulled his pants right down to his ankles.

I took off like a rabbit, darting behind machinery on the flatcar. The train slowed down and I bailed out. I remember hitting the ground and then I lost consciousness until I saw the man, who'd also gotten off the train, running back to me.

He was dragging me by the collar, slapping me around, and telling me what he was going to do to me. Next thing I knew this bunch of kids came to my rescue. There were about a dozen of them, the youngest around twelve years. They took care of my attacker, stepping on his face and beating him severely.

I had a big cut on my head. One of the kids had a needle and thread, same as you use to put on a button. They poured whiskey into the cut, washed out the gravel, and sewed it up.

These kids banded together for mutual support. They were tough and stood up for one another. That was their main strength. No one bothered them, no one threatened them sexually or any other way.

I stayed with the gang in a jungle for four days. They invited me to go with them but I didn't like their leader. He was around twenty, a bully who bossed the other kids around, told them what to do, and took part of what anyone else made.

That was the only time I was with one of these kid gangs. I didn't like the lack of freedom and having someone tell me what to do. I might as well have stayed home. But for many kids, it was the only way they could get by.

＊ ＊ ＊

Late one afternoon, I was walking along a country road way out in the boonies. It was getting dark so I looked for a place to sleep. I was about to climb into a ditch and wrap up when I saw a light flashing in the distance. I walked on and came to a roadhouse with a bar and a dance hall. There was a crowd of people out front.

"Hey, kid, you wanna make some money?" one of them called over to me.

The roadhouse was holding a marathon dance contest. A young girl about my age said that her partner had pooped out on her. "Can you dance?" she asked me.

"Well, yeah," I said.

I walked into a cavernous hall, where a juke box was playing and people were stumbling around the middle of the floor. The only dance I'd ever learned was the waltz taught to me by my grandmother's maid—the old one, two, three slide; go to the corner; then turn right angles.

"My God, can't you do anything else?" my partner asked. She got me to move a little better but it was hard going.

Every four hours we were allowed a fifteen-minute break. Other times you could catch some rest with your partner's help.

"Just keep on moving. I'm going to get some sleep," the girl said the first time this happened. She draped her arms around my neck and slept, her feet moving just enough so she'd still be dancing. During the fifteen-minute breaks we'd sit or lie down at the side of the dance floor.

There was a snack table with doughnuts, sandwiches, and Coca Cola. I was so doggone hungry that I went over to the table even before we started dancing, but the girl stopped me. I could only eat during my first break. I had to stagger around for four hours before I could get to those doughnuts.

Hour after hour we went on dancing. The fellows at the bar were betting on who would drop out next. Ninety-five percent gave up early in the contest. One woman who stopped up after many hours was seven months pregnant.

My partner and I lasted four days and nights until only one other couple remained. We'd slap each other on the face and jiggle each other to keep awake but finally she just slid down in front of me onto the floor. The other couple won the contest.

I lay down on a thin mattress and almost passed out. My feet were sore and blistered.

"How much did we get?" I remember asking a nurse.

She told me we'd earned fifteen dollars. "That's a hell of a way to make fifteen bucks," she added.

I got off a rattler and hit this burg around eleven o'clock one night. A hard north wind was blowing. I went to the Salvation Army, but it was full. Then I remembered what a hobo said when I was sitting in a jungle some days before: "If I were a baby-faced kid, I wouldn't worry. All you have to do is go to a whorehouse."

I screwed up my courage and found the red-light district. I went up a flight of stairs in a house to a dimly lit landing. Nobody was there, so I thought, "Good. I'm just gonna turn around and leave."

Then a door opened. "What can I do for you?" a woman asked. She was the madam of the place. Her name was Gail and she was a motherly type. I ended up practically crying on her shoulder.

One of the girls came up to us. "Who's this?" she asked.

"This poor kid wants food, Jackie, not what you're peddling. You'll scare him to death," Gail said. She sent Jackie to fetch food for me.

Next thing I knew all these prostitutes were coming in with sandwiches and chocolate milk.

Gail asked where I was staying. I told her I would look for an open car or some other place like that.

"No, you won't. We have a room that's about to be vacated."

A girl came along dressed in a peach-colored negligee with froufrou feathers. She was going to spend the night elsewhere. She took me to her room, where I slept.

knew where I spent the night," I thought. I did that three times when I was desperate for a place to stay.

People today ask, "Wasn't there a social worker or youth counselor you could go to?" They were available, but we didn't trust them. They were deluged by kids who were running away and roaming the country.

If you were ill and went into a welfare office, they wanted to know all your particulars. What's your name, where were you born, what's your address? If it was late afternoon, they'd feed you a meal, maybe give you an overnight. In the morning they'd march you down to the train station or bus depot and ship you back to your parents. That happened to me once but I was able to get off the train and sell my ticket.

Jan van Heé left the road in late 1938 when he enrolled in the Civilian Conservation Corps, where he spent two years before joining the U.S. Navy. He served in the navy for five and a half years before getting a medical discharge. "The doctors said I had six months to live. My first thought was that I would never have to worry about anything again. I'd lie back in the hospital and the only thing I'd have to decide would be am I going to get the Coca Cola or the chocolate when it comes around? Then I became scared: Was this all life was about?"

Van Heé checked out of the hospital two days later. The same week he enrolled in junior college, eventually becoming a teacher and later a professor and psychotherapist.

When people think of the Depression, they think of hard times, of families, of people on the bum. Few people know what we kids went through. We were always hungry. Wasn't just 'cause dinner was hours late. It may have been a couple of days late. You were hungry, cold, and miserable, with nobody to help you.

One of the sad things about kids on the road was that they

didn't know how to play. Life was earnest, life was hard. We didn't have time for ball games or anything like that. When we got off the road, we had to go to war. Five years later when we got out, it was time to go to school. Then it was time to get married. When the hell could we play?

We went from childhood to being adults. We never thought about being teenagers. All we thought about was surviving.

Clydia Williams

———•———

1932–35

*I*n 1932, when Texas-born Clydia Williams was seven, she began
hopping freights with her cousins, two boys of eight and a half
and ten years. For three years, the trio roamed Texas, Oklahoma,
Kansas, Arizona, and California, sometimes with relatives following the cotton and fruit harvests, sometimes riding boxcars for
hundreds of miles on their own.

An only child of mixed descent, Clydia went to live with her relatives in Longview, Texas, when her mother remarried. The
younger of her cousins lived with his mother in Texas; the older
boy was in Oklahoma with his father. The boys frequently hoboed
back and forth between Texas and Oklahoma, and Clydia began
to ride the rails with them.

We lived in small one- or two-room places with a well in the middle of the yard that rented for twenty-five or fifty cents a week. My
relatives would be gone for days at a time workin' someplace or
lookin' for something to do. They left my cousins to baby-sit me.
When they started riding freight trains, I went with them.

In 1932 there weren't as many people as were traveling later:
maybe ten or fifteen on a train. We saw children our age riding
alone and others who were with their families.

An empty boxcar was always our first choice for a ride. Sometimes we had to travel in cattle cars. The animals would bawl all

201

the time 'cause they were thirsty and plain scared. Hog cars were less noisy, but the railroad didn't clean them and they stank.

We were thrown off trains but avoided trouble with the railroad dicks. We watched them making their rounds in the yards. When they went one way, we'd go the other. When we rode a train we would try to get off before we reached a town. Some bulls and brakemen were mean. We saw them catch many white hoboes and beat them just for the exercise.

I tied up my hair and wore boys' clothes because a girl could get into trouble on the road. Boys could go over and ask for water or something like that. "Yeah, OK, go out to the windmill," they would be told. If a girl did that, the woman of the house might just decide to keep you. You didn't have any rights in those days. People could keep you and make you work without pay.

The good part about pretending to be a boy was that you could be your own person. There were many things boys did that girls couldn't do. For instance, my cousins could smoke. When I dressed as a boy, I tried to smoke but found it too much trouble. I chewed tobacco instead. It was sweet and tasted good until you swallowed it.

Every town that I went to had some sort of sign that you weren't welcome. The white hobos would have no problem unless somebody recognized them as a stranger. If you were black, they sure knew you didn't belong there.

We rode the trains in the spring and fall. We would stop by people's orchards to get something to eat. When we came to a town, we went to the back of hotels near the railroad yard and looked for food in garbage cans. We broke open crates and stole fresh fruit and vegetables at produce markets. We lifted milk and other items off delivery wagons. Country houses had big porches where pies and cakes were left to cool and smokehouses where they stored food. We didn't steal to sell for profit. We took only what we needed to survive.

Most of our folks were living on salt pork and hardtack biscuits. We may have had no chicken gravy or molasses, but we were eatin' better than they were.

Clothing wasn't a big problem. We'd get off the train and look for a laundry line and take what we needed. Sometimes we'd go to a black neighborhood where women took in washing. We'd wait until we saw clothes drying on a line and then look for what we thought would fit. You hopped the next train out of town with your new clothes.

We were dirty, our hair was full of lice, our scalps itched. Almost everybody went barefoot. Sometimes we joined a circus or carnival and worked for fifty cents and food. The circus people would give us shoes that were always too big or too small.

My cousins and I did many things to get money. We once found a place near a well where bootleggers hid their booze. We took liquor from them and sold it. You earn a few dollars, but what you gonna do with it? You weren't welcome in the stores. Sometimes a storekeeper invited you in but first asked you to give him your money. You handed it over and got nothing in return.

Occasionally we hit a place with a large black population. Many people weren't open to offering you any support because they felt that you'd be taking something they should have. People wanted to know about places they'd heard about and we'd tell 'em. People were always asking how things were someplace else 'cause I guess it was very bad where they lived.

You'd go to a little bitty shack where a Mexican woman lived. They were poorer than we were because they'd no way to get anything, no back porches or smokehouses to raid. They shared whatever they had with you, even if it was only a scoop of rice and beans.

On some trips my cousins carried everything they needed to shine shoes in a big box. They'd be shinin' shoes for a nickel or a dime and would hear about some fabulous deal someplace else. 'Come on, kid, we gonna go there,' they'd say, and we would up and leave—I guess everyone riding the rails was looking for a mirage somewhere.

* * *

Many people wouldn't know where the trains were going. They didn't want to end up in an area where the bulls would put them in jail. We'd show 'em cars with scrap metal on them heading over to Pennsylvania. We knew the Southern Pacific trains that ran across Louisiana to California and would warn 'em not to take the track that went through Arizona to Yuma—"Probably die before you get where you're goin'." We could tell which were refrigerator cars that weren't going to be sitting in the yard for a week but would be going out soon.

We knew many cowboys working on the range between Longview and Fort Worth. Sometimes we'd stop to get water and they'd see us in a boxcar. They would ride over to the train.

"Hey kid, next time you come through this way, there's something I want you to bring me from Dallas or Fort Worth," they'd say.

They'd give us money and we'd fetch whatever they wanted.

After the roundup, when the cowboys loaded the cattle onto the trains, they went to town to go dancing and drinking. They'd put their gear onto a flatcar and we'd ride with them. They paid us to clean and polish their saddles and boots. We knew good places in Fort Worth where they could have a haircut and get cleaned up and smell very good. When the cowboys got their pay, they'd give us tips.

It was a time when there wasn't much concern about disciplining kids or trying to mold their character. My mother didn't have any experience in raising children. My dad was never mean or strict. I lived and grew up without any rules.

Our families just let us run. You could be gone for days and nobody would miss you. Kinda like a stray dog that takes off and leaves, then comes wandering back a couple of days later.

From 1930 until 1935, I didn't know anybody who had a proper home. You were either working for somebody and staying in lodgings they provided, or you lived in a rented slum. I didn't know any kids who just stayed at home and went to school.

I went on the road because I felt I was not wanted. When welfare came in around 1935, my relatives made a place for me to sleep on the floor so that they could get money for my support. Living with them in run-down, dirty cities was worse than being on the road. I was never unhappy or lonely when I was riding the rails. I was free.

Clydia Williams returned to school in the mid-1930s. She later served in the military and worked as an X-ray technician in the U.S. Health Service. She earned a college degree in economics over nine years of study at night school and went on to do her graduate studies at the University of New Mexico's Anderson School of Business Management. Clydia remained single all her life. "I never wanted to have a family live like I had to live. If you can't see where your own future's going to be, how can you bring a child in to go the same route?"

The Way Out

---◆---

"Job—that was the magic word," says James Martin, who rode freight trains for eight years from 1932 looking for a steady job that he never found. While one road kid in five was on a summer adventure, most teenagers riding the rails left home to seek work. Some were high school dropouts, but many had graduated only to find their local job prospects were nil. They joined the mass of migrant job seekers estimated in 1933 to be as many as four million. It was a desperate world of cut-throat competition, where a boy or girl had to hustle for the lowliest job.

Some found work in New Deal programs, especially the Civilian Conservation Corps (CCC) and on National Youth Administration projects.

Many road kids followed the harvests in the West, as genera tions of hoboes had done before. Young migrants who were fortunate landed on farms where they were decently housed and paid a fair wage, though their employers might themselves be struggling to survive. Others not so lucky were cruelly exploited. Frustration and disappointment drove many back home without having found better lives.

The era of the boxcar boys and girls passed with the coming of World War II and the end of the Great Depression. Riding the rails had been a rite of passage for a generation of young people and profoundly shaped the rest of their lives. Self-reliance, compassion, frugality, and a love of freedom and country are at the heart of the lessons they learned. Their memories are a mixture of nostalgia and pain; their late musings still tinged with the fear of going broke again. At journey's end, the resiliency of these survivors is a testament to the indomitable strength of the human spirit.

Looking for Work

"When I hopped a train I didn't care if it was going north or south, east or west. I was looking for work and opportunity," says Anthony Caralla, whose home was in Geneva, New York. "I dug ditches for a pipeline from Niagara Falls to Albany, working ten hours a day for 7.5 cents an hour. I helped tear down the old Union Trust Company building in Cleveland at a dollar a day. I built roads in Texas for fifteen cents an hour. I worked in restaurants throughout the country as a busboy and kitchen helper, twelve hours a day for two dollars and meals."

From the time Thomas Rodgers first began to ride the rails in 1933 at age fourteen until he went into the CCC at seventeen, he'd had nineteen different jobs in seven states from Virginia to Utah. His mother had died from cancer in 1927, leaving Thomas and his siblings in the care of their father. In 1930, when the Depression was in full swing, his father was injured at work and became unemployed. The family received $2.50 a week from the Philadelphia City Welfare department. At age eleven, Thomas was the wage earner in his house as a shoeshine boy, hawking the *Philadelphia Bulletin* and selling gum and candy on the street.

In 1931 following a beating by his father, a juvenile-court judge sent Thomas to a foster home on a farm run by the Philadelphia Society to Protect Children from Cruelty. One hot summer day in 1933, he forgot to check the water in the chicken coops and caused the death of scores of birds. Thomas ran away with five dollars in his pocket.

Among the jobs Thomas held in this period were dishwasher, window cleaner, dairyman, truck farm laborer, factory worker, tobacco warehouse handler, harvest tramp, forest fire-fighter, circus worker, barroom help, and vacuum cleaner salesman.

"I never seemed satisfied to stay in one place very long. I was searching for something," wrote Rodgers in a family memoir. When his wanderlust ceased, he became a schoolteacher, minister, and missionary.

Dale Olson rode the freights from 1933 to 1939, going wherever he could find work. "I had the choice of putting in long hours on the family farm and having nothing to show for it or getting out to see the country," said Olson. He went from job to job not from wanderlust but because most positions available to young drifters were seasonal and temporary. His ramblings led him to jobs as varied as mining silver and punching cattle in Colorado, to operating apple-weighing scales in Wenatchee, Washington.

Youths like Rodgers and Olson had the knack of being in the right place at the right time and landing job after job. For many road kids, it was hard-going from the start. Sixteen-year-old Duval Edwards ran away from home in central Louisiana in September 1932 after realizing his parents' desperate straits. In *The Great Depression: A Teenager's Fight to Survive*, Edwards recounted his first attempts to find work in Bossier City, Louisiana: "There were signs in Bossier City restaurant windows advertising: 'Dishwashers Wanted—only college graduates need apply.' Not believing these words, I went into several cafes to inquire personally and always got the same reply: 'We mean it, sonny. We are helping those who have finished college and can't find any other work.'"

Josef Ofer graduated from the University of Detroit in 1931 with a degree in electrical engineering. Two job offers he had lined up vanished by graduation day. "A degree became an obstacle to getting a job. 'You are overqualified,' I was told. It became a struggle to earn something to eat," said Ofer. It took him ten years to finally land a promising engineering job with Lockheed Aircraft Company.

There were no limits to the resourcefulness of a boy or girl desperate for work. Runaway Denzil Stephenson left his Flint, Michigan, home in the middle of winter 1933. On his arrival in Traverse City, forty miles to the north, fourteen-year-old Denzil witnessed an accident—a restaurant worker delivering food to the local jail was struck by a car. "The next morning I reported to the restaurant and got the job. I heard nothing of the worker's fate and did not ask. I stayed all winter employed as a dishwasher for two dollars a week and my meals."

Nine months after leaving Lester, Arkansas, with $4.45 in his pocket, Braxton Ponder finished work in the vineyards of Bakersfield, California, and headed for the wheat fields of Oregon. Arriving too early for the harvest, he took a job as a rattlesnake catcher. Desert rattlesnakes, eighteen inches to two feet long, would not cross blacktop roads in the day. "They waited until sunset when the surface cooled off. I caught them while they were gathered up along the roadside and sold them to coyote trappers for bait."

At Laramie, Wyoming, Selby Norheim opened a boxcar door and saw a brakeman looking up at him.

"What do you do besides bum around the country?" the man asked.

"Look for work, sir," replied Norheim.

The brakeman had a job for Norheim. He told him that some time before, a man had come through Laramie with four silver foxes and no money. He offered a pair of foxes to the brakeman, if he would help him. The brakeman now owned twenty-one foxes and was building pens for them. Recalls Norheim:

"For the next two months I dug ditches for fencing around ten fox pens. I lived in a small shack and was given a rifle to keep mountain lions away from the foxes. Happily, no mountain lion showed up."

Clifford St. Martin and his road partner Hank Beckner, who hoboed together for four years, made a living as "junkers." They scoured city dumps for pickings, sometimes striking it lucky. On the dump at Glendive, Montana, they found discarded hospital sheets. After laundering the sheets in a jungle, they sold them to car dealers for use as cleaning rags. At Alder, Montana, they picked up so much copper wire they couldn't carry it away. They drew straws to see who would cross the foothills to the nearest junk dealer in Dillon. "Hank walked forty miles and came back with the dealer, who paid us forty dollars," said St. Martin. "We bought new shoes and overalls. We had a few good meals and slept in a bed a couple of times. Then we were broke again."

Fire Fighters

Henry Koczur, one of six children, left his East Chicago home in September 1932 at sixteen. His father was out of work and suffering from stomach ulcers. On many days the family lived on potato soup for breakfast, lunch, and supper. Henry headed for California, "a land where I didn't think anyone could starve."

At Saugus, California, he was bumming a house for food when a forest ranger drove up and ordered him to climb into his vehicle. He was going to fight a fire in the mountains. When Henry asked what authority the ranger had to pick him up, the man said that if the governor himself was on the scene, he could force him to fight a fire. Other recruits were swept up along the road to the blaze in the Caustic Canyon.

At a forest camp Henry was handed a double-bladed ax and a canteen of water, and was sent to fight the flames.

"When I got to the top of the mountain, it looked as though the whole world was burning. We built fire trails from the top to the bottom. Behind us men threw the brush to one side so the fire wouldn't leap across the trail, but it always did," recalls Henry.

A captain of the rangers sent for a water tanker. He ordered Henry to take two lengths of hose to a fire fighter wetting down the brush on a new trail.

"I was on my way when another ranger told me to drop everything and run for my life. The captain was very disappointed when he heard that I had abandoned the hoses. As soon as the fire passed, I went back to retrieve them. All I could find were four chrome-plated hose ends."

The wind changed and helped extinguish the Caustic Canyon fire. Henry and the other recruits remained on patrol for several days looking for signs of smoke and covering embers with dirt. The pay was twenty cents an hour, but when the job was over and the fire fighters went to get their wages, they learned they would have to wait thirty days for checks to be issued.

Henry bummed around California and Arizona for a month before returning to Saugus to collect his $12.50. He had no identification and couldn't cash his check. He took two pieces of cardboard, put the check between them, and stuck it in his back pocket. After four months he made it home, where he knew a man with a bank account who cashed the check for him.

Ross Coppock worked for the Forest Service at Mt. Hood National Forest in the summers of 1937 and 1938. Stationed at Hood River, a community on the railroad through the Columbia River Gorge, Coppock recalled that the local sheriff would stop freight trains and commandeer hoboes who were aboard: "They were given the choice of 'volunteering' to fight a fire or going to jail. Almost invariably they chose to fight fires. They would be fed, housed, and paid."

Coppock remembered seeing volunteers at work in the hottest part of the battle. Many had never been nearer a forest than when they rode the train they were pulled from. The fire-fighting equipment they used was mainly backpacks with water pumps, shovels, and Pulaski axes. Nothing sophisticated, only sweat and backbreaking toil.

"Fire fighting can be pure hell. It is the most draining and challenging physical and mental torture. Inevitably, I would reach a point of exhaustion and collapse—if the fire came and got me, that was going to be it. I can imagine what it must have been like for the men and boys from the freights who came to give it their all, untrained and alone and scared to death."

Keep on Moving

Wisconsin farm boy Fred Schatz, who spent two years hoboing in the early 1930s, found work on one of the railroads that had given him a free ride. Arriving in a boxcar at Mandan, North Dakota, Schatz and Leo Elder, a friend and traveling companion, were greeted by the boss of a railroad gang who offered them jobs as "gandy dancers"—track workers who shoveled gravel under railroad ties. They worked ten hours a day for twenty-five cents an hour, with ninety cents deducted for board. After two weeks during which they contracted dysentery from the spoiled meat dished up in the commissary, the pair went back on the road. Despite this experience, Schatz took jobs on "extra gangs" in South Dakota, Iowa, and Minnesota. "It was hard physical labor pumping a shovel up and down all day long, but this was one of the few jobs you could find at the time," says Schatz.

With the coming of 1933, Roosevelt and the New Deal government's $3 billion public works programs created thousands of jobs on projects ranging from flood control in the Tennessee Valley to construction of "megadams" like Fort Peck on the Missouri River. In spring 1936, nineteen-year-old Bernard Carlson completed his first year at Jamestown College, North Dakota. Like most North Dakota farmers, his parents were just getting by with no extra cash to finance his college education. Carlson rode the rails a thousand miles to Fort Peck in Montana to get a summer job.

"I was given work on the bedbug control crew at fifty cents an hour. The wage was double what was paid for farm labor," said Carlson. "We took a squirt can of kerosene and went through the barracks inspecting bunks for bugs. If we found any they were given a shot of kerosene." After a couple of weeks Carlson transferred to a crew working on the surface of the dam. He stayed in Montana until the beginning of September, when he headed back home. "I'd had the chance to work with eleven thousand men from every walk of life building one of the world's marvels of engineering. I earned good wages and had enough money to go back to college."

While public works projects created tens of thousands of jobs, it was as rare for a teenage boy to land work on a Public Works Administration (PWA) site as anywhere else when long lines of older, more experienced workers stood waiting.

"You move along the line—maybe get to be next up—only to hear them say, 'Sorry, we don't need anyone today.' In more than one place they had jobs for young people but expected you to have years of experience," said Walter Barrett, a teenager when he left Prescott, Arizona, in 1930.

Chester Siems was nineteen when he was riding the rails in the West searching for a job. He experienced these same frustrations even as the Depression was coming to an end in 1939. Two penny postcards Siems wrote to his brother reflect his mood at the time:

Storm Lake, Iowa
June 6, 1939

Dear Ted,

Am in Storm Lake, Iowa. Getting along fine although I haven't any job as yet. I am on the trail of something good so I'll keep trying. If I don't get anything I am going to Colorado on the chance of getting on a dam they're building there. I've had several small jobs but they didn't amount to much.

Be seeing you,

"Chick"

South Bend, Indiana
April 16, 1940

Dear Ted,

Well I'm on the road again. It sure takes a hero to stay out here starving. I just wanted to tell you I am all right and will be home by July. Don't try to contact me because I won't be any place you know of.

"Chick"

Herbert Teitelbaum, on the road between the ages of twelve and sixteen, faced many disappointments. "The clothes you wore were distinctive in telling people who and what you were," recalls Teitelbaum, whose experiences spanned the years 1930 to 1935. On occasion he found jobs on construction projects, fishing boats, and farms, as a bare-knuckle fighter and as a bouncer in a brothel. "Most times people came right out and said, 'Get the hell out of here.' Nothing subtle."

Finding work was no guarantee of even fleeting security. "Several times I was promised that I would be paid a certain amount when I finished a job," said Arthur Lent. "I was lucky to get a dollar or two in cash or a loaf of stale bread. 'Get going, son, before I change my mind,' I was told."

When William Hendricks found the Washington apple harvest abandoned in 1932, he drifted down to California looking for work with little success. The eighteen-year-old had some experience in meat cutting and occasionally landed a few days work with a butcher. "They could not spare a red cent but I could have meat and vegetables as pay for my work."

One day in September 1932, Hendricks was sitting with a group of hoboes in Sacramento talking about finding paying jobs. A stranger came and offered to hire them to dig a ditch at fifty cents an hour. They followed him to a toolshed where they got picks and shovels. He showed where he wanted them to dig the ditch and they set to work.

"We were happy that at last we were going to earn some money," Hendricks said. "We talked about what we were going to do with our wages."

They'd been busy for several hours when another man walked up. He demanded to know why they were digging up the yard of the local insane asylum. The man supervising their effort was an inmate who'd no authority to hire anyone.

"We were one disappointed bunch of men," said Hendricks.

Donald Kopecky hoboed through almost the entire Depression, beginning in 1931. In Colorado a farmer promised Kopecky and two companions jobs putting up alfalfa that would be ready in a week. The trio camped out in the woods and then went back to the farm. The farmer told them he had enough local men who needed the work. There was no place for them.

On another occasion in Seattle, the same three paid a recruiting agent for jobs with Alaska Fisheries. When they got to the Fisheries, they learned they had to join a union at a fee of fifty dollars each, and that they would be hired by seniority. "We had neither the fifty dollars nor the seniority. We returned to the job seller for a refund of fifteen dollars we'd each paid. The man had gone out of business," said Kopecky.

In 1940 Kopecky saved money to take a six-week course in aircraft sheet-metal work in San Francisco. The school guaranteed a job if you completed the course with good grades. Kopecky finished successfully and went to inquire about his new job. "I was to be a busboy in a college dorm. When I complained they shrugged it off: 'We guaranteed you a job. Take it or leave it.'" Adds Kopecky: "On the eve of World War II, I'd been on the road for ten years. All I had to show was my bindle and the clothes on my back."

Clemence Ruff had never been more than a hundred miles from his home in the village of Gackle, North Dakota. On his second road trip to look for work, in June 1934, Ruff went from one hobo jungle to another in the Northwest chasing rumors of jobs.

"The end of the rainbow was always somewhere else, and it kept us moving," said Ruff. After his second summer among the jobless and destitute, Ruff returned home and enlisted in the CCC.

For Richer, For Poorer

Geneva Fuqua was fifteen and her husband, Eldridge Carter, twenty-one when they married in Oklahoma in 1937. Shortly after their wedding, her husband and father-in-law were both laid off. For six months, the young couple would spend two days with one set of parents and then two days with the next, hitchhiking fifty miles between their homes in hopes of lightening the burden on their families. Finally Geneva and Eldridge began to ride freights searching for work in Oregon and California. Half a century later she recalled their struggle: "No one would even let us into their offices or accept our applications. After a while I began to feel worthless and gave up looking for a steady job. We had no decent clothes, no stable address. We were treated like the street people of today and ignored."

Twenty-year-old Allene Biby was married to her husband, Howard, in Pueblo, Colorado, in 1929. The Crash came and they were in the thick of it when Howard lost his job. He was a good dancer and had always bought the best shoes he could afford for dancing on Saturday nights. He stopped riding streetcars and wore out the soles of his shoes looking for work.

"I will never forget Howard's beautiful pair of Florsheims. To the very last step, they had class, never lost their shape or shine. They are symbolic to me yet—to be the best you can until the end," said Allene.

Howard and Allene were forced apart when he and his brother-in-law bummed their way by freight to California to look for work. It was four months before he had scraped together enough money for Allene to join him in Santa Barbara.

D. L. Young was the son of Texas sharecroppers, one of eleven children living on a one hundred-acre cotton farm near Fairlie, Texas. In December 1934, when D. L. was eighteen, six feet tall, and 125 pounds, he hopped a train to Gainesville to visit a cousin. At a New Year's Eve party, D. L. met brown-eyed, brown-haired Thelma Jones, who was fourteen and a half. D. L. began to ride the rails with a new purpose, courting Thelma all that winter and summer too. With the consent of their parents, they married in April 1935.

"We had to borrow the money to get our license. We didn't know where our next meal would come from but we loved each other and had the courage to believe we could make a living," D. L. remembered. The first job they found was in Wolfe City, Texas, where they cut wood for fifty cents a rick. "It took Thelma and me all day to cut a rick of wood. We lived on three dollars a week."

When they visited Thelma's folks at Gainesville or traveled anywhere else, the couple rode the rails or hitchhiked. By June 1937, they had a baby boy. When he was four months old they took him on his first boxcar ride to see D. L.'s parents, who lived twenty miles from Wolfe City.

"We were chopping cotton for one dollar each a day and picking it for fifty cents a hundred pounds. We saved our first fifty dollars, which we put in the bank at Wolfe City," said D. L. In December 1938, the couple took a boxcar to Fort Worth to look for work with their eighteen-month-old son. Stopping at the Santa Fe depot, D. L. got a job as a news "butch," selling papers on trains between Fort Worth and San Angelo, Texas. In 1941, D. L. began a twenty-five-year career on the railroads, rising to engine foreman.

Vagrant Ambition

Though Herbert Teitelbaum suffered repeated setbacks looking for work, he took courage from the example of others. "The will to survive was remarkable. People were desperately poor, hungry, and ragged, yet they always had hope." Nowhere did hope burn brighter than with ambitious youths riding the rails to follow a dream.

Mel Stine ran away from home in 1929 when he was seventeen and worked at menial jobs for the next three years. In 1932 he took an aptitude test at the San Francisco YMCA and was encouraged to become an airplane engine designer. He wrote to Pratt and Whitney in East Hartford, Connecticut, and received a pile of literature from the company. Over the next six months, Stine sat down to design an aircraft engine for a portfolio he hoped would get him a job with the company.

In June 1933, Stine sold all his worldly possessions, which netted him sixty dollars. He bought a money order for fifty-five dollars and arranged for it to be forwarded to him poste restante, Hartford, Connecticut. With five dollars in his pocket, he set out to cross the United States by hopping freights and hitchhiking.

Thirteen days later, Stine arrived in Connecticut with one dollar in his pocket. At the post office he found a letter from the man who was to have sent his money: Since the post office held mail for only two weeks and Stine couldn't possibly reach Hartford in that time, the man had delayed forwarding the money order. Stine had better luck when he went to fetch a trunk he'd sent ahead by express baggage. When he told the clerk his story about the money order, the man felt sorry for him and loaned him two dollars.

He checked into the YMCA for one dollar a week and immediately arranged for an interview with Pratt and Whitney. The plant superintendent was impressed with his drawings and his story of crossing the country by boxcar. He introduced Stine to the chief draftsman but every drafting board was filled. They told him to phone the factory regularly in case a position opened up.

For the next two months Stine took any part-time jobs he could find. On one occasion he had to put up a clothesline on the fourth floor of a four-story flat. The clothesline had to be attached to a forty-foot pole that had spikes driven into it for steps. Climbing the pole was frightening enough but jockeying around clotheslines at the first three levels was even more harrowing. Off balance, he had to wrap his arms tightly around the pole as he pulled a leg up and over the line.

"As I climbed I saw the three lines grow taut and realized they were all that kept the pole from falling. Finally I was at the top, strung the line through the pulley, and then started down again," said Stine.

He had been promised two dollars, but the landlady's son offered him fifty cents for his work. They were still arguing when the landlady arrived. Furious when she found out her son was trying to cheat Stine, she paid him in full.

He worked at various jobs, including handyman, busboy, and dishwasher. Every week he phoned the superintendent at Pratt and Whitney. One day two months after he arrived, he was told to report to the chief draftsman and was given a job as a tracer. Stine remembered his elation: "At last I had my big chance. I had a warm feeling toward the whole world. I'd found my first job as a designer draftsman, a career I followed for thirty-seven years until I retired."

Ambition was sometimes not enough to beat the Depression odds. After his experience digging a ditch at the insane asylum, William Hendricks decided to go home to De Queens, Arkansas.

In the fall of 1933 he enrolled in the College of the Ozarks, arranging to work four jobs to earn his way.

Hendricks spent two hours or more every day milking sixty Jersey cows with another student. He served as college butcher, slaughtering two steers and a hog on Saturdays. During the week he cut and trimmed the meat. At night he washed dishes in the cafeteria. Another part-time job involved transplanting trees from a nearby forest to the campus. He also earned fifty cents for animals butchered on the farms of his college professors. Every three months he received twelve dollars from the Arkansas National Guard, which paid one dollar for each drill attended.

After four years, Hendricks earned his B.S. degree. In the graduation line, he was given a notice telling him that he'd receive his diploma as soon as he paid the college what he still owed them.

"I hit the rails once more and sought a job as a chemist," said Hendricks. "At least twenty prospective employers asked me, 'Why should we employ you when you have only a B.S. degree? We can hire a chemist with a Ph.D. for the same price.' I couldn't give them an answer." Until he enlisted in the army, Hendricks had to fall back on his skills as a part-time butcher.

Harvest Tramps

Like earlier generations of migrant workers, boy tramps of the Depression followed the grain harvest in the Midwest. They started in Oklahoma in early summer and trekked northward through Kansas, Colorado, and Missouri; through Iowa and Nebraska; and into the Dakotas and Minnesota. A boy had to be strong and healthy and not shy of hard work and long hours. "A farmer I worked for was an eight-hour man—eight hours before lunch and eight hours after lunch," said Arvel Pearson, who was paid one dollar a day and board for his labor.

Farm boys like Willard Berg, who was born and raised in Oregon, found it natural to seek jobs as field hands not only in the grain belt but wherever they drifted. On the road for two years from 1933 to 1934, Berg traveled from coast to coast and was never turned down when he sought farm work.

In Ashfield, Wisconsin, when he asked a farmer for work the man wanted to know how much he wanted a day. "Six bits and board," said Berg, then realized this was a Western expression. "Seventy-five cents," he explained. At the time, fifty cents a day was a high rate for farmhands. The farmer was behind in his hand cultivation and agreed to the wage.

"What a glorious three weeks! Shirtless and bronzed, I hoed strawberries, potatoes, beans, corn, and carrots, working with zest ten to twelve hours a day. I reveled in the early summer sunshine and the air that breezed through the conifers on the edge of Lake Superior."

When Berg left Wisconsin, he went to Traverse City, Michigan, the nation's sour-cherry capital. Joining other migratory pickers, who slept together in a barn and cooked over camp fires, he partnered up with a worker named Frank. He couldn't understand how Frank, who picked no faster, came out with a daily tally 20 to 25 percent higher. Early in the morning Frank brought in four buckets of cherries at a time. Later, as buckets began to stack up on the receiving table, Frank would bring in three and put his hand on a fourth, accepting the tally without comment. What made an even greater impression on young Berg was a piece of advice Frank gave him:

"Get out of overalls. Nobody ever made any money wearing overalls."

At a farm outside Houlton, Maine, Berg was asked if he knew how to "stook" grain. He didn't have the faintest idea what "stooking" meant, but said he knew. The farmer took him to a field where a tractor-drawn binder was dropping off bundles of grain.

"'Well, then, start in,' said my new employer. I hesitated. The boss picked up two bundles and set them together, butts down in the stubble. I grabbed two bundles and set them smartly against the first, then grabbed two more and gave them the same treatment.

"'You have stooked before,' declared the man."

Berg didn't tell the fellow that he wasn't "stooking" grain but "shocking" it, as they said out West. After stooking grain, Berg harvested potatoes in Maine, picking eighty to ninety barrels of 160 pounds each per day. At six cents a barrel he was making good money and earned nearly one hundred dollars during the season.

Reflecting on his days as a harvest tramp, Willard Berg commented: "I still remember the shivering nights in boxcars and under filthy blankets in shelters. When I think back on the total experience, though, I regard it as one of the happiest periods of my life. Why? I believe it may be the freedom to do as one pleases and the challenge of living on the road—knowing one will survive but gleefully anticipating the revelation of 'how?'"

When the Depression came, Lloyd Jesse Veitch had already been following the grain harvest for seven years, starting as a sixteen-year-old in a time when jobs were plentiful. "When one job played out there was always another in the next farming town. You'd just sit on the curb downtown and wait for a farmer to come along and offer you work," said Veitch. A young hobo could afford to be choosy. "After asking how much a farmer would pay, a smart field hand would also inquire what kind of mattress he provided for a bed. If it was corn shucks, wait for another farmer to come along and offer feathers."

By the mid-1930s, jobs were becoming harder to obtain, as field hands uprooted from drought-ravaged states swarmed along the harvest routes. At the same time, the demand for labor decreased when agriculture began to mechanize with huge combines that could do the work of thirty men.

In August 1934, Kansas school dropout Rex Cozad saw a newspaper ad placed by the Fruit Growers Association of Palisade, Colorado: The growers needed two thousand peach pickers for thirty days from August 5. The going rate was five cents a bushel, and a good picker could harvest one hundred bushels a day.

The sixteen-year-old Cozad and four other boys left their homes in Norcatur, Kansas, and rode the rails to Colorado. Three days later, they crossed the Continental Divide and rolled into Palisades, where they expected to make five dollars a day. Cozad recalls going to the one-block-square city park and finding it elbow to elbow with people.

"The local paper estimated that five thousand people had flocked in for the harvest. Worst of all, it would be four or five days before the peaches were ready to pick. We were told that every morning growers who needed help would send a truck to the park for workers. The trucks never came so I started walking from orchard to orchard in the valley. I got the same answer at every stop: 'Our regular help comes every year.'"

Three of the boys returned to Kansas after one week in Palisade. Cozad and the remaining boy continued to roam the valley but found no work. "Money was running short. My shoes were worn out and I had to wire the soles to the uppers. After two weeks we gave up and caught a freight back home," said Cozad. Despite the failure to find work, Cozad never forgot the journey home through Glenwood Canyon, Colorado. "We rode a refrigerated train that strained and steamed up the canyon. Its whistle echoed on the canyon walls. I'll never forget the sights and sounds and the smell of coal smoke and hot steel. I decided then that the whole trip had been worthwhile."

In the orchards of central Washington, Wallace Horton found a line of men three blocks long looking for work in the 1935 fruit harvest. "I waited all day and all night so I would not lose my place in line. The next afternoon I was fifty feet from the hiring booth. A man called out asking if anyone knew how to color-pick peaches. I held up my hand and six other guys did the same." Horton, eighteen, and the men walked fifteen miles to the orchards where they were to work. On the way one of the men asked Horton what was involved in 'color picking.' When he said he'd no idea, the rest confessed they'd held up their hands thinking he knew and would instruct them.

"I told them to leave the talking to me when we got to the job. When the farmer asked if we were experienced, I said we all had different opinions on how to color-pick peaches. 'If you show us what color you prefer and how you like things done, we'll do it your way,' I told the farmer. He came up with a big smile and never said anything, but told us what he wanted done. We went all out to do a good job for him."

Living and working conditions varied from farm to farm. At Hood River, Oregon, Richard Sheil worked on one of the best fruit farms in the valley. Wages were five cents an hour higher than at most camps. The living quarters consisted of clean, comfortable cabins furnished with beds, tables, and cooking stoves.

"Lady Luck was not so kind to us after Hood River," Sheil recalled. "In the Arizona and California cotton fields the camps were utterly revolting. At Buckeye, Arizona, we had a ragged tent and the bare, hard-pan Arizona soil to sleep on. After we had bent double all day in the fields, the hard ground was too much for our weary backs. Four of us rented a tourist cabin not far from the camp for two and a half dollars a week. This extra expense, however, destroyed our margin of profit."

In winter 1934, Jack Kidwell got his first job after graduating from high school working on a farm in Michigan: "I got one dollar a week and lodging. I chopped ice out of the troughs and carried water to the sheep and hogs. What time I didn't spend watering livestock, I spent chopping wood. I left Michigan when spring came. I have never gone back, and never will."

Few field jobs took more out of you than the sugar-beet harvest. "A plow would root out the beets. It was your job to pick up each beet and whack off the green tops," said Donald McCutcheon, who was fourteen when he topped beets. "Bent over eight hours a day, you wondered if you'd ever be able to stand up straight again."

At sixteen, Elizabeth Verwolf was topping beets in Idaho in 1936. "You made $3.50 a day if you worked hard, but it was a horrible job. You had a long knife with a big hook on the end. Every now and then the hook embedded in my knees. I still have the scars to prove it."

Cotton Pickers

"Cotton picking is an honorable occupation, boys. In another week, you'll have the cotton all picked out. Stick around after that and you won't be cotton pickers—you'll be bums."

This advice was given to Edgar Bledsoe and two cousins by a farmer in southern Oklahoma. It was less than a year since Bledsoe had left his hometown of Ardmore, Oklahoma. At age sixteen, Bledsoe had found himself making less money than he'd been earning mowing lawns when he was twelve.

In late summer 1930, he joined his cousins and their families in the Oklahoma cotton fields. "Tents were set up for families with small children," recalls Bledsoe. "We teenage boys slept in the seed house. After a hard day's work, sleeping in a bed of cotton-seed was heaven."

From Oklahoma the boys followed the cotton harvest into the plains of Texas. At Indianola they went to the cotton gin, where the first farmer they talked to offered them a job. Jeff Upshaw, who everyone knew as "Uncle Jeff," was a seventy-year-old widower. He had a rickety old wagon pulled by two mules. The boys climbed in and rode thirteen miles to Uncle Jeff's property, where they stopped at the threshold of his house. It had been a chicken coop before he moved in. He invited them to spread their bedrolls on the dirt floor.

Bledsoe remembers that while they waited for Upshaw to get their supper ready, he saw his cousin John digging at something in the dirt with his toe. A lamp was a luxury Uncle Jeff did not possess, so John kicked his find into the fading light. It was a dead mouse trodden under foot for so long that it had become one with the floor. Later that night the boys spread their rolls below the stars.

Supper was the same meal they would have three times a day for the next week: salt pork and fried dough. After a week of this fare, Bledsoe volunteered to do the cooking himself, much to Uncle Jeff's satisfaction.

"The weather stayed good and we pulled bolls from sunup to

sundown. Uncle Jeff had given us the choice of fifty cents a hundred for picking or thirty-five cents for boll pulling. We opted for the latter. Not only does it weigh more when you pull the entire boll, but it goes faster."

When Upshaw's harvest was finished and they were paid, the boys rode on top of the last load going to the Indianola gin. They held a council of war, resolving that no matter how badly they needed the money, at least one of them should finish high school. The other two convinced John that since he was the youngest, he should go back to school while they continued to follow the harvest. Said Bledsoe: "When we waved goodbye to John we'd no idea we were greeting a future head of the vocational department at Penn State University. Had we known, we would have told him never to recommend the honorable occupation of cotton picking to anyone."

Few former road kids had anything good to say about working in the cotton fields of the south. Riding a freight in Texas in 1933, seventeen-year-old Hal Buffa and a friend shared a boxcar with a black man, who offered to get them jobs picking cotton. That night they ate with the man's family and slept on his porch. The next morning he took Hal and his friend to the cotton fields: "We lasted less than an hour," said Hal. "We thanked him for his offer and hopped the next train out of there."

In September 1938, three Texas runaways—Claude Franklin, thirteen; his brother Charles, sixteen; and their friend Robert Brookshire, thirteen—made for the Mississippi Delta, where they had heard cotton was tall and easy to pick. They saw themselves making a pile of money. Riding the rails to Cleveland, Mississippi, they found a farm that needed cotton pickers. They were offered seventy-five cents a hundred pounds. They would pay ten dollars a week for room and board, which would be deducted from their earnings.

Claude Franklin remembered their first morning on the job. "My back began to ache in about thirty minutes. My fingers hurt with pricks and scratches from cotton burrs. When you had a good quantity of cotton in your bag, you took it to be weighed. A good picker would weigh up forty or fifty pounds. My bag held thirty pounds. It took several weigh-ins for me to reach one hundred pounds."

Mid-morning on Friday, the trio had had enough. They decided to quit at noon and ask to be paid off. Since workers were normally paid on Saturday, they figured that if they took off on a Friday they could leave without paying for room and board.

"They weren't dumb enough to let us get away with anything like that. The man added up our weigh-ins and then hit us with a bombshell: 'Now, boys, we have to deduct money for your room and board.' Charles had fifty-five cents coming, I had thirty-five cents, and Robert was a nickel in the hole."

It wasn't only in cotton picking that a road kid could be fleeced. Elmer Beckman was paid 17.5 cents an hour for picking apples in Underwood, Washington. When it rained or when the trees were covered with heavy dew, there was no pay at all. Beckman and other harvest workers occupied a shack with broken-down beds. Water had to be fetched from an outside faucet. Except for apples that were free and plentiful, they lived on macaroni and beans, with a ration of meat once a week.

John Kercsi thought he had it made when he climbed off a freight in Georgia and went to a farmhouse to beg for food: The farmer offered him a job.

"I asked how much he paid. '$1.75,' he said. I accepted. I had to get up at 4 A.M. and work until 8 A.M., have breakfast, and then go out and work until nightfall."

At the end of the week, the farmer told Kercsi he no longer needed him.

"He handed me $1.75. I said I thought he'd offered $1.75 a day. He started yelling at me and cursed me for socializing with his black workers. I'd played cards with them on a couple of nights. While I waiting by the railroad tracks one of the black men came up and sneaked me food wrapped in newspaper for my journey."

Walter Miletich and two young friends picked grapes in Fresno, California, for a penny a box. They worked for three days and thought they had made about nine dollars. When they asked for their money, the grape contractor pulled out a pad and did some pencil work. He told them that they owed him fifty-six cents. "He charged us fifty cents a day for the ride to the grape patch and made us pay for bologna sandwiches he gave us," said Miletich. "When we protested, he didn't hesitate to let us see the .38 in his hip pocket. Being a bum, you could not complain to the local authorities."

While some farmers and growers exploited young harvest tramps, many showed compassion toward the wandering boys and girls, even when they themselves were strapped for resources.

Lee Leer was half starved when a farm woman picked him up on the road one late spring day in 1937. The fifteen-year-old had run away from an abandoned cotton farm in Olive, further south in Oklahoma. "It was a place of existence rather than a home," where his family were barely surviving from day to day. The evening before Leer had been chased out of Osage by a policeman who found him going through trash cans looking for food. He fled the town with three rotten apples, all he could find to eat. He slept the night in a ditch and was on the road when the woman stopped for him.

Leer got into the back of a truck loaded with empty milk cans. After several miles the woman stopped at a turnoff and he climbed out. Years later, Leer set down his recollections of their meeting:

"'Are you hungry, boy?' the woman asked.

"'Yes, ma'am, I'm hungry.'

"'Are you a bum or a hobo?'"

It was the first time Leer heard the question. He wasn't sure what the difference was. "'I'll work for something to eat,'" he mumbled.

"'Then you're a hobo, boy. Bums won't work but hoboes will. Ain't been on the road long enough to learn that?'

"'I guess not, ma'am, but I'd sure work for something to eat.'"

The woman told him to get back into the truck. She drove down a dirt road to a farmhouse, where Leer followed her inside. She fed him leftovers from breakfast—fatback bacon, cornbread and gravy, and glass of milk.

Leer learned that the woman was married, but she owned the

farm and was the boss. She offered to employ him at one dollar a day plus his noon meal. There was a store within walking distance where he could buy food for his supper. He was to sleep in the barn, where he was forbidden to smoke or make a fire. He would start work after dinner that day.

At noon, Leer sat down for the meal with the woman and her husband, Leer's eyes bulging at a table covered with a platter of fried ham, bowls of butter beans, black-eyed peas, potatoes, and turnip greens.

After dinner he tackled his first job: raking hay with a dump rake. When he came in from the hayfield, he helped the woman with the milking. Afterwards he turned a cream separator for two hours.

"I was ready to collapse when I got to the barn that evening. I found four eggs in the hallway. I would've fried them for my supper but had been told not to make any fires. I broke the eggs into a glass of milk and drank the mixture."

Leer began a daily routine of milking, separating cream, drawing water, and working in the fields. One evening when Leer was in the milking shed, the woman told him she'd been getting three to four eggs in the barn in the past.

"'Do you think rats may be carrying them off?'

"I hung my head and said, 'No ma'am, I'm eating those eggs.'"

"'Aren't you walking to the store to buy food?'

"'I don't have any money, ma'am, not one cent.'

"'From now on look under the water trough at the well. You'll find something for your supper.'"

True to her word, the woman always left something for him to eat, a hunk of cornbread or a piece of pie.

Then, after he'd been there six days, he was helping the woman with the morning milking when she suddenly announced that would be his last day.

"'We can't afford a hired hand. You can leave after your noon meal,'" she said.

Leer shuffled out to the hayfield, where the husband found him.

"'You and my wife aren't pulling the wool over my eyes. I know what's going on,'" he said.

Leer saw that the man was holding a big crescent wrench in his hand. He backed up, looking for a place to run.

"'I know she is feeding you extra,'" the man said and just walked off.

Leer thought about the outburst all morning. He came to the conclusion that it was part of a ploy the pair had to avoid paying him the dollar a day they'd promised.

When he went to the dinner table at noon, he saw that his plate was bottom side up.

"Here's where they're gonna spring it on me," he thought. "Stealing eggs, eating extra food, maybe a few more trumped-up charges. No pay, no money, just eat and get on down the road, boy."

The woman broke the silence. "'Well, boy, turn your plate over and let's get on with it.'

"I caught my breath and felt my heart beating. I picked up my plate. I found a pile of green dollar bills under it. Six dollar bills to be precise, a fortune to a boy who didn't have one copper penny to his name.

"Later there would be times when I found myself weak, broke, and hungry on the road. I wished I'd said I would work for nothing. 'Just feed me and I'll stay.' What I wouldn't have given to sit down at their table just one more time."

The Tree Army

Riding the rails in his early twenties, Texas-born Harry Keller occasionally found low-paying harvest jobs. Most of the time he had no work as he bummed his way around nine Western states. The Roosevelt administration introduced the Civilian Conservation Corps in 1933. Keller signed up and was sent to a CCC camp in the Tonto Basin near Globe, Arizona.

Nearsighted but without glasses, Keller was first hired as powder man on a dynamiting crew, though he had never worked with explosives before. His job was to fill drilled holes with dynamite and ready it for blasting. He got the hang of it quickly enough or he might have ended his CCC days then and there. Headaches caused by exposure to dynamite later resulted in his being transferred to a less hazardous area.

Reenlisting in the CCC year after year, Keller strung telephone poles across the Tonto Basin, repaired roads, built fish dams, planted trees, and fought forest fires. He eventually became head chef at the camp, feeding 175 to two hundred young men and youths.

"I'd never cooked in my life. I wrote home to my mother asking her to tell me how to prepare this and that," recalled Keller. He rose to be mess sergeant, a position he held for more than three of his eight years in the CCC.

"I was scared and worried before I joined the corps. The CCC taught me responsibility and gave me confidence. Never again did I worry about how I would survive."

Young men serving in the CCC were paid thirty dollars a month, twenty-five dollars of which was automatically sent to their families. Arthur Hunevan's parents were in danger of losing their home when he went into the CCC in northern California. His wages helped them make the payments on their house. Besides alleviating the financial burden on Wallace Horton's widowed mother, his year in the CCC taught him to understand and work with other people. "I learned that the world did not owe me a living. If I wanted to get ahead, I would have to earn it," said Horton. The former CCC-er went on to become a USAF electronics engineer, whose career earned him the air force's highest civilian award.

Runaway Jan van Heé's self-esteem was "down to ground zero" when he enlisted in the CCC. "I felt I was no good, unwanted, rotten, dumb, stupid. No one cared for me and no one ever would," said Van Heé. After six months in the corps, he was made foreman of a fire-fighting unit with six youths. When the fire season ended, he was promoted to a position in the ranger's office. "I was getting pats on the back. 'He's doing a good job,' my officers said. I began to feel that I was worth something."

Franklin Roosevelt's "Tree Army," as the CCC was dubbed, marched to many different drumbeats. In a personal memoir, Ernest Amundsen recalled being sent to a "spike" camp at West Yellowstone. "We worked on Forest Service roads. A dump truck hauled loads of gravel. Left-handed boys had to shovel on the right-hand side and right-handers on the left side. The boss did this with whatever tools we were using. I learned to use a shovel, ax, saw, pick, and other tools left-handed. I also learned not to drink whiskey like you drink beer, and how to play poker and how not to play poker."

Darwood Drake and other North Dakotan farm boys found themselves posted to a CCC camp at Locke, a small community in the heart of the Ozarks thirty miles from Fort Smith, Arkansas. "We had to get used to the Southern drawl, the slower way of living, the grits and corn pone. We saw poverty-stricken families in ramshackle places with livestock running in and out of the shacks." In this unlikely locale, inspired by one of the North Dakotans who could tap dance. Drake joined nine comrades in working up a "routine" for the camp show. "None of us was less than 160 pounds and several weighed over 200 pounds. It was a sight to see ten uncoordinated men jumping up and down trying to tap to 'The Sidewalks of New York.'"

Not every recruit found a haven in the CCC. Weldon Keele signed up in Utah after graduating from high school in May 1935. He was assigned to a camp in Wood Cross, Utah, where he reported in time for supper. "I didn't know that you had to put your dishes in one place and your knife, fork, and spoon in another place for washing. A big, burly guy from Kentucky who was doing the dishes called me a dumb son of a bitch and wanted to beat me up. I didn't like the guys from the East. They were too roughtalking for me. I went back to my bunk, gathered up my belongings, and headed for home."

Nineteen-year-old George de Mars had become totally discouraged working on a farm for twenty-five dollars a month in the summer and three dollars a month in winter. In February 1933 he left Minnesota in below-zero weather and rode the rails for four months. He was looking for work, but could find only menial jobs and was worse off. "Franklin Roosevelt was my all-time hero when he introduced the CCCs. The corps took a multitude of young men off the road and kept them on the straight and narrow. The pay was not great, but we had good food and clothing and comrades," said de Mars who served thirty months in the Minnesota CCC. "We were under military discipline. When World War II came, we made good soldiers."

With three hundred thousand enrollees a year, the CCC provided a way of leaving the road for thousands of young men in their teens and early twenties. In 1936, Howard Oxley, director of CCC Camp Education, reported that the previous year the corps had found jobs in private industry for 135,000 boys, about one-fourth of the total number in the camps.

The Last Ride

Finding a steady job through the CCC—or on their own initiative—ended a young hobo's often aimless wandering. For many other lost and lonely boys and girls it took far less for them to hop that last train homeward.

"Riding the rails began to scare me. I was beginning to like it too much. I realized I had another life to live and had to pay more attention to my education," said Francis Gerath, who was eighteen at the time. Between hopping trains, Gerath stuck his thumb out in Chicago and got the ride of his life. He was picked up by the noted inventor R. Buckminister Fuller, who was driving his twelve-seater Dymaxion, dubbed the "Flying-Fish." Gerath never forgot Buckminister Fuller's kindness toward him and considered the experience instrumental in leading him to a career in engineering.

Jack Cunningham was on a five thousand-mile trip from his home in Naylor, Missouri, to look for work in Spokane, Washington. "I saw a pretty stream in Spokane that made me so homesick,

I caught the first freight train I saw headed for Missouri. I didn't make even one dollar clear on that trip," remembered Cunningham.

Three months after leaving home, sixteen-year-old runaway Orrin George wrote a letter to his mother, receiving a reply with money and a picture of "Tuffy," his dog. On the photo was the caption, "Please come home—Tuffy." George used most of the cash to pay for a bus ticket.

Richard Barnes had been riding the rails for three years and was working in a logging camp in northern California in 1930. One night he heard the loggers singing sentimental songs about the people they'd left behind. "I became homesick and quit the job on the next payday," said Barnes. He bought a train ticket for home and left. "It hurt my pride to pay to ride on a train," he recalled.

A chance meeting at night in Scranton, Pennsylvania, changed L. E. DeLany's life. In 1936, DeLany had dropped out of high school in Massachusetts and spent the summer drifting around the country. On this night it was drizzling and he looked for a place to spread his "Hoover blanket" of newspapers. The only shelter he could find was already occupied by a young streetwalker waiting to ply her trade.

When DeLany said he was looking for a place to sleep, the girl suggested they go to her room. When he declined what he thought was a proposition, the girl laughed. "Not for sex, but a cup of coffee and a dry bed," she said.

The girl had a can of beans that she shared with DeLany. She told him that working as a prostitute was the only way she could care for her parents and sisters. When DeLany revealed that he had dropped out of school, she argued that he was lucky to even have a chance to go to school and find a proper job.

"The girl changed my thinking. She'd had no opportunity to make a better life for herself. I could go back and finish my schooling. When I left the next morning, I split my $2.40 with her as a friend and headed home. I graduated in 1937 at the bottom of my class, but I was eligible to take a civil service exam."

In 1939, DeLany was one of twelve candidates to get perfect

scores in a qualifying exam and became an apprentice at the
Springfield Armory. He went into the navy in 1941 as a journey-
man tool and diemaker.

"Many years later I was working offshore in the Persian Gulf. I
thought of that summer of 1936 and the girl who changed my life.
I was grateful for my good fortune."

Sometimes a returning road kid had a good idea of what greeting awaited him. Robert Keerns, who'd taken off at fifteen without approval, decided it was time to go home when he wound up
with five cents and enough Bull Durham to roll one cigarette. He
met a predictable fate shared by many young nomads: "I took a
good beating when I got home. I accepted that school wasn't such
a bad place after all," said Keerns.

In 1933, after going to the West to look for work, Theryl Gale
rode freight trains from California back to Missouri, where his
family lived. His final ride didn't stop at Willow Springs, a small
southern Missouri town close to his home. He was forced to jump
off while it was still speeding along.

"I hit a steep bank and rolled through brush and cinders. I lost
a lot of skin but broke no bones," said Gale. "It was a Saturday
and Dad was in town. When he saw me, his greeting was, 'Who
have you been fighting, son?' Dad expected that after raising six
boys alone."

Runaway Vernon Roudebush's summer adventure ended in fall
1935, when his father learned his whereabouts and ordered him to
return in time for school. When Vernon reached his home in
Chicago, his mother gave him an icy reception.

"Mother kept her distance and surveyed my miserable appearance with frosty disapproval and then called my father at
work," Roudebush remembered. "Dad greeted me soberly at
first, then clasped me in a bear hug. I knew I was home and
everything would be all right. Dad had trouble concealing his
pride in my sticking it out through some perilous times but it
took Mom a few days to forgive me for what I had put them

through. 'Did you learn anything?' Dad asked. 'Yeah, never to do it again,' I replied without hesitation."

Returning from a job-hunting trip in 1935, Harold Sparks was too dirty to hitchhike and had to walk the last fifteen miles to his home in Toledo, Ohio. As a joke, he went to the back door of his house and tried to bum a meal. A new maid slammed the door in his face.

"At that moment, my mother walked into the kitchen. She told the maid to give me breakfast. While I was eating Mother looked in several times," said Sparks. "Finally, I could stand it no longer and started to laugh. Mother recognized me and fainted dead away."

End of an Era

John Fawcett, who ran away from Wheeling, West Virginia, for adventure in 1936 and discovered an America he never knew existed, made one last boxcar trip in June 1940. Working as a seaman and temporarily on the beach at San Francisco, Fawcett hit the road for Duluth, Minnesota, to find a berth on a Great Lakes ship. In a diary Fawcett kept at the time, he noted the end of an era:

> I have noticed a big difference in the kind of people compared to the summer of 1936, when there were many thousands of hungry, homeless and desperate-looking people on the road. Okies and farm families who'd lost their homes; parents and little kids wearing no clothing but bib overalls and all barefooted.
>
> Now it's mostly migrant farm workers, runaways and workers of one kind or another temporarily unemployed like me and looking for a job. And of course the sprinkling of old-time hoboes and bums who ride the trains and live in one jungle after another and talk about the past.
>
> There's lot's of talk about Germany invading England this summer. I've heard it across the country the last couple of weeks, in the hobo camps and freight yards, wherever guys sit

around and talk. Two guys tonight were going at it. One said, "Sure the Limeys were lucky after the Frogs quit. They got most of their army out of France but they had to leave all their guns and equipment behind. Hitler ain't going to miss a chance like this. Stands to reason, all the Krauts got to do is walk right in." Others said it might not be quite so easy. It is scary to think about it all the same.

Observed Joe Cornett, a former boxcar boy who attended Officer's Training School at Fort Sill in 1942: "In the dark days of the Depression, no one would have thought much about it if I lost my life riding the rails. Twelve years later the government was interested enough to spend thousands of dollars to make me a better killer."

As World War II loomed, many young men left the road and joined up. Under fire they would be grateful for their boxcar experiences, which toughened them up for the ordeal ahead. "It gave me the strength to live and survive," said Charlie Jordan, who rode the rails for six months and served in the CCC in Emmett, Idaho. Jordan enlisted in the army and was sent to the Philippines in April 1941. Captured after the fighting at Bataan and Corrigidor, he was a prisoner of war for more than forty months, thirty of which he spent working in coal mines in Japan.

Fighter pilot James Morehead credits three years riding the rails with teaching him self-reliance and ingenuity. Operating out of Java in defense of the Philippines, Lieutenant Morehead shot down five Japanese bombers and two fighters between February 23 and August 23, 1942. On April 25, Morehead led the first decisive aerial victory over the Japanese forces—eleven Japanese aircraft destroyed by eight P-40s, three by Morehead alone, who earned both the Distinguished Service Cross and the Distinguished Flying Cross.

A Rite of Passage

In 1933, Leslie Paul traveled halfway across America from his home in Duluth, Minnesota, to Seattle, Washington, to look for work. Eighteen-year-old Leslie and a road partner were with a group of older hoboes when the freight they were riding stopped in the Seattle yards. They all jumped out, crossed three or four pairs of tracks, and sought refuge in deep grass below a bank on the edge of the yard.

Six decades later Leslie's memories of his boxcar days were prompted daily as he looked out of his living room window onto those same railroad tracks.

"One hobo had a small bag of coffee grounds: 'You two, go fetch water and you two'—my partner and I—'get some wood,' he said. Unable to find wood in the immediate vicinity, we climbed a steep embankment onto what I now know as Dravus Street. We found a fuel store with wood stacked on the porch, grabbed some, and ran back to our rendezvous. The others were there with the water. A fire was kindled and coffee made. I needed something to drink from. I remember finding a rusty can with cobwebs inside that I wiped out as best as I could. I'm sure the coffee tasted good regardless."

Few veterans of the boxcars have a constant reminder of their grand adventure. Countless lines they rode have been abandoned, and iron rails have been left to rust. When D. L. Young and his child bride, Thelma, went to retrace the boxcar route they took from Commerce to Sherman, Texas, sixty years earlier, they found the tracks had been torn up for Highway 11.

Like the names of old friends, some still with them, some gone forever, the boxcar riders recall railroad lines such as the Nickel Plate, the "Katy," the Burlington, the Santa Fe, the Southern Pacific, and the Northern Pacific. They have lived to see man walk on the moon, and they witnessed the televised spectacle of the space shuttle blasting off from Cape Canaveral. Don't try to tell them that anything can match the power and thunder of a Union Pacific fast-freight Mallett, a 250-ton colossus charging along at a blistering ninety miles an hour and making the earth tremble.

"The smell of coal smoke, the atmosphere and feel of the trains gets to be like a drug," said John Fawcett. "I remember one scene as though it were last night, racing through the Ohio countryside in the dark. Mick and I had never ridden freight trains at night. We were twenty cars back from the locomotive. The fireman opened the firebox to throw in a shovel of coal. An intermittent bright orange reflection flashed onto the smoke pouring over the cab. It lit up the landscape in a flickering glare fifty to a hundred feet around. Soon as the fire door was closed, all was suddenly dark again except for the white swath the engine's headlight cut on the tracks up ahead. It was a show I never tired of watching."

The old riders look back to their wild summers with wistful pride. "What happened to me this past half century plus ten? Except for a few high moments later on in life, everything beyond the first three weeks following graduation was anticlimactic," George Hanson noted in an address to the sixtieth class reunion of Roosevelt High School, Minneapolis. In June 1932, while their classmates were marching down the aisle to "Pomp and Circumstance," Hanson and his friend Mike Shorba hit the rails from St. Paul to New York.

"We challenged the mighty New York Central system, had at least one narrow escape every day, were arrested three or four times, and spent two nights in jail. We saw New York and returned home, red-eyed and exhausted. We proved that it could be done. I still ask myself, was it courage or just plain damn foolishness?" mused Hanson. In World War II, Hanson served in the Merchant Marine, earning six of eight service ribbons issued, including the combat ribbon with two stars. One time he survived a German surface attack on a ten thousand-ton bomb-laden munitions ship in the North Sea.

"It was my biggest experience in life," Basil Maita said simply. The son of Italian immigrants, Maita hit the rails in 1930, when he was eighteen. Louis "Red" Johnson, a Memphis boy regarded as a baseball natural, worked out with the New York Yankees in 1935. He would've been drafted but for a rule forbidding major league clubs from tampering with youngsters before they finished high school. Since 1932, when he was fifteen, Red had been riding freights in summer, leaving home to lighten the burden on his mother. "If you had ten dollars in your pocket, you could make it all the way across the U.S.," said Red. "I saw the Grand Canyon, Yellowstone Park, the Organ Mountains in New Mexico. In Hollywood, I bummed a bunch of movie stars, including George Raft, James Cagney, and Martha Raye. I had my picture taken with Max Baer. It was burned on the USS *Lexington*, when we were sunk in May 1942."

"I started out as a teenager and came back a man," said Omar McCoy, reflecting on four years on the road as a character-building experience. "There were many temptations along the way, and it would have been easy to smoke, gamble, drink, and steal. To be perfectly honest, I did lift a quart of milk from a doorstep once."

Edgar Shanholtzer spent seven summers on the road from the age of thirteen, initially as a runaway, and later with the blessing of parents. "In retrospect, this was the only time in my life that I was really free, riding in a boxcar and watching the world go by," he said.

Amid wishful yearnings for the boy beside the tracks, aging boxcar philosophers retrace a rite of passage from youth to maturity, calling back vivid memories from an impressionable age. What is remarkable about their recollections is that while they rejoice in the good memories, the "bad old days" are not forgotten.

"Most of all I remember the loneliness," said René Champion. "I'd be stranded at night in the wide open spaces of Texas and New Mexico, with not a single winking human light in sight, overwhelmed by that immense star-studded sky. The night silence is so dense that it attaches itself to you like a second skin. More than once I cried. I felt so sad, so utterly alone."

They never forgot the loneliness, dirt, and hunger attended by constant danger and hardship. Shivering nights spent wrapped in newspapers and huddled in boxcars. Scorching days hugging the walkway on a long drag through a parched desert. They can be philosophical, too, about the misadventures that befell them.

In January 1940, Dave Dawson tried to hop a fast-moving fruit train out of Memphis and fell on the tracks. Doctors amputated his right leg eight inches below the knee. Said Dawson:

"The most important lesson on my road back came from the man who built my first prosthesis. 'There's no reason you can't get along with a wooden leg, as long as you don't have a wooden head,' he told me. I'd hit rock bottom and became rehabilitated. I consider myself one of the lucky ones."

Lessons of the Road

Self-reliance and compassion were two of the most enduring lessons learned on the road that shaped the lives of the boy and girl tramps. "I was a naïve high school graduate on a lark for adventure, never dreaming that I would have a learning experience in economics, human relationships, and politics," said Manuel Krupin, who hoboed around the country in 1932 and 1933. "Although no one had any surplus, I found everyone willing to share their meager belongings. What I saw and heard taught me to look at people who were down and out with compassion rather than scorn. I would not question a person asking for food because I know the humiliation and loss of dignity one experiences when you have to beg for a handout."

Andrew Szabo never forgot the camaraderie of older hoboes and young road kids. "The hoboes of that era were a breed all their own. Their care and honest concern shown me will last until I die. I saw the frailty of human life and I learned compassion for my fellow man." Leaving home in 1934 at eighteen, when he was in the eighth grade, Doyle Yancey got his education on the road. "At that time—even before radios were numerous—people had only limited knowledge of national events. I got to know and live with people of different racial and ethnic backgrounds. My travels opened my eyes to the abuses in our system, especially the failure to administer equal justice to all. I learned what to expect and what not to expect from our legal system."

Living with the "desperately poor, hungry, and ragged," Herbert Teitelbaum was profoundly influenced by the injustice he witnessed. "Little intermingling took place among blacks and whites riding the rails, but there was a mutual tolerance of each other in an atmosphere of abject poverty. Blacks were treated appallingly by townspeople and police. Many were killed almost as a sport in the hobo jungles." Teitelbaum's experience on the road made him a "lifelong liberal: politically, morally, and socially."

In Kansas in the mid-1930s, twenty-year-old harvest tramp Chester Smith saw the ravages of the Dustbowl: sand piled up over fence posts like snow, and men and women frantically shoveling away locusts. Half a century later, he remembered a sign outside Linden, a small Kansas town: "Nigger, don't let the sun set on you here." He would also recall a degrading and dehumanizing sight seen firsthand on a freight train: a man selling his wife for sex for twenty-five cents to any boxcar rider who would have her.

"My three years on the rails made me understand and view the injustices men and women of our country have faced in a new light. We don't all have the luxury of doing what we dream of, but whatever we do should be with dignity and respect for one another," said Smith.

A road kid meeting one disappointment after another could be left deeply cynical. At nineteen, William Aldridge searched for a job for a year with no success. "I thought the land of opportunity lay beyond our isolated village in North Carolina. I had the idea that somewhere down the road I would miraculously be offered a wonderful job with food, clothing, and housing. I realized that dreams are great, but that's all they are. Just dreams."

"I have a clear feeling a black cloud constantly hovered over my generation, but at the time I luckily didn't know it," says Gordon Bredersen.

Ralph Jones found life on the road was "very real, very basic— the wrong decision at the wrong time could have devastating consequences. You learned to keep a low profile and keep your mouth shut for the most part. You tried not to antagonize anyone, but if you had to fight, you did."

A lasting effect was to make many road kids frugal and fearful of being broke again. Chester Clever rode the rails for six years from 1933 until he joined the army. He remembered the constant hunger and fear as he traveled alone. When he settled down and married, Clever insisted on having copious stores of food in his house and would be upset if the stock got too low.

Raised in an orphanage in North Carolina, Robert Lloyd had begun riding freights in 1929 at seventeen, looking for a job. He saw more than one hobo just give up and drop from a train to his death. A time came when hunger made him think of following their example, said Lloyd. "Pride or maybe the lack of guts to do so kept me from it, but it wasn't easy. I was so desperate I worked for ten cents an hour cleaning outhouses. No one else would take the job. The hard knocks of the Depression leaves me with a fear for the future when I think of the myth that people believe in— that the Federal Reserve can keep us from falling into the same pit. Should the banks fail, the Federal Reserve can also fail.

"We used to have a saying: 'Hoover blew the whistle, Mellon rang the bell. Wall Street gave the signal and the country went to hell.' Today, as it was in 1929, most of our wealth is on paper. Wall Street controls us as it did back then."

In 1934, Philip Bonosky's older brother Walter, twenty-two, fell between two freight cars on his way to Buffalo, New York. Walter became a double amputee, losing one leg below the knee and having his other foot cut off across the instep.

Philip Bonosky himself took to the freights in a futile search for a job in 1935. He had finished high school at in the steel town of Dusquene, Pennsylvania, graduating with distinction as class poet and playwright. Observed Bonosky: "Those years left a deep and permanent impression. It was one of those rare moments when life affords you a glimpse of the truth. What I learned then, though infinitely varied and fleshed out, endures to this day."

One of the impressions that stayed with Bonosky was that, as the Depression deepened, people's clothes began to change from store-bought items with style and color to "relief clothes"—cheap gray cotton pants, thin coats, badly made socks and stockings. "All those years have for me the color of gray, only gray—though there was summer and winter too," he said.

In winter 1935, when he was still seventeen and without work, Bonosky sat down and wrote a letter to first lady Eleanor Roosevelt. He told Mrs. Roosevelt he wanted to go to college but his parents couldn't afford to keep him in clothes, let alone send him to school. What could Mrs. Roosevelt do to help him?

"One day the mailman dropped a letter into our mailbox. The return address was the White House. I opened it with burning cheeks of shame and excitement. Shame because I'd sent what seemed to me now a begging letter, and excitement because of the possibility that what I had begged for had been granted."

Mrs. Roosevelt had been moved by Bonosky's appeal. She told him he should not lose heart; he was young and the world was before him. She could do nothing about getting him into college beyond suggesting he try for a scholarship. She also recommended that he apply for the Civilian Conservation Corps.

When Bonosky tried to get into the CCC, he was rejected because of a preexisting condition of osteomyelitis. Back on the rails in 1936, he finally had a change of luck when he checked into a Transient Bureau in Washington, D.C. Ann Terry White, a social worker at the bureau, helped Bonosky gain admission to Wilson Teacher's College, now a part of the University of the District of Columbia. After two years of college, Bonosky worked on a WPA writer's project and became a leader of the Worker's Alliance in Washington, a union of the unemployed. It was the beginning of a lifetime involvement as a labor activist and author that would see Bonosky blacklisted in the McCarthy era—a "victim of the dry guillotine," as he calls it.

"Ours was one of those pivotal generations one sees in periods of crisis. We taught our fathers and we taught our sons, for what we learned between 1929 and 1941 was the truth. We saw the ruling class on the defensive. We saw breadlines and thousands of workers rioting to get a dozen jobs. We saw cops raising fountains of blood on the heads of ex-servicemen and workers in steel towns and coal towns.

"There is a parallel between the plight of the Depression kids and the plight of kids today, particularly unemployed black youths. In the thirties, sooner or later kids knew who was blame. It wasn't them, for they wanted to work. It was the system that was at fault. Today young kids find it difficult to discover who is causing the problem. In the thirties we escaped on the freights and looked for hope. Today, I find it incredible to hear a black kid say he doesn't believe he will live beyond his middle twenties. It's an indictment of all society.

"The Depression wasn't simply an episode that came and went. It colored the American point of view permanently. I see people who have lost their jobs for the first time with that stunned look of disbelief that they're outside of society. It's quite a shocker to them, but it connects right to the Depression."

"It was a time of confusion and loneliness, yet bonds of love flowed through the majority of people," said Blanche Stovall, who recalled hoboes, young and old, sitting down to eat with her family in their Colorado home. Road kid L.E. DeLany never forgot the kindness shown toward him in summer 1936: "We didn't need cynical politicians to promise kinder, gentler times before they raid public funds. People were already kinder and gentler."

"It was a terrible way to live. It was rough and dangerous but there was also a mystical quality," said Don Snyder, who rode the rails for three years from 1933, when he was fifteen. "The sound and moan of a whistle in the silent darkness echoing through the hills. The smell of the cars and the clicking of the rails. The ding, ding, ding at the crossings. The excitement of avoiding the bulls and brakies. The open prairies, the mountains, and the clear skies above you. For all the hardships, you feel a faint longing to hit the road again. I wouldn't do it for anything."

Charley Bull

———•———

1930

*C*harley Bull was a high school student when he came face to
face with the Depression in 1930. Overwhelmed by debt, the
owner of a gas station where Charley worked part-time shot himself. Charley rode the rails for two and a half years in search of a
job, working on farms, in tramp steamers, as a cub reporter at the
Toronto Daily News, and as a barker and waiter at the Chicago
World's Fair. At the World's Fair, he met the chancellor of Lincoln
Memorial University in East Tennessee, who gave him a chance to
work his way through college.

From 1939 to 1941, Charley was an education adviser in the
CCC. After Pearl Harbor, he enlisted in the army, serving in the Pacific and in Europe and becoming an army reporter. At the end of the
war, he spent several years as a teacher in civilian life before returning to work for the army in 1951. He served at home and in Europe,
Korea, and Vietnam until his retirement in 1973. He has since been
active in the Huntsville, Alabama, chapter of Veterans for Peace.

Here's how my day went in my senior year at Burbank High in
1929. My alarm clock would wake me at 4:30 A.M. I made myself
breakfast, grabbed my schoolbooks, and walked a mile to my job
at the gas station. I worked there until Hal Blackwell arrived at
8:30 A.M., when I left and ran a mile to school. During the noon
hour I worked in the cafeteria for my midday meal.

After school I hurried on down to a drugstore and jerked sodas

246

from four to ten o'clock. I would get half an hour off to have dinner and would go a block down the street to the Greek's, where I could buy a good meal for twenty-five cents.

There were five kids in our family. In 1924 we had been living in Reno, Nevada, where my father, Charles Edward Bull, served as constable and justice of the peace. One night Dad came home with the news that a Hollywood producer had called long distance. He had been invited to try out for the part of Abraham Lincoln in *The Iron Horse,* a movie about the building of the first railroad across the United States.

Dad was a long and lanky drink of water, six feet four inches tall, and had himself been born in a log cabin. When he put on a beard, stove pipe hat, and dark cut-away coat, he bore a striking resemblance to the Great Emancipator. He would march in parades in Reno, Sparks, and Carson with another character dressed as Uncle Sam.

Dad walked into Fox Studios in his Lincoln costume. He read for them and asked if he could speak a few words. "You sure can, Judge," they said. Dad recited the Gettysburg Address. John Ford himself walked over and told him he had won the part.

We thought Dad was launched on a new career. The pay was tremendous—two thousand dollars a week—but all told Dad worked five or six weeks. No one told us and now it seems we should've figured it out for ourselves: They don't make a Lincoln film very often, not one a year or even in five years.

When the picture opened at Grauman's Egyptian Theatre, Dad appeared as Lincoln in the prologue that preceded every performance. He helped pack in the crowds for twenty weeks, and then that job folded too. Mama and us kids thought, "Well, now our dad will go out and get a regular job."

Dad didn't look for a job but wrote a play, *The Lincolns in the White House.* He went back east, traveling the Orpheum and Chautauqua circuits, performing on high school and college stages.

We moved from place to place in California until 1927, when a successful season enabled Dad to buy a house in East Whittier.

Since my sophomore year in high school, I'd been helping out with part-time jobs. I worked in the citrus groves in winter, lighting smudge pots to raise the temperature above freezing. The job paid a dollar an hour. Several school friends and I went out every night for three weeks. We'd shower and change our clothes before school but soot and smoke clung to our hair, eyelashes, nostrils. We didn't care. We'd just say, "Hell, man, I'm getting rich, ain't I?"

Hal Blackwell and his wife had been married eighteen months. Her father helped them finance the Union gas station out on San Fernando Highway and gave them a down-payment on their house, furniture, and car. Hal hired me so he could catch the big eighteen-wheelers running out of Los Angeles early in the morning en route to San Francisco. I'd get two or three truckers a week, and they'd be good for a forty- or fifty-gallon purchase. That helped but Hal's daytime business never picked up. I could see they were hurting for money.

One spring morning in 1930, in my third period class, a student office worker came and said the principal wanted to see me.

"Come in, Charles," the principal said when I knocked on his door. His voice sounded pleasant and that was reassuring. When I stepped inside, I saw two uniformed policemen and a detective. My reassurance vanished completely.

"Charles, these men are Burbank city policemen. They'd like to ask you some questions," the principal said. I just nodded my head. My God, I thought, what do they think I've done?

"Do you work for Hal Blackwell?" one asked.

"Yes, sir," I said.

"You worked at the station this morning?"

"Yes, sir."

"How was Mr. Blackwell when he came to work?"

"What do you mean, sir?"

"What did he say or do? What time did he get there?"

"About 8:30 A.M., maybe three or four minutes late. Sometimes he comes three or four minutes early, so we don't worry about that.

I had two customers. I showed him a slip of paper with the gas readings on the storage tanks. 'OK, Charley,' he said, and I took off."

"Is Hal all right?" I asked. I guess they weren't ready for my question 'cause they ignored it.

"Does Mr. Blackwell keep a gun at the station?"

"Yes, sir."

"Did you see it this morning?"

"No, sir, he keeps it in the safe."

"Did you ever fire the pistol?"

"Last October or November, we were all firing it. Hal and I and some guys who were painting the station tried to hit a five-gallon gasoline can one hundred yards out on the prairie. It's a very old pistol and isn't much good."

"Did you fire it this morning?"

"No, sir." I was becoming anxious and fearful. "Tell me, please, has something happened to Mr. Blackwell?"

"Did you kill Hal Blackwell this morning, Charles?"

"Oh, God!" I said. "I would never do anything to hurt him. He is a dear, dear man."

Suddenly, the questioning ended. The police walked out. I sat down and put my head in my hands and sobbed quietly to myself.

The Depression had finally caught up with me. Everyone who ever read a newspaper or listened to a news broadcast knew about men who'd been jumping out of windows on Wall Street. Men all across America—businessmen, farmers, laborers—were shooting themselves or turning on the gas, drinking poison or drowning themselves in lakes, rivers, oceans. Most pitifully some disconsolate souls were taking their wives and children with them.

Hal and his wife were well-mannered, intelligent people from upper-middle-class families in Pasadena. Hal had gone to UCLA and had a degree in business administration. He was well equipped for life in the business world. The Great Depression just plowed him under.

It was a hell of a time! I began to feel a sense of loss for all those folks who had died.

* * *

The Depression delayed my dreams of going to college for two and a half years. The only dreams I had were to keep myself together and have three meals under my belt a day. I didn't succeed every day.

My first summer out of high school I worked in the hayfields around Johnsonville and Susanville in California. When I finished pitching hay I caught a freight down to New Orleans. I worked as a deckhand on tramp steamers in the Gulf of Mexico and on a shrimp boat out of Gulf Port, Mississippi.

When I couldn't get a job, I bought a bucket and a squeegee and went house to house and washed windows. I'd do 'em inside and out for ten to fifteen cents a window. Sometimes I'd spend half an hour on a big window and charge twenty-five cents.

I drifted up to Canada, where I worked on a ranch one hundred miles out of Toronto in the dead of winter. I earned the slave wage of six dollars a month for a twelve- to thirteen-hour day. The family's adopted son and I milked fourteen to sixteen cows every morning before breakfast. We then worked all day cutting and logging pine trees. In the evening, we milked the cows again.

This was one of the few jobs I quit during the Depression. On what turned out to be my last day on the ranch, I broke an ax handle. The rancher's wife growled at me, "You broke it on purpose, that's what you did."

I said it was an accident and apologized. The son backed me up but the woman insisted that I pay for the handle. The next morning she counted out my wages for the month. "Ax handles cost eighty cents," she said. She gave me $5.20 instead of the $6.00 that was due to me.

I was young and I felt nothing could defeat me. Some of the older men you met on the road had been unemployed for two or three years and had lost hope. I didn't think of myself as a bum or a tramp but just a vagabond. There were times when I had not eaten for two or three days and I became discouraged too. But I never gave up because deep in my heart I knew that I would eventually get to where I was going.

* * *

I hooked rides one hundred miles back to Toronto. I was cold, dead tired, and damn near starved when I applied for the job of cub reporter on the *Toronto Daily News*. The guy on the desk said, "I don't know if you can write but I'll say this for you, Yank, you've got guts. The job is yours."

That was in the fall of 1932. I loved my work as a reporter. Unless you lived at home and had few expenses, you couldn't survive on the fifteen dollars-a-week salary. It was just slow starvation.

The Chicago World's Fair was opening in spring, 1933. I walked across Niagara Falls that February, the first time the falls froze over solid in a hundred years. My first job on the midway was as a barker at Ripley's "Odditorium," describing the characters we exhibited. I remember particularly Johnny Eck, the 'half-boy'; Blystone, the Rice Writer, who penned the Lord's Prayer on a grain of rice; and Lady Leona, a perfect beauty only twenty-seven inches tall.

After a month I moved to a better job at Victor's Vienna Café, where the pay was fifteen dollars a week plus tips and three meals a day. Going to college was still only a dream but then one day I met the man who would help me get there.

John Wesley Hill, a lawyer and preacher, was chancellor of Lincoln Memorial University. I got talking to him when I served him a beer and told him of my ambition to attend college. Chancellor Hill offered me a job at the college that would pay for my tuition and board.

I was so happy and exhilarated that I could have hugged Dr. Hill. I grabbed his hand and wrung it like an old dishrag. Appreciation and hope welled up in my heart. It was as though the agonies of despair, deprivation, hardship, and heartache were all washed away.

In early September, I rode freight trains down the winding roadbed to Cumberland Gap in the Great Smoky Mountains. I walked and hooked rides over to Harrogate, Tennessee, and arrived at Lincoln Memorial University carrying all my possessions in a small paper-pressed suitcase.

John Wesley Hill was as good as his word, and his word for
me was gospel. Enrolled at LMU, I worked on the college farm,
slopped hogs, fired furnaces, dug ditches, shoveled a hundred
tons of the best cow manure in the Tennessee Valley. In the summer, when other kids went home for the vacation, I worked ten
hours a day plowing corn and cutting and pitching hay, all at
twenty cents an hour. I quit the ten-hour shift the day before
school took up in the fall, by which time I was almost even with
what I owed the college.

Depression? Yes, God knows there were depression days but do
you know what? Almost no one ever mouthed the threat of anar-
chy. There were thirteen million people unemployed and some of
us had been without a steady job for years, but very few people
hated our country, or our government, or our president.

President Roosevelt talked to us from time to time over the
radio. We could tell by the hurt in his voice that he cared. He held
up hope and the promise of a better day, and he implored us to
keep on trying. And we did.

There were some who joined the communist party in the U.S. I
used to attend meetings of a group who called their movement
"Technocracy." I never joined but I did explain to a girlfriend,
"I'm just sitting in there wearing out some old clothes." Old
clothes was about the only thing I had plenty of.

Poor as I was, I wasn't the poorest by a long way. I saw people
who were without jobs and hungry doing everything they could to
sustain themselves and support their families. They weren't shift-
less and lazy but simply lacked the opportunity. I had compassion
and sympathy for them.

After attending Lincoln Memorial, I went to Arizona State University, where I got a B.A. degree. At different times during those
years I worked for the WPA and the Public Works Administration
(PWA) building roads and bridges and fire trails. I earned my master's degree from Boston University. I secured my first good job in
1939 as education adviser in the Civilian Conservation Corps.

The CCC was one of the best programs of the New Deal. Roosevelt's detractors said the CCC would bankrupt the treasury, but it didn't. The CCC was a salvation for tens of thousands of young men and their families.

I enlisted in the army in World War II. I'll never forget an April day in 1945 when my company was marching back to Fort Gordon, then known as Camp Gordon, from two weeks stay in bivouac. Though it was April the sun was blazing down on us as we marched twenty-two miles through the Georgia hills. We were within a mile of camp when a car drove by our marching troop line and someone yelled out, "The president is dead."

Our company commander brought us to a halt. We stood sweat-drenched in the sun, just looking at each other, waiting and wondering: Had we heard right? God, it must be wrong, we thought. He's a good man. He can't be dead.

Soon another car came along. The captain stopped it and asked the occupants, "Is our president dead?"

The man at the wheel seemed reluctant to say the words, but finally did: "He's dead."

We all stood there like we were struck dumb, as though we'd just heard our mom or our dad was dead. Some guys just cried softly, not making a sound 'cause they were soldiers. Some stumbled away by themselves 'cause their hearts were breaking and they couldn't hold it in.

I remember watching the captain's face. A meadow lark trilled its springtime song in the distance and every man heard it. The captain looked in our eyes again and a wan smile crossed his face. Maybe he too was wondering, as Walt Whitman had wondered when Lincoln fell, how a little old bird would have the courage and impudence to sing a note on such a day.

Then the captain called to us and we all stood to and marched the long last mile back to camp. No one counted cadence anymore or spoke a word. It was a quiet reverence that we felt for a dear friend—our president, lying dead somewhere.

A thousand boots hitting the pavement in perfect step was the only sound that broke the awful stillness of that day. Not a man among us would ever forget.

We who loved Roosevelt are legion. For his courageous leadership, his effect on history, and the changes he wrought in our lives, and for his great and noble and caring heart I would rank him second only to Abraham Lincoln. To paraphrase a line from Winston Churchill, for it could be equally true of us in America: Those days and months and years with Roosevelt through the Great Depression and most of the war may well have been our finest hours.

Jim Mitchell

---•---

1933

When his father lost his job in 1931, Jim Mitchell saw his family slide to rock bottom in the "undeclared war of the Dirty Thirties," as he calls the Great Depression. The Mitchells lived in Kenosha, Wisconsin, where Jim remembered pulling a little red wagon through the streets to collect the family's relief food. In his sophomore year at high school, humiliated and taunted by classmates who derided his circumstances, Mitchell persuaded his buddy Peter Lijinski –"Poke"–to run away with him in winter 1933. The pair set their sights on Texas, where they wanted to work as cowboys. From the moment they hopped their first train in the Kenosha yards, the runaways experienced the best and worst of life on the bum in America.

Dad worked ten hours a day for six days a week before the Depression, and things were fine. I remember the morning it happened. I was in the basement fooling around with my crystal set before school when Dad came home. "I lost my job. I'm out of work," he told Mother. It was the first time I saw my father cry.

Dad had to stand in unemployment lines. He'd get a job for a day or two and earn a buck or so. You could see his suffering. Dad wasn't a banker, he wasn't a machinist, he was a common laborer like hundreds of thousands of others. He put pieces of metal in a machine that went clunk. That's what my dad did but he had his pride. Take away a man's pride and he's skin and bones. He is nothing.

255

Things went downhill. You lived off your relatives. You went to eat at grandma's and here and there until you hit rock bottom and went on relief.

Mother had to leave the house and find work. She did cleaning jobs and was a pastry cook in a restaurant.

Never once were my father or mother mean to me. I saw their struggle was slowly squeezing the life right out of them. They were going nowhere. It tore the living hell out of you.

Those days you didn't get a check in the mail. You took a little red wagon and dragged it around and waited in line. The relief people threw in food as if they were feeding dogs. It was the most humiliating experience in the world for a fourteen-year-old kid.

You couldn't do things in school that other kids did. You had to buy milk but couldn't afford it. You wanted to belong to the Boy Scouts but didn't have fifty cents to join.

Everything closed in on me. One day I decked the principal and ran out of school. I sat down and said to myself, You're no damn good to your family or anybody. I was just another mouth to feed at home. I'd lighten my parents' burden if I took off.

The quickest and easiest way to get out was to jump a train and go somewhere. We thought it was the magic carpet—the click of the rails—romance.

That winter morning I climbed out on the roof and down the apple tree, and went to meet Poke. I don't think we were twenty miles down the road, cold and miserable, and I knew right then I had made a mistake. You are young and foolish and don't go home crying. You are going to see it through as far as you can.

Our first ride from Kenosha was on the blinds of a passenger train. A couple of stops down the line, a gaunt, scruffy guy swung on, holding a bag tied with rope. He reeked of rotgut whiskey. With no space in the blind, his only option was the ladder at the back of the tender. "Watch my bag, kid," he growled at me, throwing his belonging up onto the tender. I'd all I could do to take care of myself.

The wind caught the bag and sent it crashing down, splitting apart against the side of the car and scattering its contents beneath the wheels.

"Damn you, kid, I told you to watch my bag."

The bum snatched a switchblade from his pocket. As it snapped open Poke grabbed the man's wrist. He slammed the man against the door of the car. The knife clattered to the rails.

The guy went white with fear. Quickly he slipped back to the tender ladder and never moved. At the next stop, he got off.

That was my first experience on the road. There were not many mean people, but sometimes you ran into that sort of thing. It was not a safe or happy place, and no place for a kid to be.

The freight out of Sioux City, Iowa, started rolling. I spotted an empty car and made a beeline for it, grabbed the door guide, and pulled myself up, then rolled back to give Poke a hand. My heart pounded frantically. We rested a while to get our breath and collect our wits.

Poke put his rucksack under his head and dozed. While he slept, I sat in the door and dangled my feet over the side of the car. For an all-too-brief moment, I put aside the seamy side of bumming and took time to enjoy our journey.

The early afternoon sun occupied a cloudless sky. The trees and shrubs were fresh and green. This country had been spared the horror of the dust storms. I basked in the warm summer sun. As I looked across the prairie I recall thinking, God, but America is big!

For a while the tracks ran along the Missouri River. We rumbled through vast stretches of farmland. To my citified eye, the corn looked as if it couldn't miss being a good harvest.

Sleek horses pulling cultivators plodded slowly over the earth. In adjoining fields, well-groomed teams briskly pulled mowers, while farm workers laid the freshly cut hay in neat rows. I was puzzled. I knew times were rough on the farm. Why, then, did the animals all look so fit? Later I was to learn that although farmers were making little money, they didn't stint on feeding and caring for their animals.

The smell of fresh-mown hay swirled past. A girl about my age, bringing water to the field, waved. She, no doubt, had never been in the city. For sure, I'd never been on a farm. At that moment, I little realized that her life was as dire as mine.

You thought it would be a glamorous life—"By God, we're going to find our fortune. Someone out there needs us." The hell they did. You went on the road and exchanged one misery for another. If you could hold body and soul together you were doing a good job.

You never lost the basic virtues your family passed on to you. You wanted to remain honest and be decent to other people. You tried to keep yourself clean but could rarely take a bath. You were always filthy and constantly hungry.

You'd take whatever odd jobs you could. We did everything, from mowing lawns to cleaning grease traps in restaurants. It was humiliating but sometimes you panhandled. "If they've got extra cash, they'll give it to you. If they don't, you won't get anything." That was Poke's attitude. "You're not stealing from them. You're just asking for a loan until better times come along."

We'd go to missions to get free meals. All your life you'd gone to Sunday school and you knew those people were speaking from their heart. They were preaching to me because they wanted to save my soul, which probably needed saving. I was there only because I wanted something to eat. I felt as though I were an interloper, and I was ashamed.

Probably the most heartbreaking thing was seeing whole families on the road together. We ran into a mother and two or three children. We found out that a couple of days before the father had been killed two hundred miles down the road. They'd been on their way to California. The mother and children had gotten on a boxcar and the father was trying to climb on. He slipped and fell in the path of an express train.

I don't know if I laid awake and cried that night, but it just gripped at your guts. It was another chink in the armor of the so-called great adventure.

As long as you kept moving you were all right, but you were going nowhere. You were just drifting. Nothing was happening and there was no direction in your life.

Sometimes you'd meet kids your age in a town and start talking with them. Their mothers would call them. They didn't want their kids talking to bums.

I remember once I was cutting a lawn. I started talking to this perfectly nice girl and her mother called her away. Boy, that really hurt. I was as good as her or anyone else.

I didn't want to live on the road and become a bum. You had to do something with your life. You couldn't roam around like a damn dog eating out of garbage cans. That's about what you were, a damn dog roaming the road.

Poke and I ran into an army officer in Lake City, Iowa. We told him we were on the road and had taken up with a carnival. "That's no life for kids," he said. "Why don't you join the CCC?" Poke was easily persuaded. I balked at the idea of having some army guys push me around. But I was sick to my guts of being footloose and went back to Kenosha with Poke. My grandfather talked me into joining the CCC.

Company 2616 was stationed at Camp Norwood on the banks of the Wisconsin River, nine miles north of Merrill, Wisconsin. We were trucked from a railroad depot to our new home, which consisted of a group of long, low buildings covered with tarpaper in a clearing in the pines. Little did we realize that this stark encampment was the haven thousands of boys like ourselves needed.

There was a wonderful social mixture in the CCC. We lived forty men to a barrack. Two bunks down there would be a farm kid who couldn't read or write. If he got a letter from home, somebody read it to him. You could go up a couple more bunks and find a medical student who'd dropped out of the University of

Wisconsin. Another boy's father had had an automobile dealer-ship that went bust. Some kids were literally hoods from the cities.

You had every race, every creed and color mixing in. Don't get me wrong; we had our personal problems, but it never became a major factor. Once I remember that race was an issue. They called the white guys in camp together. "We can send these guys off to a colored camp if you want us to," we were told. We said that would be ridiculous. "They're our buddies. They live and work with us and it is no problem. We want them to stay."

I found out what discipline was about. Captain Entringer, who ran the camp, held inspection every morning. Your bunk had to be neat. You had to be able to bounce a quarter off your blanket. Your footlocker had to be in a precise place. There had to be no dust on your shoes. If you failed inspection, when you got off work that day you would have extra duty. You'd work in the kitchen or chop wood until ten o'clock.

On the road you lived for yourself and to hell with everyone else. In the CCC you not only learned to live with other guys, you had to go out with a crew and haul logs together. You learned to work as a team.

You worked alongside state foresters who took no nonsense from you. They wanted a day's work and they got it. We had a thousand and one different jobs, from climbing trees to surveying parks. You learned to do a job and do it well. It gave you confi-dence when you started to become accepted by your peers and to fit in with them.

You had three square meals a day with good food and a good place to sleep. On the road you spent all your time wondering about whether you were going to eat. If you worked it wasn't use-ful work but just for food. To this day I can go and see parks that we built in the CCC. I can see trees that we planted. It's a living legacy. You didn't have a living legacy on the road.

A cold fall day in 1934, they sent our crew to work in a tama-rack swamp. Our job was to drag twenty-foot long tamarack logs out of the muck and mire of five hundred-year-old loon dung. The day started with our getting wet to our belt buckles, and it never got any better. It was a messy, dirty business. We slogged back to camp that night bone-weary and whipped.

As we passed the dispensary, Lt. Kuehl, the camp doctor, barked, "You!" I looked at him and he nodded. "Yes, you. Come here."

The last thing I wanted was a reaming from a shavetail. I strutted over to him. "Yes, sir," I said sullenly.

He looked me over for a moment and then said in a concerned tone, "Where are you working, son?" I told him.

Our crew chief got a tongue-lashing for letting us work on the tamarack detail without hip boots. It was a solid lesson in comradeship and responsibility to your men.

I remember thinking to myself, Thank God somebody cares about me.

The CCC shaped my life, which had had no direction. Back home I'd had no role models to measure my life against. In the corps there were well-educated fellows whose goals had been interrupted. I wanted to be like them and knew I had to get an education to do so.

I stayed in the CCC for two years getting thirty dollars a month. At last I could bring some help to my family. Ma's first letter gave me a big boost:

> Dear Son,
>   I want you to know how grateful we are to you and proud, too. The $25 we get each month goes a long way in holding us together. It's good to look Dimitri in the eye and plunk down cash for groceries, and not to be obliged to Merriweather for the rent.

For the first time I felt good about myself.

The CCC was to my mind the poor man's West Point. We learned everything a West Pointer learned about duty, honor, and obligations, and got thirty bucks a month in the bargain.

I was nineteen when I went back to finish high school. I had classmates of thirteen who were pulling in A's while I was struggling to get a C. I didn't let it bother me because I wanted to get a hold on my life. I wanted to go to college, though at the time I didn't have a prayer. I didn't let that bother me either. I knew I would get there somehow, and I did.

Jim Mitchell went on to study at Ripon College, in Wisconsin. After his service in World War II, the GI Bill enabled him to earn a master's degree from the University of Wisconsin. His professional life was spent producing promotional films for the auto industry.

To put the Great Depression in proper perspective one must bear in mind that most of the parents of my generation were fresh off the boat. America was the land of opportunity. Working in a factory for five dollars a day was heady stuff for an immigrant who, but a few months ago, left a homeland where poverty and destitution were the norm. The world was his oyster. All he had to do was work hard, obey the law, and go to church on Sunday, and he had it made.

All of a sudden the bottom fell out. Why? No one had the answer. All too often one would hear, "There is work out there if only they will go looking for it." Many thought that it was they who had failed.

Our country was on the brink of hell. I ran into two types on the road. One type firmly believed in the American system: "By God, this is gonna work." The others, honest to God, I swear they were Marxist revolutionaries. They wanted to start the revolution now. Communism looked very attractive to people. "We are going to share everything. We are all going to be one big happy family." That was a lot of baloney, but people were ready to believe anything. We were looking and searching for anything to get us out of that mess.

Then Franklin Roosevelt stepped in, this extremely wealthy man with his big smile and his cigarette holder. Back in my youth, aviation was a big thing. When Roosevelt came to Chicago, what did he do? He flew to the city. Can you imagine? The president-elect of the United States getting into an airplane and flying to Chicago. Wow! Things are going to happen with this guy, we told ourselves.

So when Roosevelt says, "My fellow Americans, you have nothing to fear but fear itself," we believed it. His fireside chats on the radio were never the folksy thing. You knew he was president... "My fellow Americans I would like to talk to you about banking. I want to tell you what we have done this week, why we have done it and what the next stage will be."

Roosevelt's attitude had the biggest effect on the country. Unless you were a dyed-in-the-wool Republican, you thought he was the greatest guy since Galahad. The Depression hung on until the Second World War but people were going out and putting in a day's work on the WPA, in the CCC and other programs.

The youth of those fateful years were taken from the steamy streets of cities in economic turmoil and from our ravaged farmlands. In the CCC camps we learned values that gave meaning to our lives. When the Axis threatened all we had worked to preserve, we stood ready to serve again.

Despite all the horrors of the Depression, there was never a time that we didn't have hope. We didn't live in terror but looked ahead. We knew that down the road things were going to get better.

Robert Symmonds

———•———

1934–42

*R*obert Symmonds—"Guitar Whitey"—saw his family go from *"middle-class gentility to scrabble-ass poor overnight." His father's security business collapsed in 1938 and they lost everything, including a home in Seattle. Robert and his three sisters moved with their parents to a cabin that a relative owned in the mountains of western Oregon, with three small rooms and no electricity or water. His father tried to start a new business but never earned another dime in his life.*

Robert hopped his first freight in 1934 at age thirteen. In 1938, he became a summer tramp, riding the rails to follow the fruit harvests from Oregon to southern California. Some years he would earn two hundred dollars, which would carry the family through winter. Between harvests in 1939 and 1940, he served two six-month stints in the CCC in Montana. In 1942 he joined the navy and when he left the service stayed at sea as a merchant seaman. He eventually settled in California, married, and raised four children.

In 1972, after a hiatus of thirty years, Guitar Whitey felt the urge to hop a train again. He began riding the rails for a few weeks every year. In the late 1990s, when he was in his seventies, he was still riding freights in California and singing the old hobo songs, the last of the boxcar boys on his own path of glory.

I first started riding freights when I was thirteen years old. I was living in Seattle, a wild reckless kid looking for adventure. Whenever you saw a train it was crowded with hoboes. Some would come to our back door for a handout and my mother would feed them. I'd talk to them while they ate their sandwiches. I started hanging out in "Hooverville," a huge shanty town just south of King Street Station in Seattle. The King Dome stands on the site today. I'd sit around the hoboes' fires and listen to stories of their journeys. Hoboes became my boyhood heroes, not cowboys.

Hollywood made a movie about kids traveling on the trains in 1934—*Wild Boys of the Road*. Kids loved the movie. It put ideas in your head. There's a scene where a kid gets his leg cut off by a train. Nothing was going to happen to you, you thought. I was nearly killed on my very first trip.

In June 1934, when school ended, a friend and I went down to the jungle to catch our first train out. We'd seen hoboes getting on and off trains but didn't really know how it was done. When the train comes at you, will it stop? If it doesn't stop, what do you do? Are you going to be like those guys you see and run alongside, catch onto a ladder, and climb to the top? All you gotta do is make one mistake and that's the last one.

We found a boxcar with about twenty guys in it. They had to help me up because I couldn't even reach the floor. The train was a Great Northern hotshot that we rode all night down to Portland, Oregon, five hundred miles away.

The next night, when my friend and I hopped a train back to Seattle, our first ride took us no further than Vancouver, Washington. Our second ride was on a tank car that had a two-by-twelve-foot wooden running board. We scooted down to the middle and held onto a metal grab.

That was fine as long as the train was going slow. Trains ran as fast as they do today. We picked up speed, fifty, sixty, maybe sixty-five miles an hour.

You looked down and saw the wheels and the ties flashing by. You felt the wind tearing at you. All you gotta do is hang on.

She's goin' faster and faster. The plank started to vibrate like a springboard tossing us up in the air. All I could think of was that

I shouldn't have gotten on that train. If I lose my grip I'm gonna die. I'm gonna go under the wheels. I'm going to hit the ties or rails and bounce off. At the speed she's goin', I'll be killed.

What will my mother think? She doesn't know I'm out here. I told her a lie that I was goin' to stay at another boy's house. She'll get word that her darling son was found mangled along the railroad tracks.

"Oh, my God, why am I doing this?"

We managed to hang on long past the point we thought we couldn't bear it one moment longer. Finally the train stopped for water at Centralia. We climbed off so weak and scared, we could hardly walk.

We went back a couple of cars and got into an empty boxcar. By the time we got to Seattle, we were like conquering heroes again. You snapped back real quick.

My father was an outstanding businessman. It hurt him bad when he went broke and all his friends deserted him. He did the best he could but never recovered his self-esteem or his pride.

When we moved out into the country there was no income at all coming in and no way of getting any. I was the logical breadwinner so I had to go out and fruit tramp. I did that clear up until World War II.

In winter I would work out of our cabin in the Oregon mountains cutting wood and doing odd jobs for local farmers. As soon as spring came, I'd leave for the harvest.

We'd start with strawberries and work clear on through apples, beans, and hoeing hops. We'd till potatoes in the fall in California and end up shaking walnuts.

You'd hear people talk and say, "Well, where you goin'?" "I'm goin' up to Wenatchee, Washington. I know a guy who owns an apple orchard." "Would there be room for me?" "Yeah, I think I could get you on."

You'd take a train over to Wenatchee. You might pick apples for three weeks to a month, maybe even six weeks, then hop another train down into Portland, Oregon, or Eugene and take another job. You weren't just riding for kicks.

We'd run the whole gamut, maybe six or seven months on the fruit tramp. I would earn around two hundred dollars. It was enough money to buy groceries that would see the family through the winter.

In the city I'd been growing up to be a wild rebel getting into trouble. I had to drop out of high school when we moved to the country, but it was probably the best thing that could happen. I had to learn how to go out and make it day after day. There was no way you could quit. You had to hustle and dig and push and saw. If you didn't work, you didn't eat.

You wouldn't get half a block asking for a handout in a town today and the phones would start ringing. "There's some dirty old guy with a pack at my door. Says he wants something to eat." The squad cars would be there in a minute.

Back in the thirties everybody had an uncle, a brother, a son, or someone else they knew who was riding the rails. Today the closest to the old hoboes are Mexican migrants out looking for work. On the highways they'll quickly be picked up by the authorities, but on the trains they have a chance to sneak through.

There is a new breed of rider today, including Vietnam vets and young guys out for adventure. They hit the road equipped with scanners, they have cash in their pockets and trail mix in their packs. They are self-reliant and resourceful and know exactly which railroad you have to take to get to a certain place. Sometimes you'll also see homeless people lugging all their gear in plastic sacks like the old bindle stiffs.

The thirties' steam-drawn trains were slower getting out of the yards. Today if one of those four- or five-unit diesels gets a car length ahead of you, you just kiss it goodbye or you'll be taking a terrible chance. The railroads have everything zipped up so that there is hardly any place to ride anymore. Used to be you could get into a boxcar and there might be ten or twenty guys waiting to give you a hand up. Today if somebody is there you first ask if he minds if you ride with him. Chances are he'll say, "There's plenty more down that way." Mostly he's just doing that because he's scared of you.

There's guys out there that hang around division points. "Streamline Jack Rollers" we call them, because they don't carry any gear. They're just combing the trains looking for some old hobo to rob of his sleeping bag, food stamps, or any money he might have.

The jungles of today are a disaster area littered with broken glass, tin cans, and other rubbish. Transients don't have to cook up because in every town there's a welfare kitchen where they can get a hot meal. People go to the jungles to drink and pass out. In the past it was common to have clean pots and pans, a shaving mirror hanging up in the branches of a tree, sometimes even small take-one-put-one-down libraries. The old spirit of leaving the place ready for the next guy is a thing of the past. Today's jungles are a sad sight.

I was in my late fifties and in good physical shape when I decided to go back and ride again. I've ridden more freight trains since I retired than I ever did as a kid. I'll do maybe ten thousand miles in a summer. It's against the law, it's dirty, cold, and miserable but it's the last free, red-blooded adventure.

I didn't tell my wife, Joyce, when I started riding again. I'd catch a passenger train out of San Luis Obispo to Dunsmuir, where I'd pick up a freight. I'd spend two or three weeks on the trains and then come back riding the cushions. I'd walk into our mobile-home park wearing a pack and boots. The other residents would give me strange looks. 'What's he up to?' they'd ask. I didn't tell them.

My wife didn't learn what I was doing until a reporter asked me a bunch of questions at a mission shelter in San Luis Obispo. I answered off the cuff while I played my guitar. The paper came out with the whole story.

It didn't do my reputation any good, living in a mobile-home park filled with retired high school principals and insurance agents, people on two and three pensions playing golf in their white bucks and red pants. And here, in the midst of them, a secret hobo!

My wife overheard a group of women talking about me. "Do you know Joyce's husband is a bum?" My wife felt they were putting us both down and was devastated. The best thing I did was to take Joyce to the annual hobo convention held in Britt, Iowa. She was overwhelmed by the kindness of people she met and now accepts my hoboing.

"Where's Bob?" people ask.

"Oh, he's on a trip. He's traveling."

"Oh, yeah, how does he travel?"

"By train," Joyce says. They think it's by passenger train but my wife knows better now.

There are not many guys from the old days left. I don't ride trains in any heroic fashion anymore. I don't like to have to catch out in a hurry. I don't care for it in winter when you have to spend nights on a steel boxcar floor. I like it in the sunshine when everything is going just fine. It's hard to explain why I do it. It's something that got into my blood years ago. I guess it's a freedom thing.

References

━━━━•◆•━━━━

Page   **Preface**

9   "Boxcar Boys—and Girls," Etcetera, *Modern Maturity* (October–December 1992) 22.
10 Walter Miletich, American History Project (AHP*), Arizona, October 1992.

Introduction

12 Arvel Pearson, interview transcript, April 15, 1994.
Jim Mitchell, interview transcript, April 23, 1994.
John Fawcett, interview transcript, April 14, 1994.

13 Grace Abbot, chief of the Children's Bureau, Washington, D.C., statement on Relief for Unemployed Transients, *Hearings before a Subcommittee of the Committee on Manufactures on S. 5121,* United States Senate, 72nd Cong., 2d sess. (Washington: Government Printing Office, 1933) 23–35.
A. Wayne McMillen, University of Chicago, Relief for Unemployed Transients, 30–50; A. Wayne McMillen, "An Army of Boys on the Loose," *The Survey Graphic* (September 1933) 389–92.
C.C. Carstens, Child Welfare League of America, New York, statement on Federal Aid for Unemployment Relief, *Hearings before a Subcommittee of the Committee on Manufactures on S5125,* United States Senate, 72nd Cong., 2 sess. (Washington: Government Printing Office, 1933)

---

* The American History Project (AHP) was the organizational name under which letters and interviews were solicited for the *Riding the Rails* documentary. The AHP archives identify the letter writers by the state in which they were living when they contacted the project researchers.

271

160–61; Maxine Davis, "200,000 Vagabond Children," *Ladies Home Journal* (September 1932) 8–9, 46–48.

14 Grace Abbot, Relief for Unemployed Transients, 23–35.

R.S. Mitchell, chief special agent of the Missouri Pacific Railroad, Relief for Unemployed Transients, 35–38.

Pelham D. Glassford, Relief for Unemployed Transients, 125–34.

15 A. Wayne McMillen, "An Army of Boys on the Loose," *The Survey Graphic* (September 1933) 389–92.

A. Wayne McMillen, Relief for Unemployed Transients, 30–50.

16 Mario E. Lapenta, Letter to the Editor, *New York Times*, October 25, 1932.

Herman J.P. Schubert, supervisor of research and vocational guidance, *Twenty Thousand Transients—A One Year's Sample of Those Who Apply for Aid in a Northern City* (Buffalo, NY: Emergency Relief Bureau, 1935).

Lowell Ames Norris, "America's Homeless Army," *Scribner's Magazine* (May 1933) 316.

17 Grace Abbott, Relief for Unemployed Transients, 23–35.

John Levy, Columbia University, "The Homeless Boys Retreat," *Mental Hygiene* (July 1933) 369.

18 Nels Anderson, "The Juvenile and the Tramp," *Journal of the American Institute of Criminal Law and Criminology* (August 1, 1923) 290–312.

Henry Knibbs, *Songs of the Outlands: Ballads of the Hoboes and Other Verses* (New York: Houghton Mifflin Company, 1914).

19 Jack London, *The Road* (New York: The MacMillan Company, 1907).

Obituary of Jim Tully, *The New York Times*, June 23, 1947.

Ray Hinkle, *Polk County Vagabond* (Hinkle 1991); Hinkle, Letter to AHP, October 1992 (OK).

20 Obituary of Richard Halliburton, *The New York Times*, October 5, 1939.

Charley Bull, interview transcript, March 24, 1994.

Frank Bunce, "I've Got to Take a Chance," *The Forum* (February 1933) 108–12.

21 Kingsley Davis, *Youth in the Depression* (Chicago: University of Chicago Press, 1935).

Otto Mullinax, representative of the Progressive Democrats of Texas, statement on American Youth Act, *Hearings before a Senate Committee on Education and Labor on S3658,* 74th Cong., 2 sess., Mar 19-21, 1936. (Washington: Government Printing Office, 1936) 120.

Daniel Robert Maue, *Detroit News*, December 13–16, 1932.

22 John Levy, "The Homeless Boys Retreat."

Nels Anderson, "The Juvenile and the Tramp."

Beulah Amidon, "Schools in the Red," *The Survey Graphic* (June 1934) 266–69, 295–96.

Leonard Mayo, New York School of Social Work, "What Are We Doing to 7 Million Children?" *The Survey* (August 1934) 245–47.

Celeste Strack, national high school secretary of the American Student Union, American Youth Act, 49.

23 William Manchester, *The Glory and the Dream* (Boston: Little Brown & Company, 1974) 22.

"Educators Urge a National Plan," *New York Times*, February 26, 1933.

Eleanor Roosevelt, "Facing the Problems of Youth," *Journal of Social Hygiene* (October–December 1935) 393–94.

Leonard Mayo, "What Are We Doing to 7 Million Children?"

24 Celeste Strack, American Youth Act, 49.

Homer P. Rainey (American Youth Commission) *How Fare American Youth?* (New York: D. Appleton-Century Company, 1937).

Phil Schiff, head worker at Madison House, Long Island, American Youth Act, 17.

Clinch Calkins, *Youth Never Comes Again* (New York: The Committee on Unemployed Youth, 1933).

25 Coral Brooke, Cook County Bureau of Public Welfare, Chicago, "Youth Engulfed," *The Survey* (January 1935) 10–12.

Homer P. Rainey, *How Fare American Youth?*

26 Donald Newhouser, letter to AHP, December 1993 (IN).

Thomas Amlie, Representative, U.S. Congress, Wisconsin, American Youth Act, 23.

27 Jim Mitchell, interview transcript, April 23, 1994.

Earnest L. Best, *The Hobo's Trail Through the Depression* (North Little Rock: The Heritage Press, 1988).

George Phillips, letter to AHP, October 1992 (CA).

John Fawcett, interview transcript, April 14, 1998.

28 Thomas Minehan, *Boy and Girl Tramps of America* (New York: Farrar & Rinehart, 1934).

A. Wayne McMillen, Relief for Unemployed Transients, 30–50.

William Fields, Untouched Youth of America, American Youth Act, 227.

29 A. Wayne McMillen, "Migrant Boys: Some Data From Salt Lake City," *Social Service Review* (March 1933) 64–83.

Nels Anderson, Relief for Unemployed Transients, *Hearings before a Subcommittee on Manufactures on S. 5121*, 72nd Cong., 2d sess. (Washington: Government Printing Office, 1933) 63–71.

Thomas Minehan, *Boy and Girl Tramps of America*.

30 Mary Heaton Vorse, "How Scottsboro Happened," *The New Republic* (May 10, 1933) 356–58.

31 Olive Vassell, editor, "The Scottsboro Boys," http://www.afroam.org/.

Clarence Lee, interview transcript, April 6, 1994.

Herman J.P. Schubert, *Twenty Thousand Transients*.

32 "Speaking of Pictures—Primer for Hobo 'Gaycats,'" *Life Magazine* (October 1937) 14–17.

Grace Abbot, Relief for Unemployed Transients, 23–35.

Gene Wadsworth, letter to AHP, October 1992 (WA); Wadsworth, *My Life as a Hobo*, unpublished mss.

33 A. Wayne McMillen, "An Army of Boys on the Loose," *The Survey Graphic* (September 1933).

Janet Vezolles Ress, letter to AHP, October 1992 (MS).

Pelham D. Glassford, Relief for Unemployed Transients, 125–34.

John Fawcett, interview transcript, April 14, 1994.

Thomas Minehan, *Boy and Girl Tramps of America*.

William Fields, American Youth Act, 227.

34 Paul Ernest Anderson, "Tramping with Yeggs," *Atlantic Monthly* (December 1925).

Nels Anderson, "The Juvenile and the Tramp."

Thomas Minehan, *Boy and Girl Tramps of America*.

James Pearson, letter to AHP, October 1992 (VA); Pearson, *Steel Rails, Smoke and Cinders*, unpublished mss.

35 A. Wayne McMillen, Relief for Unemployed Transients, 30–50.

36 Henry Hill Collins, Jr., *America's Own Refugees—Our 4,000,000 Homeless Migrants* (Princeton, NJ: Princeton University Press, 1940).

John Kazarian, "The Starvation Army," *The Nation* (April 26, 1933) 472–73.

The Book of Vagabonds and Beggars, with a Preface by Martin Luther, 1528, edited and translated by John Camden Hotten (J.C. Hohen, 1860).

H.T. Roach, letter to AHP, November 1993 (AK).

37 Henry Hill Collins, Jr., *America's Own Refugees—Our 4,000,000 Homeless Migrants*.

Henry Koczur, letter to AHP, October 1992 (IN); Koczur, unpublished autobiography.

John C. Lint, letter to AHP, October 1992 (VA).

Roger Brown, letter to AHP, October 1992 (OH): Cathy McCullen, "Kindness Remembered for 59 Years," *Fargo Forum* (March 15, 1992) 16.

38 Richard Sheil, "On Trek," *The Outlook of Missions* (February 1940) 57–59.

Burton Williams, letter to AHP, October 1992 (CA).

39 Lurene Irwin, American Youth Act, 256.

Frank Bunce, "I've Got to Take a Chance."

John Levy, "The Homeless Boy's Retreat."

Otto Mullinax, American Youth Act, 120.

40 Kingsley Davis, *Youth in the Depression*.

Alfred C. Oliver, Jr. and Harold M. Dudley, *This New America: The Spirit of the Civilian Conservation Corps* (New York: Longmans, Green and Co., 1937).

41 Percy H. Merrill, *Roosevelt's Forest Army: A History of the Civilian Conservation Corps, 1933–1942* (Montpellier, VT: P.H. Merrill, 1981); Leslie Alexander Lacy, *The Soil Soldiers: The Civilian Conservation Corps in the Great Depression* (Radnor, PA: Chilton, 1976); Howard Oxley, director of CCC camp education. American Youth Act, 189–97.

Gene Lamb, letter to AHP, September 1992 (CO).

Facing the Problems of Youth:, The Work and Objectives of the National Youth Administration (Washington, D.C.. U.S. Government Printing Office, 1937).

Celeste Strack, American Youth Act, 17.

Edward Strong, National Negro Congress, American Youth Act, 84.

42 William Hinckley, Chairman of American Youth Congress, American Youth Act, 2.

43 John N. Webb, *The Transient Unemployed*, Works Progress Administration, Division of Social Research, Research Monograph III, Washington, 1935.

George Outland, "The Federal Transient Program for Boys in Southern California," *Social Forces* (March 1936) 427–32.

George Outland, "The Federal Transient Service as a Deterrent of Boy Transiency," *Sociology and Social Research* (November–December 1937) 143–48.

44 George Outland, "Should Transient Boys Be Sent Home?" *Social Service Review* (September 1935) 511–19.

Gertrude Springer, "Send 'em Back Home," *The Survey* (December 1935) 364–65.

Catching Out

46 Janet Vezolles Ress, letter to AHP, October 1992 (MS).

47 Among the most useful works consulted: John Kenneth Galbraith, *The Great Crash 1929* (Boston: Houghton Mifflin Company, 1955); T.H. Watkins, *The Great Depression* (New York: Little Brown & Company); Robert S. McElvaine, *The Great Depression: America 1929–1941* (New York: Times Books, 1984); Robert S. McElvaine, ed., *Down and Out in the Great Depression: Letters from the "Forgotten Man"* (Chapel Hill: University of North Carolina Press, 1983); Studs Terkel, *Hard Times: An Oral History of the Great Depression* (New York: Pantheon Books, 1970, 1986); Caroline Bird, *The Invisible Scar* (New York: David McKay, 1966); David A. Shannon, *The Great Depression* (Englewood Cliffs, N. J.: Prentice Hall Inc., 1960); Isabel Leighton, ed. *The Aspirin Age: 1919–1941* (New York: Simon and Schuster, 1949); Arthur M. Schlesinger, Jr. *The Coming of the New Deal* (Boston: Houghton Mifflin, 1958); Glen J. Elder, Jr. *Children of the Great Depression* (Chicago: University of Chicago Press, 1974); John Modell, *Into One's Own: From Youth to Adulthood in the United States 1920–1975* (Berkeley: University of California Press, 1989); Glen H. Elder, Jr., John Modell, Ross D. Parke, *Children in Time and Place: Developmental and Historical Insights* (Cambridge: Cambridge University Press, 1993); Robert Coles, *Children of Crisis*, 1967 (Boston: Little Brown and Company); Ruth Shonle Cavan and Katherine Howard Ranck, *The Family and the Depression: A Study of 100 Chicago Families* (Chicago: University of Chicago Press, 1938); William Manchester, *The Glory and the Dream* (Boston: Little Brown & Company, 1974); Richard Wormser, Hoboes: *Wandering in America, 1870–1940* (New York: Walker and Company, 1994).
Edgar Bledsoe, letter to AHP, October 1992 (AZ).

48 Leo Truscon, letter to AHP, December 1992 (CA).

49 James San Jule, interview transcript, April 5, 1994.
William Wallace, letter to AHP, October 1992 (CA).

50 Christine Wolfrum, letter to AHP, September 1992 (OH).
Lee Leer, letter to AHP, October 1992 (AR); Howard Underwood, *Hobo Boy*, unpublished mss.

51 Coyle Case, letter to AHP, October 1992 (TX).
Harold Dropkin, letter to AHP, October 1992 (CA).

52 Duval Edwards, letter to AHP, October 1992 (WA); Edwards, *The Great Depression: A Teenager's Fight to Survive* (Gig Harbor, WA: Red Apple Publishing, 1992).

Leslie Paul, letter to AHP, October 1992 (WA); Paul, *Jock and Duke*, unpublished mss.

53 Clarence Lee, interview transcript, April 6, 1994.

54 Robert Chaney, letter to AHP, December 1992 (OH).

Berkeley Hackett, letter to AHP, October 1992 (FL); Hackett *Boxcar*, unpublished mss.

Daniel Elliot, letter to AHP, October 1992 (AZ).

55 Thomas Minehan, *Boy and Girl Tramps of America*.

"What Next for Transients," *The Transient* (September 1934) 6–8.

"The Transient Boy: Who and Why," *The Transient* (January 1935).

"Boys and Girls Who Have Been Returned Home," *The Transient* (March 1935).

Gene Wadsworth, letter to AHP, October 1992 (WA); Wadsworth, *My Life As A Hobo*, unpublished mss.

James Pearson, letter to AHP, October 1992 (VA); Pearson, *Steel Rails, Smoke and Cinders*, unpublished mss.

56 Betty Stone, letter to AHP, January 1993 (NC).

Richard Myers, letter to AHP, November 1992 (CA).

John Gojack, letter to AHP, September 28, 1992 (NV); John Gojack, "On One Particular Christmas," *Gazette-Journal*, Reno, Nev. (December 24, 1978) 5.

57 Gy Thomas, letter to AHP, October 1992 (CA).

Robert Schmelzle, letter to AHP, October 1992 (FL); Harriet Gustason, "Summer of '31 with the five 'Boes." *Freeport Illinois Journal-Standard* (Mar. 16-17–Apr. 13-14, 1985) 2–3.

James Carroll, letter to AHP, October 1992 (PA).

58 Claude Franklin, letter to AHP, November 1992 (TX); Franklin, *Adventures of a Young Texas Boy*, unpublished mss.

Hank Kaban, letter to AHP, October 1992 (CA).

Edgar Shanholtzer, letter to AHP, October 1992 (FL).

Harlan Peter, letter to AHP, October 1992 (NV).

59 Glen Law, letter to AHP, October 1992 (IN); Law, *The Hard Way*, unpublished mss.

Ina Máki, letter to AHP, October 1992 (WI).

Dobie Stadt, letter to AHP, October 1992 (OR).

60 Joseph Rieden, letter to AHP, October 1992 (CA).

Clay Nedblake, interview transcript, April 26, 1994.

Violet Van Meter Perry, letter to AHP, October 1992 (IN).

Edith Ely Walker, letter to AHP, December 1992 (FL); Walker, *Memoirs of the Depression*, unpublished mss.

61 Norma Darrah, letter to AHP, January 1993 (WA); Darrah, *Westward to Casper*, unpublished mss.
Harold Kolima, letter to AHP, October 1992 (FL).
Naomi (Smith) Trout, letter to AHP, October 1992 (OR).

62 Lucille Asney, letter to AHP, November 1992 (CA).
Edward Kaufmann, letter to AHP, October 1992 (CO).
William Aldridge, letter to AHP, March 1993 (NC).
Berkeley Hackett, letter to AHP, October 1992 (FL); Hackett *Boxcar*, unpublished mss.

63 Weaver Dial, letter to AHP, October 1992 (WA).
René Champion, interview transcript, March 25, 1994

64 Kermit Parker, letter to AHP, October 1992 (CA); Parker, *Railroading at Fifteen*, unpublished mss.
Ted Baer, letter to AHP, October 1992 (CA); Baer, *Boxcar Odyssey*, unpublished mss.
Weaver Dial, letter to AHP, October 1992 (WA).

65 Vernon Roudebush, letter to AHP, October 1992 (FL); Roudebush, *Knights of the Road 1935 — "Boxcar Bummers,"* unpublished mss.
Glenand Spencer, letter to AHP, April 1993 (CA).
Arvel Pearson, interview transcript, April 15, 1994

66 Leslie Paul, letter to AHP, October 1992 (WA); Paul, *Jock and Duke*, unpublished mss.

John Fawcett

67ff. John Fawcett, interview transcript, April 14, 1994; Fawcett, *1936: Awakening of Conscience*, unpublished mss.; Fawcett, "Hobo Memoir, 1936," *Indiana Magazine of History* (December 1994) 351–64; "In Tribute: John and Ellen Fawcett," *ACLU Newsletter*, vol. 28 (December 1995) 7.

Arvel Pearson

82ff. Arvel Pearson, interview transcript, April 15, 1994; Pearson, "*Sunshine the Hobo*," unpublished mss.; Pearson, *The Way It Was, The Way It Is* (Pearson, 1993); Mike Nemeth, "'Sunshine' sheds light on his travels," *Skagit Valley Herald* (February 27, 1995) 1.

Phoebe Eaton DeHart

90ff. Phoebe Eaton DeHart, interview transcript, April 16, 1994; DeHart, *Chronicles of a Western Family*, unpublished mss.

Hard Travelin'

100 Van Rance, letter to AHP, January 1993 (CO); Rance, *Flight by Night*, unpublished mss.

Ted Baer, letter to AHP, October 1992 (CA); Baer, *Boxcar Odyssey*, unpublished mss.

101 George Rex, letter to AHP, October 1992 (OH); Rex, *Thorns and Roses*, unpublished mss.

Ross Crane, letter to AHP, October 1992 (AZ).

102 Donald Davis, letter to AHP, January 1993 (PA).

L.W. "Red" Barber, letter to AHP, September 1992 (OK).

Ralph Shirley, letter to AHP, October 1992 (MT); Shirley, *Grabbing a Handful of Boxcars*, unpublished mss.

Joseph Watters, letter to AHP, September 1992 (WI).

Leslie Paul, letter to AHP, October 1992 (WA); Paul, *Jock and Duke*, unpublished mss.

103 Ralph Shirley, letter to AHP, October 1992 (MT); Shirley, *Grabbing a Handful of Boxcars*, unpublished mss.

Rudy Ursic, letter to AHP, October 1992 (WI).

William Martin, letter to AHP, October 1992 (FL).

104 Stanley Cole, letter to AHP, October 1992 (WA); Cole, *Hobo*, unpublished mss.

Ken Leabo, letter to AHP, October 1992 (OR).

Frank Dunn, letter to AHP, October 1992 (NC).

Chester Siems, letter to AHP, December 1992 (MI).

105 Howard "Bud" Holmes, letter to AHP, September 1992 (CA).

Manuel Krupin, letter to AHP, October 1992 (CA).

Paul Swenson, letter to AHP, October 1992 (TN); Swenson, *Family and Personal History*, unpublished mss.

106 Samm Coombs, letter to AHP, October 1992 (AR).

107 Verne Smith, letter to AHP, October 1992 (CA).

Bill Lawrence, letter to AHP, January 1994 (OK).

Herbert Rand, letter to AHP, December 1992 (FL); Rand, *16th Summer*, unpublished mss.

108 H.T. Roach, letter to AHP, November 1993 (AK).

Rev. Graham Hodges, letter to AHP, January 1994 (NY).

Clifton Fitzgerald, letter to AHP, August 1993; Fitzgerald, *Carlsbad Caverns Here We Come*, unpublished mss.

109 Chester Dusak, letter to AHP, November 1992 (CT).

Howard Oriel White, *North Carolina Trooper* (July 1992) 39–44.

110 Clemence Ruff, letter to AHP, October 1992 (CA); Ruff, *Recollections*, unpublished mss.

Peter Salzman, letter to AHP, October 1992 (KS).

William Creed, letter to AHP, September 1992 (WA).

111 Virgil Thomsen, letter to AHP, October 1992 (NH); Thomsen, *Boxcar Journey*, unpublished mss.

Kermit Parker, letter to AHP, October 1992 (CA); Parker, *Railroading at Fifteen*, unpublished mss.

Willard Berg, letter to AHP, October 1992 (OR); Berg, *Hit the Road*, unpublished mss.

112 George Rex, letter to AHP, October 1992 (OH); Rex, *Thorns and Roses*, unpublished mss.

Robert Hamilton, letter to AHP, October 1992 (FL).

Archie Frost, letter to AHP, September 1992. (MO).

113 Harry Christian, letter to AHP, October 1992 (CA).

Gordon McCarty, letter to AHP, February 1993 (IL).

H.J. Heller, "Hobos' Boxcar Rides a Journey into Life," *Pittsburgh Press* (December 23, 1979); Julia Oliver, letter to AHP, September 1992 (MD).

Harold Jeffries, letter to AHP, October 1992 (IL).

114 Harry Christian, letter to AHP, October 1992 (CA).

Glen Law, letter to AHP, October 1992 (IN); Law, *The Hard Way*, unpublished mss.

Byron Bristol, letter to AHP, September 1992 (AR).

115 Willard Berg, letter to AHP, October 1992 (OR); Berg, *Hit the Road*, unpublished mss.

116 John West, letter to AHP, October 1992 (TX); West, *Two Ways of Looking at a Hobo*, unpublished mss.

117 Michael Cleary, letter to AHP, February, 1993 (CA).

Margaret Dehn, letter to AHP, September 1992 (CA).

Weaver Dial, letter to AHP, October 1992 (WA).

118 Gene Wadsworth, letter to AHP, October 1992 (WA); Wadsworth, *My Life As A Hobo*, unpublished mss.

Carl Johansen, letter to AHP, October 1992 (IL).

Donald Kopecky, letter to AHP, October 1992 (CA).

119 Robert Chaney, letter to AHP, December 1992 (OH).

John Kercsi, letter to AHP, October 1992 (OH).

Thurston Wheeler, letter to AHP, October 1992 (UT).

Claude Franklin, letter to AHP, November 1992 (TX); Franklin, *Adventures of a Young Texas Boy*, unpublished mss.

Harlan Peter, letter to AHP, October 1992 (NV).

Ben Fowler, interview transcript, April 4, 1994; Fowler, letter to AHP, September 1992 (CA).

120 William Wallace, letter to AHP, October 1992 (CA).
Gordon Golsan, letter to AHP, October 1992 (ALA).
Jack Jeffrey, letter to AHP, September 1992 (AZ).

121 Arthur Payne, letter to AHP, October 1992 (FL).

René Champion

122ff. René Champion, interview transcript, 25 March, 1994; Champion, letter to AHP, September 1992 (CO); "Denver W.W.II Hero Honored," *Le Canard* (Summer 1994) 6.

Clarence Lee

131ff. Clarence Lee, interview transcript, April 6, 1994.

Tiny Boland

138ff. Tiny Boland, interview transcript, March 30, 1994; Boland, letter to AHP, October 5, 1992 (AZ); "John Edmund Boland, Riverman," recollections as told to Bert Hall, *South Dakota Historical Collections*, Vol. XXIII (Pierre, SD: State Publishing Co., 1947).

Hitting the Stem

146 William Csondor, letter to AHP, September 1992 (PA).

147 Clay Nedblake, interview transcript, April 26, 1994
Archie Lawson, letter to AHP, October 1992 (CA); Archie Lawson, *Freight Trains West* (Sacramento: Lucas Publishers, 1980).

148 Ben Fowler, interview transcript, April 4, 1994.
Ross Quinton Reager, letter to AHP, October 1992 (CA).
Harold Hoopes, letter to AHP, October 1992 (FL).
Norma Darrah, letter to AHP, January 1993 (WA); Darrah, *Westward to Casper*, unpublished mss.

149 Peter Pultorak, letter to AHP, October 1992 (MI).
Sol Tucker, letter to AHP, October 1992 (CO).
H.B. "Doc" Harmon, letter to AHP, October 1992 (CA).
Clifford St. Martin, letter to AHP, October 1992 (NV).

150 Robert Engle, letter to AHP, October 1992 (FL).
Jery Basham, letter to AHP, October 1992 (CA).
William Hendricks, letter to AHP, October 1992 (OR).
Burland Webster, letter to AHP, October 1992 (CA).

151 Harold Kolima, letter to AHP, October 1992 (FL).
Fred Hess, letter to AHP, October 1992 (IL).
Peter Chelmeldos, letter to AHP, September 1992 (WA); Chelmeldos, *Peter, the Odyssey of a Merchant Mariner* (Seattle, Odyssey Books, 1992).

152 Giles Wilkins, letter to AHP, February 1993 (MS).
Harry Fisher, letter to AHP, October 1992 (CO); Carolyn Taylor, *Harry Fisher's Stories from His Life*, unpublished mss.

153 Edward Warr, letter to AHP, October 1992 (NJ).
Ed Shanholtzer, letter to AHP, October 1992 (FL).
Geneva Fuqua, letter to AHP, October 1992 (OR).
Paul Gould, letter to AHP, December 1993 (TX).

154 James Overby, letter to AHP, September 1992 (CA).
Donald Kopecky, letter to AHP, October 1992 (CA).

155 Louis Vincent, letter to AHP, September 1992 (CA).
C. D. White, letter to AHP, October 1992 (CA).

156 William Aldridge, letter to AHP, March 1993 (NC).
Paul Booker, letter to AHP, October 1992 (CA); Booker, *High Adventure During the Great Depression*, unpublished mss.
Daniel Elliot, letter to AHP, October 1992 (AZ).

157 Edward Palasz, letter to AHP, October 1992 (NY).
Alvin Svalstad, letter to AHP, November 1992 (MT).
John Gojack, letter to AHP, September 28, 1992 (Nevada); John Gojack, "On One Particular Christmas," *Gazette-Journal*, Reno (December 24, 1978); Gojack, "A Long Way from Hungary," *Magyar Szo* (New York) (September 1986–July 1987).

158 Edgar Bledsoe, letter to AHP, October 1992 (AZ).

159 Harry Kaban, letter to AHP, October 1992 (CA).

160 Sidney Kaufman, letter to AHP, November 1992 (CA).
Myron Overland, letter to AHP, September 1992 (ND).
Ben Fowler, interview transcript, April 4, 1994.
Otto Oliger, letter to AHP, October 1992 (FL).
Russell Morrison, letter to AHP, January 1993 (MN).

161 Channing Smith, letter to AHP, October 1992 (WA).
Van Rance, letter to AHP, January 1993 (Co); Rance, *Flight by Night*, unpublished mss.

162 Max Sarnoff, letter to AHP, November 1992 (PA).
Dorothy Gavin, letter to AHP, October 1992 (WI).

163 Wallace Horton, letter to AHP, October 1992 (OH).

164 Charles Doty, letter to AHP, October 1992 (OK).
Charles Bishop, letter to AHP, October 1992 (CA).
Parley Jensen, letter to AHP, October 1992 (ID).
James Pearson, letter to AHP, October 1992 (VA); Pearson, *Steel Rails, Smoke and Cinders*, unpublished mss.

165 Albert Tackis, letter to AHP, October 1992 (AZ).

166 Manuel Chavez, letter to AHP, October 1992 (FL).

167 William Loft, letter to AHP, October 1992 (ID)
"Hobo Names, Language, Markings," *Hobo Guide—A Guide to the National Hobo Convention and Britt*, 4th Edition (1990) 8.

168 Patricia Schreiner, letter to AHP, October 1992 (MI).
Pat O'Connell, letter to AHP, October 1992 (MT).
Glenna Emlenger, letter to AHP, October 1992 (OH).
Vivian Holland, letter to AHP, October 1992 (AZ).

169 Betty Glover, letter to AHP, November 1992 (VA).
Fr. Roger La Charite, letter to AHP, October 1992 (AL).
Rev. Jack Kidwell, letter to AHP, October 1992 (TX).

170 Alexander Gretes, letter to AHP, September 1992 (MD).
Mary Coulter, letter to AHP, October 1992 (IA).

171 Ann Walko, letter to AHP, October 1992 (PA); Walko, *I Will Never Again Steal to Eat*, unpublished mss.
Everett Childers, letter to AHP, October 1992 (WA).
Freddie Pate, letter to AHP, October 1992 (IL); Pate, *Hobo Travels—1932*, unpublished mss.

172 Ulan Miller, letter to AHP, October 1992 (MO).
Ernest Blevins, letter to AHP, January 1993 (NC).
Casimir Brzeczek, letter to AHP, September 1992 (PA).
Edward Palasz, letter to AHP, October 1992 (NY).

173 Vernon Chadwick, letter to AHP, October 1992 (CA).
Carl Boden, letter to AHP, January 1994 (AZ).
Jack Butler, letter to AHP, October 1992 (PA); Butler, taped interview, October 1992.

174 Herbert Ganger, letter to AHP, October 1992 (FL).

175 Dominick Grella, letter to AHP, October 1992 (FL).

176 Charles Samz, letter to AHP, October 1992 (GA).
Roy Taylor, letter to AHP, October 1992 (CA).

177 Werner Wirth, letter to AHP, September 1992 (CA); Wirth, *Hobo!*, Windsor Country Club newsletter (June 1992).
King Henderson, letter to AHP, September 1992 (CA).

Arvo Niemi, letter to AHP, October 1992 (MA).

178ff. Steve Hargas, letter to AHP, October 1992 (CA).

Alvin Svalstad, letter to AHP, November 1992 (MT).

Fred Schatz, letter to AHP, October 1992 (OR); Schatz, *Some Thoughts on the Great Depression*, unpublished mss.

180 George Nelles, letter to AHP, November 1992. Nelles, *The Way It Was*, unpublished mss.

Gene Wadsworth, letter to AHP, October 1992 (WA); Wadsworth, *My Life As A Hobo*, unpublished mss.

181 Berkeley Hackett, letter to AHP, October 1992 (FL); Hackett *Boxcar*, unpublished mss.

Gene Wadsworth, letter to AHP, October 1992 (WA); Wadsworth, *My Life As A Hobo*, unpublished mss.

Gene Tenold, letter to AHP, September 1992 (WA); Tenold, *It's A Jungle Out There*, unpublished mss.

182 Kermit Parker, letter to AHP, October 1992 (CA); Parker, *Railroading at Fifteen*, unpublished mss.

183 Fredrick Watson, letter to AHP, December 1992 (WA); Watson, *Riding the Rails*, unpublished mss.

Tennys Tennyson, letter to AHP, October 1992 (OR); Tennyson, *Railroad Days*, unpublished mss.

Robert Foster, letter to AHP, December 1992 (OR); Foster, *Hitting the Rails*, unpublished mss.

184 Howard Kemp, letter to AHP, September 1992 (AR).

Murray Simkins, letter to AHP, October 1992 (AZ).

Donald Davis, letter to AHP, January 1993 (PA).

James San Jule

185ff. James San Jule, interview transcript, April 5, 1994. San Jule, letter to AHP, September 1992 (CA).

Jan van Heé

191ff. Jan van Heé, interview transcript, April 11, 1994. Van Heé, letter to AHP, October 1992 (OR).

Clydia Williams

201ff. Clydia Williams, interview transcript, March 27, 1994. Williams, letter to AHP, December 1993 (NM).

The Way Out

207 James Martin, letter to AHP, September 1992 (KS).

208 Anthony Caralla, letter to AHP, October 1992 (NY).

Thomas Rodgers, letter to AHP, March 1994 (CA); Rodgers, *The Adventure Begins*, unpublished mss.

209 Dale Olson, letter to AHP, October 1992 (IA).

Duval Edwards, letter to AHP, October 1992 (WA); Edwards, *The Great Depression: A Teenager's Fight to Survive* (Gig Harbor, WA, Red Apple Publishing, 1992).

Josef Ofer, letter to AHP, October 1992 (CA).

Denzil Stephenson, letter to AHP, November 1992 (MI).

210 Braxton Ponder, letter to AHP, January 1993 (AZ); Ponder, *Wandering Over the Highways and Byways of America*, unpublished mss.

Selby Norheim, letter to AHP, October 1992 (MN).

Clifford St. Martin, letter to AHP, October 1992 (NV).

211 Henry Koczur, letter to AHP, October 1992 (IN); Koczur, unpublished autobiography.

212 Ross Coppock, letter to AHP, June 1993 (OR).

Fred Schatz, letter to AHP, October 1992 (OR); Schatz, *Some Thoughts on the Great Depression*, unpublished mss.

213 Bernard Carlson, letter to AHP, October 1992 (CT); Carlson, *Riding the Rails to Work on the Fort Peck Dam*, unpublished mss.

214 Walter Barrett, letter to AHP, October 1992 (FL).

Chester Siems, letter to AHP, December 1992 (MI).

Herbert Teitelbaum, letter to AHP, October 1992 (NY).

215 Arthur Lent, letter to AHP, October 1992 (NV).

William Hendricks, letter to AHP, October 1992 (OR).

Donald Kopecky, letter to AHP, October 1992 (CA).

216 Clemence Ruff, letter to AHP, October 1992 (CA); Ruff, *Recollections*, unpublished mss.

Geneva Fuqua, letter to AHP, October 1992 (OR).

217 Allene Biby, letter to AHP, October 1992 (IA); Biby, *Holes in Our Shoes*, unpublished mss.

D.L. Young, letter to AHP, September 1992 (AZ).

218ff. Herbert Teitelbaum, letter to AHP, October 1992 (NY).

Mel Stine, letter to AHP, October 1992 (NV).

220ff. William Hendricks, letter to AHP, October 1992 (OR).

Arvel Pearson, interview transcript, April 15, 1994.

Willard Berg, letter to AHP, October 1992 (OR); Berg, *Hit the Road*, unpublished mss.

222 Lloyd Jesse Veitch, letter to AHP, June 1993 (CA).

Rex Cozad, letter to AHP, September 1992 (KS); Cozad, *My Hobo Days*, unpublished mss.

223 Wallace Horton, letter to AHP, October 1992 (OH).

224 Richard Sheil, letter to AHP, October 1992 (PA); Sheil, "On Trek," *The Outlook of Missions* (February 1940) 57–59.

Rev. Jack Kidwell, letter to AHP, October 1992 (TX).

Donald McCutcheon, letter to AHP, October 1992 (IA).

Elizabeth Verwolf, letter to AHP, October 1992 (ID).

225 Edgar Bledsoe, letter to AHP, October 1992 (AZ).

226 Hal Buffa, letter to AHP, October 1992 (CA).

Claude Franklin, letter to AHP, November 1992 (TX); Franklin, *Adventures of a Young Texas Boy*, unpublished mss.

227 Elmer Beckman, letter to AHP, October 1992 (MN).

John Kercsi, letter to AHP, October 1992 (OH).

Walter Miletich, letter to AHP, October 1992 (AZ).

228ff. Lee Leer, letter to AHP, October 1992 (AR); Howard Underwood, *Hobo Boy*, unpublished mss.

230 Harry Keller, letter to AHP, September 1992 (TX); Keller and Candace Noriega, *The Depression Years*, unpublished mss.

231 Arthur Hunevan, letter to AHP, October 1992 (CA).

Wallace Horton, letter to AHP, October 1992 (OH).

Jan van Heé, interview transcript, April 11, 1994.

232 Ernest Amundsen, letter to AHP, September 1993 (WA); Amundsen, *My Train Trips*, unpublished mss.

Darwood Drake, letter to AHP, October 1992 (CA); Drake, *Looking Back* (Chicago, Adams Press, 1989.

Karen Beebe, letter to AHP, October 1992 (AZ); Weldon Keele, *Hoboing*, unpublished mss.

George de Mars, letter to AHP, November 1992 (MN).

233 Howard Oxley, director of education, Civilian Conservation Corps, statement on American Youth Act, *Hearings before a Senate Committee on Education and Labor on S3658*, 74th Cong., 2 sess., Mar 19–21, 1936 (Washington: Government Printing Office, 1936) 189.

Francis Gerath, letter to AHP, October 1992 (ME).

Jack Cunningham, letter to AHP, October 1992 (CA).

234 Orrin George, letter to AHP, October 1992 (CO).

Richard Barnes, letter to AHP, November 1992 (TX).

L.E. DeLany, letter to AHP, October 1992 (VA).

235 Robert Keerns, letter to AHP, September 1992 (MO).

Theryl Gale, letter to AHP, January 1993 (IA); Gale, *My Hobo Days*, unpublished mss. Clancy Strock "Listen in on the Old 'Party Line.'" *Reminisce Magazine* (May–June 1992).

Vernon Roudebush, letter to AHP, October 1992 (FL); Roudebush, *Knights of the Road 1935 — "Boxcar Bummers,"* unpublished mss.

236 Harold Sparks, letter to AHP, October 1992 (VA).

John Fawcett, interview transcript, April 23, 1994. Fawcett, *1936 — Awakening of Conscience*, unpublished mss.

237 Joe Cornett, letter to AHP, October 1992 (NH).

Charlie Jordan, letter to AHP, October 1992 (MS).

James Morehead, letter to AHP, September 1992 (CA).

238 Leslie Paul, letter to AHP, October 1992 (WA); Paul, *Jock and Duke*, unpublished mss.

D.L. Young, letter to AHP, September 1992 (AZ).

John Fawcett, interview transcript, April 23, 1994. Fawcett, *1936 — Awakening of Conscience*, unpublished mss.

239 George Hanson, letter to AHP, September 1992 (MD); Hanson, "God bless you, Big Joe," *The Evening Sun*, Baltimore (May 18, 1983) A12.

Basil Maita, letter to AHP, October 1992 (CA).

Louis Johnson, letter to AHP, February 1993 (FL).

240 Omar McCoy, letter to AHP, October 1992 (NJ).

Edgar Shanholtzer, letter to AHP, October 1992 (FL).

René Champion, letter to AHP, March 25, 1994. (CO).

Dave Dawson, letter to AHP, November 1992 (AK).

241 Manuel Krupin, letter to AHP, October 1992 (CA).

Andrew Szabo, letter to AHP, November 1992 (OH).

Doyle Yancey, letter to AHP, October 1992 (MO).

Herbert Teitelbaum, letter to AHP, October 1992 (NY).

242 Chester Smith, letter to AHP, October 1992 (WA).

William Aldridge, letter to AHP, March 1993 (NC).

Gordon Bredersen, letter to AHP, December 1992 (MI).

Ralph Jones, letter to AHP, October 1992 (KS); Jones, *Adventures to the West, 1937 — 1939*, unpublished mss.

243ff. Chester Clever, letter to AHP, October 1992 (CA).

Robert Lloyd, letter to AHP, October 1992 (CA).

Philip Bonosky, interview transcript, March 14, 1994; Letter to AHP, September 1992 (NY); Bonosky, "A Letter to Mrs. Roosevelt," *Mainstream* (January 1963) 3–22.

245　Blanche Stovall, letter to AHP, October 1992 (KS).
L.E. DeLany, letter to AHP, October 1992 (VA).
Don Snyder, letter to AHP, October 1992 (OH).

Charley Bull

246ff.　Charles E. Bull, interview transcript, March 24, 1994; Bull, letter to ASP, November 1992 (AL); Bull, *The Vagabond*, unpublished mss.

Jim Mitchell

255ff.　Jim Mitchell, interview transcript, April 23, 1994; Mitchell, *A Nickel for Bread* (Jasper, MN: Prairie Grove Books, 1990).

Robert Symmonds

264ff.　Robert Symmonds, interview transcript, April 10, 1994.

Acknowledgments

I am indebted to the former boxcar boys and girls whose personal remembrances are at the core of this book. Many who put their memories down on paper in 1992 were already in their seventies and eighties. Many have taken their last ride in the intervening years. It was a rare privilege to journey back with them and stand for a moment in time in the boxcar door, rolling through the heart of America. May this book stand as a tribute to the fortitude and fearlessness of one and all.

I should like to acknowledge the work of the documentary makers, Michael Uys and Lexy Lovell, my son and daughter-in-law. Through four years of unflagging dedication, they produced their award-winning film, *Riding the Rails*, hailed as Best Documentary of 1997 by both the Director's Guild of America and the Los Angeles Film Critics' Association. The film also won a 1998 Peabody Award for broadcast and cable excellence as part of the acclaimed PBS series, *The American Experience*.

The wealth of information gathered for *Riding the Rails* made this book possible. Peter Kaufman and his colleagues at TV Books had the inspired notion of developing books from the exhaustive background work that goes into making documentaries and might otherwise be lost.

Jay CJ Chiarito Mazzarella scrutinized the contents for errors of fact and interpretation (any that remain are the sole property of the author). His *North American Hobo Phenomenon: A Bibliography of Sources from 1878–1999* (Chiarito Mazzarella, Jay CJ,

1999) is an invaluable guide to the subject. A special word of thanks to Sam Birger, who devoted long hours to vetting early drafts of the manuscript.

On the road itself, I have been accompanied by my wife, Janette, as always with unstinting support and courage, for which I am ever grateful.

Index

Pearson, Arvel, *cont.*
King of the Hoboes, 82, 88
passing as railroad man, 85
reflections of, 88–89
techniques explained, 84–85
work, finding, 85–88
Pearson, James, 34–35, 55–56, 164–65
Pearson, Luther, 87
Pendleton, Oregon, 64
Perry, Violet, 60
Peter, Harlan, 58–59, 119
Peter, the Odyssey of a Merchant Mariner (Chelmeldos), 152
Philadelphia, Pennsylvania, 208
Phillips, George, 27
Pine, W.B., 50
Pocatello, Idaho, 182–83
Ponder, Braxton, 210
Portland, Oregon, 119–20
Powers, Tom, 37–38
Pratt and Whitney, 218, 219
Price, Victoria, 30
prostitution, 163–65, 198–99, 234–35, 242
Public Works Administration (PWA), 213–14, 252
Pultorak, Peter, 149

R
Raft, George, 240
railroad bulls, 37, 64–66, 69, 93, 94, 99, 101, 116–21, 142–43, 160, 163, 166, 175, 176, 202, 204

African Americans, treatment of, 114
Cheyenne bulls, 117–18
Texas Slim, 37, 65, 118–19, 156
Rainey, Homer P., 25
Rance, Van, 100, 161–62
Rand, Herbert, 107–8
Rand Corporation, 129
Rasnick, Pearl, 125–26
rattlesnake catcher, 210
Raye, Martha, 240
Reager, Ross, 148
red ball, 85
reefers, 105, 107, 109, 189
religious missions, 33–34
Rex, George, 100–101, 112
riding the rods, 84
Rieden, Joseph, 60
Rieden, Ralph, 60
Roach, H.T., 36, 108
Road, The (London), 19
Rodgers, Thomas, 208–9
Roosevelt, Eleanor, 23, 244
Roosevelt, Franklin D., 11–12, 23, 40–41, 44, 190, 213, 232, 233, 252–54, 262–63
Ross, Barney, 159–60
Roudebush, Vernon, 65, 235–36
Royal Road to Romance, The (Halliburton), 20
Ruff, Clemence, 110, 216

S
safecracking, 34
St. Martin, Clifford, 149, 210–11

Wilkins, Giles, 152
Williams, Aubrey, 23–24
Williams, Burton, 38
Williams, Clydia, 201–5
Williams, Eugene, 31
Willis, Irene, 91–96
Wirth, Werner, 177
Wise Stiff, 39
Wolfrum, Christine, 50
"wolves," 34–35, 110
women and girls. *See* girls and
    women
work
  ambitions on the road, 218–20
  Civilian Conservation Corps
      (CCC), 40–41, 42–43, 44,
      105, 199, 207, 216, 230–33,
      244, 252–53, 259–61, 263
  cotton picking, 225–28
  farm labor, 220–30
  fire fighting, 211–12
  harvest work, 38–39, 61, 87,
      125, 140, 142, 150, 151,
      220–24
  looking for work, 85–88, 207,
      208–11, 213–16

married couples on the road,
    216–18
moving on, 213–16
New Deal programs, 35–36,
    40–41, 42–43, 44, 46, 49,
    105, 141, 199, 207,
    213–14, 230–33, 244,
    252–53, 259–61
railroad work, 212–13
Worker's Alliance, 244
Works Projects Administration
    (WPA), 35–36, 41, 46, 49,
    141, 244, 252
World War II, 44, 80, 128–29,
    136, 143, 199, 200, 236–37,
    239, 240, 253–54

Y

Yancey, Doyle, 241
yeggs, 34
Young, D.L., 217–18, 238
Young, Thelma, 217–18, 238
Youth Never Comes Again (pamphlet), 24–25
Youth Pilgrimage on Jobs and
    Education (1937 march), 42

About the Author

Errol Lincoln Uys is a successful writer and editor with thirty years' experience in the United States, England, and South Africa. Uys (pronounced "Ace") was editor-in-chief of *Reader's Digest*, South Africa, and senior international editor with the US edition. Having worked for two years with James A. Michener on *The Covenant*, he was inspired to write the critically acclaimed historical novel *Brazil*. This book is his first work of non-fiction.

Visit the author's website at: http://www.erroluys.com